Living and Dying
on the Internet

ALEX DAY

Living and Dying on the Internet
by
Alex Day

Published in Great Britain in 2018 by Alex Day after extensive distraction

You only get one shot; do not miss your chance to blow
This opportunity comes once in a lifetime
You better lose yourself in the music, the moment
You own it; you better never let it go
You only get one shot

ISBN: 978-0-9930204-2-1

CONTENTS

To Hazel and Eric,
even though one of you couldn't read
and the other wouldn't have made it more than two pages in
without falling asleep;

To Flawn,
in the hope that you might have finished reading this book
by the time I publish my next one;

And to Georgia,
who's already read this book three times
and kept it — and me — from drifting.

THE EARLY INTERNET

Twelve years have passed since I loaded up my online diary and typed: 'Last Sunday, I had a brilliant idea.'

It was March 2006, and the idea I'd had was to make a video series. I wanted to watch a movie, cut out the bits I found funny and insert myself between them making witty remarks about the footage. This was a brilliant idea, as for years I'd seen the comedian Harry Hill do the same thing with television shows to much success and acclaim. What I should have written in my diary was, 'Last Sunday, I had Harry Hill's brilliant idea'.

My 'Harry Hill with films (and me)' series was to be called *The Random Touch*; I was seventeen and that seemed the appropriate sort of wacky title for a hilarious individual like me. I got to work watching the first episode of *Star Wars*. My diary reminds me it took me ages 'cos I had to burn all of *Episode 1* on to my computer and cut the funny bits out, then show it to my mum and delete the ones she didn't find funny'.

It was me and my mum against the world. I grew up living with her in Essex, an hour away from London on the District Line, where the drink is cheap and the drinkers are loud. We were often broke, but I never went without. My dad came to visit once a week or so (and still does). I'm not sure of the full impact of not having him around in my daily life, but I can tell you I've spent my life brainstorming ideas for stories, songs and videos, and that he spends his as a writer, musician and video editor.

My mum cackles at her own jokes, my dad draws a smiley face into the 'R' of his name and I am in every way the son of both. As I understand it, my mum and dad were already on their way to over by the time I was born. My mum declared herself the designated driver by giving me her surname instead of his; my dad had dominion over the middle names and made as much of a mark on those as possible, gifting me with George (after his dad) and Richard (after himself).

I called my mum 'Tracy' instead of 'Mummy' for the first few years of my talking life and she liked it that way, having taken to the task of raising me with straightforwardness and respect. I have a scar on my back from a time I jumped up and down on my bed near a boiling radiator, the most physical proof of my mum's outlook:

'Alex, don't,' she said. 'You'll fall between the bed and the radiator and you'll burn yourself.'

'I'll be fine!' I said, continuing to jump.

'Okay,' she shrugged, 'see what happens.'

It was in this way that I grew to learn from direct experience. It wouldn't do to make judgments on hearsay or someone else's opinion.

'What's that you're drinking?' I asked.

'It's called sherry,' she said. 'Would you like a bit?'

I had a sip and pulled a face. I never understood alcohol, despite a few more samples over the years. By the time I was of legal age to drink, it held no allure over me and I was happy to go without it. I told people, 'I'm happy to look like a twat sober.'

'Can I stub out your cigarette?' I asked on another occasion. My mum's cigarettes held a kind of morbid allure, like waving one's fingers through a candle flame. Again, she let me and watched as I prodded the burnt stick against the bottom of a glass ashtray. The stick felt warm and my fingers smelled for hours. I never touched one again.

There was no topic too taboo for my mum to discuss with me. One day in the car home from school when I was about ten, I described a video the teacher had shown us.

'They were fixing cars,' I said. 'The man was doing a blowjob.'

My mum looked at me. 'A what?'

'A blowjob,' I said.

'Alex, what do you think a blowjob is?'

So I explained. 'When they put a big mask on, and they use that thing to fix the car — a blowtorch.'

My mum smiled. 'That's not what a blowjob is.'

'Oh right,' I said. 'What is it then?'

'Well, it's when someone puts your penis in their mouth.'

'Ugh,' I said. 'That sounds horrible.'

'You won't always feel that way,' said mum.

'What a bean!' I said. In my school, kids called each other a 'bean' when they did something silly (a way to avoid swearing in front of the teachers). I didn't have enough friends to do that, and no siblings either, so I called my mum a bean instead. My mum had asked me once if I wanted a brother or sister, I told her not at all, thank you very much, and that was the end of that. Being an only child, the closest thing I had to a sibling was my older cousin Danny but I only saw him on the rare occasions he visited from Leicester (a city in the Midlands, about six days from London by horse and cart, which was how people got around in the days before the internet). I socialised with my mum and her friends rather than other children, who often bored me. When I was older, my evenings with mum would revolve around reruns of *Sex and the City*, so I ended up being raised by not one but five strong women: Carrie, Samantha, Miranda, Charlotte and Tracy.

I hated secondary school. I only got on with the teachers and didn't understand the kids, who talked about football, gelled their hair and sniffed each other's fingers.

'Do you think you're smarter than me?' one kid challenged, puffing his chest out as we walked out of class.

3

'Relatively,' I said, thinking this a diplomatic answer.

'What the fuck does "relatively" mean?'

'Well, if you don't know...' I said, strolling off to the library, where I spent most of my time. (I'd just begun reading a new book series called *Harry Potter* — three books had already been released.) The other kids didn't get that, either. I was once walking home from school, nose-deep in a young adult novel, and a girl yelled at me from across the street, 'Oi! Bookworm! What the fuck you readin' a book for?' (I grew up, as I said, in Essex.)

I shuffled along with my head down, ignoring heckles. My survival strategy for school was to do everything I could to deflect attention from myself. If I was late for a class, I'd skip it. I didn't want everyone looking at me as I walked through the door. I was stung by a wasp once while sitting in an assembly with the entire school and, true to form, didn't make a movement or a sound about it until the boy sitting next to me — after hissing at me to get someone's attention — raised his hand and interrupted the headteacher in the middle of her Bible sermon.

'Miss, Alex has been stung by a wasp,' he proclaimed, at which point every student and teacher in the assembly hall turned and watched me stumble outside, clutching my neck like I'd escaped a horde of zombies. In the following week's assembly the headteacher gave me an award for bravery and self-control. In fact it was the complete opposite: the collective gaze of the student body was far scarier than a wasp sting.

I didn't realise the kids who don't like drawing attention to themselves often end up attracting loads of it. I was once at the front of my French class being quizzed with a few other kids and needed the toilet but didn't want to say so for fear of making a scene, and when the teacher asked me what the infinitive of the verb 'to be' was, I wet myself. My classmates, to their credit, were so mortified that they never teased me about it or brought it up again. Thank goodness I grew up a few years before every kid had a camera in their pocket or I could have been humiliated on the world stage.

The standard advice when you're being picked on is to ignore it, which I took literally, turning my head to look the other way and pretend my classmates didn't exist. I didn't realise it made me an even more entertaining target. I think kids pick on you to test you, to figure out what you're made of, and they couldn't figure me out. I don't blame them. I still can't figure me out.

In my last year of school, I decided to own my weirdness and bleached my hair blond (probably because of Eminem, or Spike from *Buffy the Vampire Slayer*). I was being judged either way so I figured I might as well do what I liked. Provoking people's criticism gave me ownership over it. I dared them to give me their worst and was almost disappointed when their insults ended up so tame. I learned I could assert myself and the world would keep on spinning.

I was of the first generation who had experience with computers all their lives. When I was six, my mum bought me a VTech IT Keyboard, a grey plastic keyboard and mouse I plugged into my little square TV to create a simulated computer. It came with 128 kB of storage space, which is about as much data as the first eight seconds of 'Never Gonna Give You Up' by Rick Astley. The VTech was a kids' machine designed with adults in mind: it had a crossword puzzle generator, a calendar, a word processor, a phone book and even a tool to learn software programming. By the age of seven I was catching Pokémon on my Game Boy, watching old episodes of *Mighty Morphin Power Rangers* on VHS tapes and tapping out lines of code in my bedroom.

My favourite thing in the VTech, a typing 'game' called WordZap, helped my touch typing skills to flourish. In primary school I took a touch-typing book out of the library to hone my skills, and when I went back to visit years later, the teachers showed me the inside cover of that book. I remained the only person, student or teacher, who'd ever borrowed it. I have always loved typing; with the keyboard at my fingertips, I can write as fast as I can think.

Mum's boyfriend, Jamie, worked with computers, so we had one in the house when few others did, a thick, unwieldy box filled with lights and fans that seemed to take up two-thirds of the living room. Jamie made his living fixing computers and spent his evenings buying and selling spaceships in an online game called EVE. I would sit next to him for hours in silence, watching him navigate the wild space of the early internet. On my tenth birthday, my family traded the VTech for my own desktop computer connected to the new digital world. I would have been fully liberated if it weren't for the internet and the phone sharing a physical wire out of the house, meaning my solo voyages online were limited by the time my mum spent chatting to her friend Lynn. Our phone plan provided free evening calls as long as they were less than an hour long, and my mum outsmarted the system by hanging up at minute 59 and ringing back to reset the clock; I would listen for the sound of the plastic handset thudding against its base and take the opportunity to dial in for a precious few seconds of connectedness. My mum would pick up the phone only to be assaulted with a series of loud whirrs and cracks — the sound of the internet itself, clawing its way through the pipes.

'Alex,' my mum would say, 'can you turn off the internet? I want to make a phone call.'

Apple would have you convinced the most magical thing about a smartphone is the high-definition screen, the fingerprint payment technology or the voice recognition assistance; I'm still amazed I can use the internet and be on the phone at the same time.

What I remember best about the internet circa 1999 is a lot of websites made by individual people for no money. Everyone planted their own gaudy flag in some nook or cranny of the web, with a bright green background and a low-quality instrumental version of their favourite song playing, their bad poetry and lists of favourite movies surrounded by flashing cartoon cats and tiny animated fireworks. They were complete shit, but they were expressive and brimming with personality. You would never find two websites that looked the same. Also, porn was everywhere. I don't mean that there were a lot of porn sites (like I've heard there are now), but that porn would pop out at you whenever you attempted to load *any* website, the photos loading at a snail's pace because fast connections weren't a thing back then. You'd end up seeing an inch more skin every few seconds, as though the internet were putting on a striptease for you.

My map through these uncharted lands was a new searching service that carried me to websites on any topic I could imagine. It could deliver so many results that they named it after a 'googol', the number one followed by a hundred zeroes. When I first used it, Google was less than a year old. I was thrust into a world where it seemed anyone could say, do or be whatever they wanted with no fear of reproach. This unfiltered land became my home.

At the same time, music technology was leaping forward. My mum raised me to a soundtrack of Prince, The Police and Bon Jovi. We loved Queen most of all, with their bombastic hits and flamboyant performances. I went from a Sony Discman when I was a kid — a slab of kit that carried and played a single CD — to an iPod that put several thousand songs in my pocket at once. With the online iTunes Store, you could get any track you wanted without even having to buy a whole album.

I sat in the school music room during lunch hours and listened to Evanescence songs on loop, picking out the notes by ear to teach myself the piano parts. I sold my collection of Yu-Gi-Oh! trading cards and used the money to buy an electric guitar on which I cranked out Green Day's *American Idiot* album over and over again. I had an electronic keyboard to write my own songs and a computer keyboard to write my own stories. I couldn't wait to be old enough to have them taken seriously.

By the time I was finishing college, I felt I'd wasted my school life proving I'd learned things by parroting them back under timed conditions. I knew I understood the work and came to be indignant about demonstrating it, especially when a six-point exam question would only award two points for the correct answer (the rest being allocated to embellishment and a quote). Things came to a head when I received an A on a free-wheeling essay about Friedrich Nietzsche's book Beyond Good and Evil (which I loved), then sat a single-question exam on the same book and got a U, which is even worse than an F. It means Ungraded. It's so bad they don't even want to look at it. I found it preposterous that I could sit two exams on the same topic but get the highest possible grade on one and the lowest on the other.

I stormed to my Philosophy teacher, Bonnie, a self-declared anarchist.

'Do you know what the labour rights movement used to say?' she asked me. 'It was their rallying cry. "Don't mourn, organise."'

This motto changed my life. It helped me see the futility of complaining when you don't have a plan for making things better. It turned my negative listlessness into positive action. I decided I would never get stuck in a job I didn't want. I would never sacrifice all my time in exchange for money. Money's only useful if you have the time to spend it, yet everyone around me was spending the bulk of their short, singular lives working at — or preparing for — things they didn't want to do.

I started reading all sorts of books on business, finance and productivity. I listened to self-help hypnosis tapes for wealth and confidence. I learned about the 'rat race' and how to escape it by buying assets, creating multiple streams of income and managing money. I practised skills to be more charming and persuasive by improving my posture and paying attention to my body language. I found inspiration in artistic entrepreneurs like Walt Disney and Steve Jobs. 'Your time is limited,' Steve had said a couple years earlier, 'so don't waste it living someone else's life.... Don't let the noise of others' opinions drown out your own inner voice.'

To make my voice heard, I turned to the internet.

If my mum were telling this story, this is where she would tell you about a tarot reading she'd had before I was born in which she was told she would have a son who would be good with computers. She likes to remind me of this at family get-togethers.

'Spooky, isn't it?' Mum always says.

'No,' I reply, 'it was the 1980s. *Every* child who was about to be born would end up being good with computers.' She frowns at that, but loves me anyway.

I'd already been expressing myself online, writing stories for years about Digimon — a cartoon similar to Pokémon, although Digimon fans will have me executed for saying so. The most popular Digimon, Agumon, was a small orange dinosaur, so I made mine, Nerimon, a small *red* dinosaur. (This is the same creative mind that later invented 'Harry Hill with films'.) I wrote eight stories, each on a webpage more garish than the last, all in Comic Sans, and ended each story with 'The End...?'

Not many people wrote Digimon fanfiction online — not many people did anything whatsoever online — so I got some attention. I received fan art, for example, which I catalogued and listed on my site with descriptions like 'computer image of Nerimon, by Jennifer' and 'the same computer Nerimon as before but on a fiery background, by Jennifer'. (Jennifer was an enthusiastic contributor in the field of online Digimon writing. We still keep in touch.)

I didn't stop at Digimon. The internet made it easy for me to share things under any kind of persona, separate from my real life. I fought the Sailor Scouts and scored points for the Ravenclaw Quidditch team all in text from my bedroom. I made friends I'd never met who collaborated with me on stories; we would write a chapter each and email them back and forth, telling the tale to each other. Offline, I spent my time devising novels and TV shows and composing songs and poems, all of which were awful. The first song I remember writing, at thirteen, was titled 'No-One Understands Me'; I'm grateful the title is the only bit I can remember. I wrote a poem about a girl at school called Katrina and learned the hard way that my classmates were more internet-savvy than I realised when they found it online, printed it out, and distributed it around the school. I was humiliated for about twenty-four hours, after which point everyone moved on and talked about something else. I'm sure it was more embarrassing for Katrina, who I never got anywhere with, though I worshipped her for our entire five years of school together. (I spoke to Katrina recently and she said she still has the poem; being a true friend, she spared me a reading of it.)

When my dad bought me a MacBook for my sixteenth birthday — with free iMovie editing software, and a webcam built into the frame — I used it to make variety shows of me telling jokes and performing magic tricks to my patient family. I was ten years old when the first season of *Big Brother* aired on Channel 4, mesmerising a nation with 24-hour access to real people playing out their dramas on a national stage; the idea of being on camera didn't faze me.

I was, by then, in a band. We wanted to sound like Slipknot, dressed like Sum 41, listened to McFly, and were — without irony — called 'Identity'. With my new tools, I embarked on an eight-part documentary series called *Forging an Identity*, a VH1-style behind-the-scenes series showcasing our progress as we struggled to learn the bass riff of 'Seven Nation Army'. To make this 'documentary' — which I put in quotation marks because nothing we were doing was worth documenting — I shot all the footage with a single camera, running around the room getting close-up shots from different angles so it looked like a whole crew was following us around.

I only ever finished the first episode of *Forging an Identity*, twenty-six long minutes of me and my mates telling the camera how much we liked the idea of being in a band. A lengthy section is devoted to my best mate Sam musing on his keen interest in golf, a sequence made even less relevant with the knowledge that he wasn't even *in* the band.

The first episode of *The Random Touch* — my aforementioned 'brilliant idea' to make jokes about movies — ended up with a similar runtime of eighteen minutes. I had no awareness of what might hold an audience's attention online; 'internet content' wasn't a thing back then and, in any case, I didn't consider this an online project. As far as I was concerned, I was making independent low-budget documentary and comedy television shows. The internet was just the distribution method. At some point, I was sure some TV boss would pick up on my obvious skill for making fun of the first episode of *Star Wars* and give me a career and that would be the end of it.

To share my video with the world I set up a podcast, a new form of digital media akin to an on-demand radio show (named after the iPod with which people listened to them). My first experience with podcasting was when Ricky Gervais released an irreverent and podcast called *The Ricky Gervais Show* (which set a Guinness World Record when it became the most-downloaded podcast ever). Ricky's turn to podcasting followed a career that had already included writing, acting, directing and stand-up comedy. I've always struggled to answer the question, 'What do you do?' because, like Ricky, all the people I admire have done whatever they wanted. I watched singers write comic books, comedians act in sitcoms and actors invest in tech companies. What I wanted to do was be myself, professionally. *The Random Touch*, I hoped, would gain huge online traction and be my way into financial freedom and creative revelry.

Up the podcast went and I shared the link on my MySpace page, 'emohemian'. (I know.) MySpace was the first big site for 'social networking', linking people's individual websites together under a common framework. It was easy to set up your own page with customised colours and backgrounds. Users had their own customisable profiles to share things about themselves and post messages and photos to other people. You knew you'd fallen out with someone when you were no longer in their Top Friends, a showcase of eight people on each page that could be changed at a moment's notice.

A couple weeks after the podcast went live, I got an email from a guy who worked at the podcast hosting company: 'I passed the URL to your feed around the office, and everyone else who watched it —

including my boss! — loved it too. So rest assured that if you care to continue, you'll have an audience.'

That was all I needed to commit myself to making one episode a week, just like TV; that's how they did it, so that's how I would too. It escaped my notice (or maybe I just didn't care) that Harry Hill doesn't turn the cameras on, run to his desk, film all the jokes himself, import and edit all the footage to a laptop and submit it to ITV single-handedly while writing mock essays for upcoming Philosophy A-Level exams. I started shutting myself away in the college's IT centre to complete my homework each day, giving me the time I needed to make the show when I got home. Time was of the essence; I still hadn't done anything meaningful with my life and I was already nearly eighteen. I was trying everything to get the world's attention and I didn't limit myself to the podcast. When Danny came to visit from Leicester, we developed a card game called Sopio. (I wanted a word that sounded like 'Uno' but meant something completely stupid; *sopio* is the Latin word for *penis*.) I designed a Boy Scout-style badge system to reward life achievements like going to the theatre or singing karaoke, hoping to start a craze throughout college; I designed real physical badges, ordered them online and gave them out to friends. I even wrote twenty thousand words of a memoir about my life called *Those Days of Innocence* (including such musings as 'the chapter when I saw S Club 7 live').

I made seven episodes of *The Random Touch*, diversifying into *Harry Potter* movies in addition to the *Star Wars* films. Few people watched them; back then you were lucky if your internet connection was good enough that you *could* watch them, which might have been why my audience consisted largely of the employees at the video hosting office. Among everyone I knew, I was the only one who was enthusiastic about the internet. While my classmates chatted on MSN Messenger, I was the first among them to rave about a new app called Skype which provided long-distance communication for free, with audio and video and even the ability to make phone calls from your computer.

Skype became essential for me to talk to the occasional person who found my work and enjoyed it. One viewer, a Canadian girl called Heather, chatted with me almost every day. I found her pleasant, entertaining and good company, as I found to be true of my 'fans' in general. They weren't adoring, hyperventilating, shaking wrecks, because why would they be? I didn't even like calling them fans. I was just like them. They liked what I was doing and I liked doing it; we were equals. (I'm still in touch with Heather, too, as it happens.)

The internet helped me connect with people. It was unregulated, so no-one told me I couldn't do things or that I wasn't old enough. Nothing was censored. If I didn't want to engage with someone, it was easy to avoid them. This was a space where I was treated like an adult, and I, in turn, treated others with kindness and respect.

Well. Mostly.

BROADCAST YOURSELF

It took me a long time to understand what the Super Bowl was. What Americans call 'football' is nothing like it, right down to the fundamentals: you use your hands far more than your feet and the thing you're throwing isn't ball-shaped, so there's nothing 'foot' or 'ball' about it. Due to these etymological stumbling points, I thought the Super Bowl was an annual ten-pin bowling competition that, for reasons I didn't understand, the entire United States of America went insane over, even getting the biggest pop stars in the world to come out in the middle of the game and entertain the crowd. We care a lot about football in the UK, but Adele's never wandered out during an England match and busted out a medley of her greatest hits.

During the halftime performance of the 2004 Super Bowl, Justin Timberlake performed with Janet Jackson and, during his respectful lyric, 'Gonna have you naked by the end of this song,' whipped off part of her costume. According to reports, the plan was to take off her bustier and reveal a red lace bra beneath, but the stunt was cooked up so late in the planning of the show that no-one had an opportunity to rehearse it; the first time trying it would be live on the night itself. When the time came, Justin sang his line, grabbed the costume, pulled back the bustier, took the bra with it, and revealed Janet Jackson's breast to 143 million people watching the Super Bowl around the world.

The next day, a Californian called Jawed felt frustrated. He wanted to see this very important footage of a woman's naked body being accidentally exposed to the world by an unrehearsed man singing about getting her naked, but he had a great deal of difficulty finding the clip online.

The following year, inspired by this hardship, Jawed co-founded YouTube.

My thirteen-year-old cousin doesn't know what a 'videotape' is. When I was her age I had lots of them on a shelf in my bedroom, reels of tape contained in black plastic cases, stored in cardboard with the titles written on the side in felt-tip pen. The last physical videotape was made in 2006 — the year I started making videos online.

Google had moved beyond internet searches in the eight years since it began. In 2002 it launched Google News; two years later it debuted an email service called Gmail; and the year after that saw the release of Google Earth, Google Maps, and Google Video, an online space designed in part to host 'amateur media' (things made by people like me). Videos of up to 100 MB could be uploaded, enough to fill the storage space of my old VTech keyboard 781 times.

Less than three weeks after Google Video launched, a few guys — including Jawed — got together to discuss a service of their own (having just left their jobs at PayPal, a worldwide money transfer website). In the same way Google modernised the word *video*, these guys took another old word and gave it new meaning: *tube*. For much of its history, people have referred to television as 'the tube' because the screen was just the end of a bulky electronic device called a cathode-ray tube. The goal of Jawed's new site was, like Google Video, to host videos anyone could upload. *You* were the television. You were the 'tube'.

YouTube launched with the slogan 'Broadcast Yourself' and Jawed became the first to broadcast himself when he uploaded the first video ever on the site. It's a nineteen-second clip of him at the zoo. It's called 'Me at the zoo'.

'Alright, so here we are in front of the, uh, elephants,' Jawed says as he realises he has nothing of interest to say (foreshadowing the many future YouTube stars who would fail to realise the same thing). 'The cool thing about these guys is that, is that they have really, really, really long, um, trunks, and that's, that's cool. And that's pretty much all there is to say.'That's the whole video. At the time of writing, it has fifty million views.

I discovered YouTube about a year after 'Me at the zoo'. It was the middle of 2006 and I'd been using the site for about a week to watch clips of *Family Guy* when I came across some footage of children playing, overlaid with narration and sound effects to make it look like a nature show. It was a homemade amateur clip, the best that whoever had made it could do, and I couldn't stand it. I was about to leave my first hate comment.

YouTube requires you to sign up with them before messing the site with your opinions, so I did what any reasonable internet user does: I registered an account just to express my fury at a stranger about something of no consequence. I needed a unique username, so I made use of my old Digimon friend and called myself 'nerimon'. I knew it would be free because it was a word I'd invented. (And we can all agree it improved on the last word I'd invented, 'emohemian'.)

Seconds later, I posted under the video, 'what a waste of my life'.

The next day, I got a message from the guy who made it: 'fuck you!'

'Well then don't waste my time posting shit on the internet,' I shot back, and then I blocked him, and with that, I became a YouTuber.

YouTube already had a reputation for their comments section by the time I discovered it. When *TIME* declared 'You' their Person of the Year in 2006 due to the rise of online self-expression, they saw fit to mention that 'some of the comments on YouTube make you weep for the future of humanity just for the spelling alone, never mind the obscenity and the naked hatred.' Yet, in this environment, the most popular user on the site was a soft-spoken English pensioner in his seventies called Peter, or 'geriatric1927'.

Peter used his YouTube channel to recount stories of his life direct-to-camera. He called himself 'the internet grandad'. His videos had attracted subscribers, users who choose to be notified whenever one of their favourite creators puts up something new. Peter had twenty thousand subscribers and, in 2006, that made his the biggest channel on YouTube.

Peter's videos hit a soft spot for me because they reminded me of my nan. When I first burst forth into the world, my nan was the first person who held me and the first I ever saw myself; the bond was instant and mutual. When I was young I enjoyed goading her into telling me I was her favourite person, and she always played along even though I was being unreasonable as all hell, giving me a knowing smile as she confirmed that yes, of course, dear, I was her favourite person, more than her own daughters, or her husband, yes, of course, dear. My nan visited us a few times a week, always with a few Walkers crisp packets and chocolate bars and, in later years, a copy of that week's issue of *Nuts*, which I'd asked her to pick up for me on her way over and which she did without complaint. (That is, at least, until my mum overrode her and said I'd have to get them myself. 'I don't mind,' she smiled as Mum lectured her.) Along with my mum, my nan and grandad rounded out my social circle. I spent most of my evenings with them playing card games or sitting with them by the CD player listening to McFly's debut album (which reminded my nan of the Beach Boys).

I used to play weekly gigs in a pub in Romford, giving me the chance to bother people with my original songs. The week after I signed up to YouTube, my nan came to see me play.

'We have a special guest here tonight,' I announced, gesturing to her. She smiled and struggled to her feet. 'Right,' I said, 'now you need to give her a cheer, because not only has she come down tonight to support me, but she just stood up for you and she's got bad knees.' The room erupted in an approving holler.

My dad filmed the gig but I didn't think to put it on YouTube. I didn't put anything there for about six months, even when Google spent over a billion dollars to buy YouTube that November. My reluctance came from a fear of YouTube's unfiltered monsters turning their gaze on me, but I came to realise it might be useful in the same way my bleached hair and terrible gigs were: inviting the harshest available criticism into my life would be an opportunity for growth. I threw the first episode of *The Random Touch* up on my channel and soon received my first ever YouTube comment:

'I want to vomit in terror at your ugliness.'

'How many views has it got, mate?' asked a school friend a few days later.

'About thirty,' I said.

'That's amazing!' he said. 'That's thirty different people that aren't you and they all watched it!'

I can't remember how I got thirty views to my video. I can only conclude YouTube was so underground back then that I stood out simply by being there. On Google Video, you used to be able to type in 'Star Wars' and get me as the first result, prattling on about the prequels in my pants from the armchair in my dining room.

I also got some positive comments, just as extreme as the negative ones. People wrote things like, 'This is genius!!' and 'You are the funniest person in the world.' Internet love felt just as fleeting as internet hate; I let it all roll off me like water off a leaf. My mum thinks this attitude means I'm humble, but it's not that. It doesn't make sense to dismiss the negative stuff while clinging to the positive, especially when it's all coming from people I've never met and who have never met me.

I put my new video series to good use: for my Media Studies exam in college, I was tasked with studying a piece of media to analyse its effectiveness and I picked *The Random Touch* as the subject. This meant I was claiming to my teachers — and the British government — that videos of me in my living room making jokes about *Star Wars* counted as 'media'. To my surprise, I was not only allowed to proceed but got an A for an analysis of my own work.

Whilst making my next episode, I started uploading 'vlogs' (video blogs) about my life, like Peter did. I started them all with an apology: 'Sorry this isn't a proper video,' meaning an episode of *The Random Touch*, 'but I just want to tell you about what happened the other day…' I didn't have a well of life experience to draw from, but I had college anecdotes, things teachers said or badly-worded homework questions I found funny. I took the bits of my life I thought entertaining and shared them in little vignettes.

I'd been feeling a bit bad about wasting their time with such amateurish stuff — these videos were just what happened when I procrastinated from what I was meant to be doing — yet it turned out they were what my audience liked the most. This was a plus, because *The Random Touch* took weeks of editing and required me to watch a whole film, and a vlog is just me rambling off the top of my head and takes about an hour to make from start to finish.

Liberated, I started sharing funny conversations I'd had with friends, newspaper headlines that made me laugh, things I'd overheard on the bus. I used to keep a 'comedy diary' of things I'd thought or noticed, and made a twenty-minute video reading it all out (getting comments from people saying 'I watched the whole thing!', wearing their endurance as a badge of pride). I spent one vlog searching for homoerotic themes in the *Harry Potter* books: 'We all know the phrase "coming out of the closet". Well, he literally lives in a closet before becoming a so-called "wizard",' I said (amongst other such nonsense about broomsticks allowing him to enjoy the feeling of wood between his legs and his glasses making him look a bit like Elton John).

My nan wandered into my room as I finished filming one video.

'Hey, it's my nan!' I said, pointing the camera at her. I flipped the screen 'round so she could see herself. 'Look!'

My nan laughed at her own face. 'Look at that!' she said, grinning at me. 'Washed out old faggot.'

'Washed Out Old Faggot' became my newest video — with a thumbnail of my nan's beaming face — and got hundreds of views and comments.

Recognising my audience's propensity for commenting on my work, I made a video called 'YouTube's Pet Guinea Pig' inviting them to set me challenges I could carry out in future vlogs. Within twenty-four hours people asked me to shave my head, send them money and eat soap. My subscribers were enthusiastic but unhelpful.

As the weeks went on, I uploaded more and more videos to YouTube (or, as I pronounced it in my Essex accent, 'YouChoob', driving my mainly-American audience mad). I also subscribed to other users and watched their work with interest. My favourite creator on the site, an Australian teenager called Caitlin, earned around ten thousand subscribers for her funny, sarcastic videos. She was one of the top hundred most-subscribed users on the site and was featured in her local newspaper. I made a video about Caitlin saying we should be friends and was overjoyed when she messaged back and subscribed to my videos two days later, complimenting me and my work. She became a fan of my videos as I was a fan of hers; I was happy to discover that, online, you get to be the fan *and* the creator.

I knew of few people vlogging in the UK besides Peter and a quirky kid in a lion hat called 'amazingphil', but I thought the whole thing was cool and that, if my videos went well, I could get into my local paper too. Still, they couldn't be my main focus. Who ever heard of someone being successful for chatting about random stuff on the internet?

Instead, I used my videos to help push my main interests forward. I started a series singing original songs and covers, which was much better than gigging at the pub; more people saw it, I could retake the performance as much as I liked and I didn't have to leave the house or put any pants on. The chattier videos were like the banter between tracks and gave people something to watch even if they didn't rate my music.

Once I had enough tracks online, I put the songs on iTunes as an album with the optimistic title *YouTube Tour, Vol. 1*. On a few scattered laptops across the world, a few people still have distorted covers of me warbling my way through Snow Patrol, Coldplay and Oasis songs.

I got this review of the album on iTunes:

> Alex Day is a smashing young chap with a clear rising talent in this industry. His cover tracks are unique and rather nice to listen to; his original acoustic music simply superb. When this boy is a famous man, rubbing noses with people he shouldn't be getting that close to, these tracks will stand as the mark of his humble beginnings, and will be treasured for years to come.

I wrote that. I submitted it to iTunes myself. Always good to start your own balls rolling.

Most of my friends had grown out of MySpace, with its lurid hues and fonts, and my college friend Natalie recommended a new site called Facebook, which did much of the same stuff as MySpace but in a mature dark blue. Facebook made it easy for anyone to share photos, blog posts and videos, as well as play games together and meet people in special interest groups. It was like the internet itself had been distilled and presented in one place.

Launched as a tool for university students, Facebook then swept up an older crowd put off by MySpace's untamed design aesthetic, but the trade-off for elegant design was not being allowed to change it. Every person's page looks the same. You're allowed a little box for a picture of yourself which is the same size and shape as everyone else's little face box, all in the exact same place next to your name (which is written in the same tasteful font and displayed in the same size and colour as everyone else's name). It was far from the wild space of my early days online. Nothing was garish. Nothing was disorganised. Nothing had any individuality. It's not much more than a form you continue filling out. Facebook had designed a uniform for the internet, and the masses were signing up to wear it.

It was 2007 and every smartphone at the time had a physical keyboard and a wheel, or arrow buttons, to navigate a baby-version of the internet called WAP (an acronym for something too boring to bother explaining). The world seemed fine with this, apart from one man who decided it wasn't good enough: in January, after years of rumours filling the pages of the tech media, Apple CEO Steve Jobs took to a Cupertino stage and announced he was going to 'reinvent the phone'. In front of the world's press he unveiled what he called the iPhone, doing away with all the buttons in favour of a giant touchscreen. He swiped to unlock for the first time and revealed the device's tagline: 'The Internet in Your Pocket'.

In the early eighties, when most computers were black screens with lines of code, it was Steve Jobs who introduced the Macintosh, the first home computer with graphics. Instead of the green lines of code, the Mac resembled an office desktop, complete with documents, folders and a trash can. In 1984, Steve introduced the world to the mouse, having to explain concepts like 'cut', 'copy' and 'paste'. I streamed the iPhone event online and watched live while he rewrote the world a second time.

'There are no buttons,' Steve said in mock horror to the assembled crowd, 'so how are we gonna scroll through our music? How do we do this? Well, we just take our finger...' he flicked his finger across the screen, '...and we scroll.' The audience reacted to a man scrolling through his iPhone with a rapturous roar of worship. It might as well have been presented to them by Moses.

Despite the hype, early reviewers of the iPhone bemoaned its lack of Flash support, physical buttons and 2G speed. It didn't matter that we could have Google in our pockets, they said; the internet wasn't fast enough to use it. I wasn't bothered. The only mobile phone I'd ever had was a Nokia 3310 with a tiny green screen and harsh monotonous ringtones. When I dropped it, it wouldn't just crack — the whole thing would smash into several pieces, leaving me to pick up the battery here, the buttons there, the case somewhere else, while the body of the phone lay naked like Darth Vader with his mask off. From that, I queued up to buy the original iPhone on the day of release and found it nothing short of magic that I could now reply to emails while sitting on a bus. Apple had also worked out a deal with Google: the original iPhone shipped with a YouTube player built-in. Overnight, millions of people now had YouTube in their pockets wherever they went. It was a game-changer. Apple has since sold over a billion iPhones around the world.

I finished college that year and my mum drove me to pick up the results. I decided it would make a good video for my mum to read them out to me, so I gave her the document and flicked the camera on while she broke the news that I received an D in Philosophy (bad) and an E in Psychology (worse), propped up by a B I earned in Media Studies by writing about myself for a large part of the exam. The video — which I didn't upload — ended with my mum telling me to work hard and get a degree at university, to which I said I would only go for networking: Ricky Gervais and Stephen Merchant had met at university, as had the members of Coldplay.

My Psychology result was fair (I skipped classes to play Guitar Hero 2) but I was bitter about my Philosophy grade — the combination of the A I got for my essay and the U I got for my exam, both on the same topic — and made a video about it called 'Spoken Exams', detailing an idea I'd had that would solve everything. (It didn't involve me working harder.) I argued for exams to be based on a one-on-one vocal assessment from the teacher, a bit like oral language exams. The science test (for example) would begin with the teacher saying, "Susie, tell me about science" and then diving into areas of Susie's knowledge with follow-up questions based on what she said. Aside from solving the problem of broad understanding going unrecognised due to a poor performance on a narrow question, it would encourage confidence and other social skills from an early age, something I could have done with when I was growing up.

The front page of YouTube at the time had no recommended or sponsored content. It was nothing but a search bar and a playlist of about six videos. YouTube employed a bloke in London called Theo to watch videos all day and select the best and most varied to feature on the front page. Every day, one video would be added to the top of the list and the bottom one would be removed. I know this because after I uploaded 'Spoken Exams', it appeared on the front page of the site.

Although the internet was still growing, YouTube was taking charge of it, overtaking BBC News to become the most viewed website in the country. While the BBC reported on Gordon Brown's sudden takeover as prime minister, more people online wanted to watch clips of *Robot Chicken* and music videos by OK Go. Through the whole of 2007, YouTube alone used more bandwidth than the entire internet had used seven years earlier, and for a few days, everyone who visited it saw me on the front page.

Over the next twenty-four hours, my video got sixty thousand views. My diary entry that day was as follows:

> I have a video on YouTube called Spoken Exams. No need to link to it... YOU CAN JUST GO TO THE FRONT PAGE OF YOUTUBE AND WATCH IT COS THAT'S WHERE IT FUCKING IS!! That's right you cunts, I HAVE JUST BEEN FEATURED!!!!!!!!!

The 'cunts', I assume, were all the people I felt never supported me, people I kept inviting to my acoustic gigs or encouraging to watch my videos but who never bothered. I felt vindicated. After writing that humble acceptance speech, I went to my local newsagent with the pretence of buying a bottle of water, lingering at the counter in the hope he'd exclaim, 'Oh goodness, you're the YouTube guy!' (He didn't. Obviously.)

I've learned over the years that internet rage is like road rage in that they both arise in people with a few screens of glass between them. The sense of detachment leads otherwise kind people to forget each other's humanity and spew the most toxic guff all over the other person's life. We're all capable of it. The dangerous difference is that we're ourselves again once we get out of our cars, whereas these days, the internet's in our pockets. We take the rage into our homes with us.

Having said that, internet hate is a time capsule, preserving a moment of rage that might have dissipated as quickly as it arrived. Getting ten hate comments only means ten people reacted to something with such anger that they felt the need to express it. It doesn't mean ten people hate you right now. Hate can seem permanent online, but only in the sense that a footprint can seem like a boot. When I get hate, I like to imagine my hater is ten years old. For one thing, because it's the internet, they very well could be, but it's effective even if you know they're not. I stepped in front of a businessman on a Tube escalator the other week and he made a point of huffing behind me, so I imagined he was ten, all grumpy with a little suitcase like Bugsy Malone. It cheered me right up.

I tried to bear all this in mind as I found myself on the front of the most popular website in England, with large unkempt hair because I couldn't be bothered to get it cut, wearing eyeliner and an unwashed shirt, blathering into a muffled webcam in low light about how I could reinvent public education. I had four hundred new emails in my inbox to notify me of every new subscriber, message, and comment I'd received — and there were a lot of the latter.

'Cut your hair.'

'Shave.'

'You really think a petition like this would work?'

People were not only commenting to tell me I was an idiot but were making whole video responses to get the message across. A lot of people decided I was gay, which some were against, writing to tell me to stop being so gay, spurring others to reply in my defence: 'He's gay, yeah, so what, leave him alone!'

Random people were adding me on Skype:

> Anonymous: hey stupid cunt
> Anonymous: answaer u fuk
> Anonymous: ur vids r shit
> Me: did you want anything apart from telling me that?
> Anonymous: no
> Anonymous: thats it

I quite liked all of this. Having such a strong impact on people that they made whole videos to tell me I was stupid was a source of great amusement, given they didn't know me at all. It was like watching people stomp over to a portrait of Vincent van Gogh and tell him it's rude to stare. I read most of it without reacting, but I did flare up at a few things.

'Big-headed arrogant twat,' someone wrote.

'But I was on the front page of YouTube,' I couldn't resist retorting, 'so you can suck my penis.' As I read these quotes from my past, I feel embarrassed, but not because I've changed so much I can't identify with my former self. It's embarrassing because I haven't changed that much at all. I almost admire my earlier self for being so brash and exposed, even though I now realise how little is helped by inviting unsupportive or abusive people to suck me off. (Which, now that I think about it, *is* a bit gay.)

Things died down once my video left the front page a week later. To get away from it all, I decided to visit New York, a place I'd always dreamed of visiting. My mum had saved £2 a week for me since I was born and gifted it to me when I turned eighteen — just under two grand — and I wanted to do something memorable with it. I didn't know anyone there, so I made a YouTube video saying I was going and did anyone want to join me? Sure enough, a vlogger called Josh replied and drove to Manhattan for a week to hang out. I met him for the first time in the hostel where we stayed; we had a right laugh sightseeing and gossiping in taxis and bagel places. On Independence Day we went to a pier overlooking the Hudson River and danced to pop music together like idiots for so long that a circle of strangers formed around us. When the lavish fireworks display was over, an American shook my hand and said in his most patriotic voice, 'Happy Fourth of July, man' (presumably not realising I was British and therefore the enemy).

The internet scrutiny machine rolled away from me and on to its next target.

One of my favourite new vloggers was a shy and earnest teenager from Bath, called Charlie, who vlogged about Zelda games, wrote songs about haircuts, and made funny videos about how to make tea. In Charlie's newest video, 'How to get featured on YouTube', he listed the popular video styles of the time — celebrity gossip, dangerous stunts, and 'arty farty stuff', to name a few — and ended with a tip: Make a video about getting featured and hope it gets you featured.

'I don't know if this idea actually works yet,' he said.

It did.

The response to Charlie's video far exceeded the one to 'Spoken Exams'. Because of his superior video editing talent (along with his cute little face in the thumbnail) his video got hundreds of thousands of views, his audience exploded, and his newfound following led to an immediate backlash from other creators on the site, all within a few hours. A thoughtful guy called Myles led the charge, saying it was unfair for hard-working vloggers like him to be overshadowed by someone thrust into the spotlight off the back of one video, discussing at length 'what it means for the community'.

Charlie had a different way of dealing with the attention he was getting; shocking though it might seem, he didn't tell any of his viewers to suck his dick. Instead, as his subscribers grew by the thousands, he took down all his videos and disappeared from the internet. Charlie was a shy boy trying to express himself; carrying on wasn't worth the onslaught it brought.

Charlie's burgeoning creative career might have ended there if it weren't for Myles having a change of heart, reaching out to Charlie and convincing him to return to the site. The two boys decided to organise a public YouTube gathering in London the following month to foster a sense of togetherness. I say 'organise' in the loosest sense. It was as simple as making a video and saying, 'We'll be in Leicester Square at this time if you want.'

About a hundred of us turned up. Almost all of us had cameras; the rest had guitars. Everyone ran around chatting to each other, brainstorming fun things to make, or asking each other to say, shout or sing things for each other's vlogs. People included me in their videos, asked me to collab with them (vlog slang for 'collaborate'), to narrate one of their videos or to help them with new ideas. It felt like my brain had come to life.

Charlie was wearing a grey striped hoodie and an expression of dread. He hovered at the sidelines watching people and was mostly left alone despite the occasional person wanting a chat. Right before his online world blew up, I'd sent him a MySpace message complimenting his work and suggesting that we do something together. I was fortunate that he remembered it and agreed we should hang out.

I'd been asking everyone what superpower they would most want and filming all the responses for a montage video, so that's what I said to Charlie when we first met in-person.

'I'd want the power to edit myself in real life,' he said.

When I got home, I cut all the footage into a twenty-minute video overnight and showed it to my dad (who was astonished at the speed with which I'd cobbled it together) the next day.

'The people I met today are so fucking cool,' I wrote in my diary, 'and it's just hard to watch some of your closest friends leave on trains and planes.' It was the first time I'd experienced people from the internet as more than badly-pixellated faces and blocks of text. We were live and unedited. The screens had been removed. I could see their legs and how far back they went. How had I ever left a hate comment?

Those people on the internet are real.

RELATIONSHIP STATUS

Laura was three inches taller than me. She had back-combed hair, punk badges on her college bag, a dry sense of humour and a drive to do good in the world. She was studying Classical Civilisations and I was studying Philosophy. I fancied Laura and wanted to know if she fancied me, so — suave as ever — I asked a mutual friend to find out if she liked me while I watched from across the room. This he did with a commendable lack of subtlety:

'Are you into Alex?' he asked.

'Why?' said Laura.

'Why do you think?' he grinned. With any trace of mystery removed, Laura and I first kissed on the escalator overlooking Romford car park.

That evening, I logged on to MSN Messenger (my friends still weren't using Skype) to seek counsel.

'I like Laura,' I typed to a friend, 'but I don't know if it's a good idea. I don't know her that well. I wanna take it slow.'

My friend replied, 'You should check Laura's MySpace page.' I loaded it up, scrolled to her 'About Me' box and saw Laura had changed her relationship status from 'Single' to 'In a Relationship'.

'Right,' I typed, 'well that sorts that out then.'

Laura and I got to know each other very well over the summer. Like me, she didn't see the point in giving up all her time to work at a traditional job but, while I was determined to work for myself, her passion was in charity and volunteer work. She spent her time reading online articles about every topic she could think of and would start conversations with things like, 'I just learned this great fact about meerkats.' We teased each other but we never fought. I had stumbled into an easy, happy relationship.

The media were taking notice of YouTube, though their stories amounted to 'Look at this strange thing the kids are doing'; it was still derided by the majority as the 'dogs on skateboards' website (after a 2007 video of a dog on a skateboard racked up over twenty million views). It didn't help that most users at the time were filming themselves reacting to a scat porn video called '2 Girls, 1 Cup', which doesn't scream 'credibility'. I'd heard a news story a month earlier on national radio about a vlog called 'Leave Britney Alone' in which a YouTuber had made an impassioned plea to the media to... well, to leave Britney alone. His hysterical plea garnered millions of bemused viewers laughing at his histrionics. This is why I was so surprised to find Charlie interviewed on *BBC Breakfast* about his videos and featured the following day in *The Telegraph*. I texted him about his newfound media interest, eager to understand how he'd got their attention.

'I just contacted my local paper,' said Charlie. He'd told the *Bath Chronicle* what he was up to and wondered if they'd be interested in writing about him. After they published his story, he was featured on the BBC's local radio station, which led to *BBC Breakfast* inviting him to the studio for a live feature, which led to national radio and press outlets covering him. It's a media tactic called 'trading up the chain'; he had utilised it without even trying.

That afternoon I phoned my local paper, the *Romford Recorder*, telling them I made videos online and had two thousand subscribers, which was more than *The X Factor* had.

'We'll send someone 'round!' said the operator and, to my shock, a photographer turned up at my house twenty minutes later.

'Can we put your YouTube videos on the screen?' he suggested as he snapped me in front of my computer. I loaded the page.

'Maybe hold the mouse?"

I turned back to my desk, placing my hand on the mouse, and he said, 'No, just face me and hold it.' I cupped the mouse in my hand, like a pet, and turned toward him.

'And the keyboard,' he said.

'Hold the keyboard?'

'That's it.'

It seemed he wanted it to be as obvious as possible that this story was computer-related.

I was in the *Romford Recorder* a week later and after the story was published, my nan phoned the paper and asked them to send her their photo of me. She wanted to frame it and put it on her wall. They obliged and up it went. Since then, every time I've been to my nan's house I've had the joy of looking at a photo of myself at age eighteen with mad hair, grinning into the lens, holding my computer mouse up in one hand and my keyboard in the other like I'd just won first prize at a raffle, sat in a tiny room in front of a screen filled with an image of my own face.

Just like Caitlin, I had achieved my dream of being in a newspaper. The article described me as 'website nut Alex Day'.

It was tempting, as one of her viewers, to believe I was important to Caitlin. It's strange to have developed such an attachment to someone who has no real idea who you are. Like me, Caitlin was nothing special; just an awkward teenager. Her journey into the top hundred most-subscribed was no grand scheme. Her story was the same as mine: she didn't take the site seriously and got lucky, making some fun videos that did well and connecting with the right people at the right time.

Caitlin had just uploaded a video about an invite-only party YouTube were throwing in Australia to launch their new regional version of the site. To be considered for entry you had to upload a video explaining what would make you a good choice for a swanky VIP event.

I made my video and, nineteen minutes later, got this message:

> Hey there Alex! Thanks for your response and interest with regard to the YouTube Australia Party in Sydney. You have been officially selected to attend so congrats!

I was surprised it was that easy, and that none of my friends had done the same, until I realised I would still have to pay for my flights and accommodation.

Since our first gathering, the same group of YouTubers were meeting in different parts of the UK about once a month and we were all becoming good friends. The two grand my mum saved for me had largely gone on gatherings in Manchester, Portsmouth and Glasgow, as well as the trip to New York. I had enough left for a trip to Australia but it would be tight.

'I don't suppose I can stay at yours anytime around the party on the 23rd?' I asked Caitlin on MSN.

'Sure,' said Caitlin, 'Come on down. I'll be in Sydney; you can stay with me. PARTY!'

I watched the money roll out of my account as I confirmed my flight and sent Caitlin the details. She agreed to pick me up at the airport.

'I AM IN TERMINAL 1 EXIT D. HOPE TO SEE YOU SOON :)
ALEX X'

That was the message I sent Caitlin when I touched down in
Sydney and it is perhaps the most insecure message I have ever sent. I
wrote 'hope to see you soon' because I didn't know how to turn the
caps lock off and didn't want her to think I was shouting at her; I
wrote the smiley face because I realised 'hope to see you soon'
sounded sarcastic; I wrote my name in case she didn't know who the
text was from; and I wrote the 'x' because signing off with my name
felt too formal. It was a litany of overcompensation.

To further feed my lack of confidence, I waited in the airport a
further two hours before trying Caitlin again. This time, she picked up.

'Hey Alex!'

'Hey, where you at?'

'Well, you know I'm not flying out till tomorrow, right?'

'Well, no,' I said. "I didn't know that.'

There was a short silence.

'Y'know,' I continued, 'seeing as I sent you an email telling you I
was coming this morning and you said to get in touch so you could
meet me.'

'I did?'

'Oh yes.'

'Oh,' said Caitlin. 'Well… welcome to Australia!' she tried. She
was trying even harder than I did in my capitalised insecurity text. 'But
anyway, you've got accommodation sorted, right?'

'No…'

'Oh, Alex!' said Caitlin, as if to say, 'How did you not prepare for
me to fail you like this?'

'I'll just hang out in the airport and wait for you to get here
tomorrow,' I said.

'But where do you plan to stay for this week?'

'With you — you said I could!'

'Did I?'

There was obviously a huge contrast between our respective memories, but Caitlin ended up phoning the guy who organised the event to explain things. A few minutes later, I was talking to the community manager of YouTube.

'Hey, so we've got your accommodation sorted for tonight,' he told me.

'Great,' I said. 'Thank you so much.'

'No problem! So you can just pay them when you get there. It's 118 Australian dollars.'

'Oh.'

I traipsed back to the airport the next day. I walked towards Caitlin as she stepped off the plane and saw in her eyes the fear you reserve for people you don't recognise. At the last second, as I got far too close to be a stranger to her, I saw her memory kick in and the fight-or-flight instinct wash from her eyes. Caitlin opened her arms, greeted me with a warm hug, and said:

'Hey, Adam!'

We went to her room at the Hilton and she played me the *Avenue Q* soundtrack ('The internet is for porn!', a character barked in one chorus) and showed me photos of her friends on her laptop. I had a shower and sang 'Hallelujah', assuming she couldn't hear me; when I emerged, Caitlin was playing the track on her iPhone.

When we got to the party, it was clear YouTube wanted us to feel like we were the future of broadcasting. Caitlin and I were welcomed with a red-carpet entrance, complete with barriers and security. I found this hilarious, loving the idea of walking a red carpet for something as silly as video blogs, while Caitlin rolled her eyes, scoffing at the pomposity. She'd bought a black dress for the party but didn't bother wearing it and ended up going in an oversized *Empire Strikes Back* t-shirt. On a stage, the creator of 'Evolution of Dance' (YouTube's most-viewed video at the time, with a hundred million views) performed his routine live to an appreciative crowd.

Every now and then someone would scream Caitlin's username at her from across the room and she would sigh or murmur, 'Oh god,' scrunching her face up. It all felt a bit unearned.

I was a hit — the guy who came all the way from London. We were in a cordoned-off VIP section, but I wanted to meet as many people as I could, so I wandered off and chatted to everyone I could. One guy I ran into, 'Juanmann', said he'd made a video of himself in Sydney holding a sign saying 'FREE HUGS'. Once he'd uploaded it, the video was shared all over the world and sparked the global 'Free Hugs' phenomenon. Juan had been on the Oprah Winfrey Show to talk about his experiences and he told me, to date, he'd hugged half a million people. He said he wanted to 'put more love into the world'. (Full disclosure: He gave a great hug.)

Twenty-four hours later (at least according to my internal clock), I was in Glasgow for a YouTube gathering. Eager to resist the pedestals and special treatment I'd seen at the party, I got a fun intro for my next video of about twenty people all yelling at my camera lens, 'We hate you, Nerimon!' I wanted to encourage as much equality between my audience and myself as possible. We all went to a park and I played frisbee with a guy called Liam, an exuberant Scotsman who looked and sounded like a teenage David Tennant and seemed to bounce with excitement from foot to foot like Gene Kelly, grinning at all the possibilities life had to offer. (Swigging from two-litre Coke bottles that had been enthusiastically pre-mixed with alcohol, I ended up — to my shame the following morning — telling him I thought we were 'kindred spirits'.)

We all decided to crash at the home of a girl called Mhairi and even though we were strangers, she let every single one of us through the door. I slept in a double bed with eight other people that night.

'So who did you stay with in Glasgow?' my nan asked when I got back.

'A girl called Mhairi.'

'And she's someone you met on eBay?' she asked.

Mhairi was born on Valentine's Day. She was tiny, with dyed red hair, a lip piercing and a loud chirping laugh. I kept going up to Glasgow to visit Mhairi and she came down to visit me in Essex. I wrote her song after song, inspired by her loves of Kate Nash and The Libertines, until I realised something was starting to happen that needed to be addressed.

The next time I saw Laura, I burst into tears on her sofa. She held me and asked me what was wrong. She said I could tell her and that we could get through it no matter what. I was terrified of telling her the truth but I knew I had to. I heaved each word out, rasping for breath:

'I have feelings for Mhairi.'

Laura backed away from me. Her eyes widened. She ran upstairs to her room and I heard the door slam behind her.

Neither of us knew what to do next, so I called my mum.

When she arrived, Laura chatted to her in the living room and I sat upstairs on Laura's bed, taking in her Johnny Depp calendar and her Beanie Baby collection. Then I heard the clomp of Mum's feet coming up the stairs.

The door burst open and Mum hissed, 'What did you do that for?'

When I was younger, my mum was cheated on by her boyfriend Jamie (the computer-fixer). It was part of the reason they split up, but my mum always wished she'd never learned the truth. She found it a struggle to bear the pain of knowing what had happened, so she didn't understand why I'd told Laura about my feelings for Mhairi.

'She was happy,' Mum said. 'And now you feel better because you've done "the right thing", but *she* feels like shit.'

Laura and I broke up, and I dated Mhairi for all of two weeks before calling it off. Her extroverted playfulness felt too invasive at close range. She is a Gryffindor; I am a Hufflepuff. The episode helped me appreciate Laura's chilled-out Ravenclaw inquisitiveness all the more and we soon found our way back to each other, considering the experience a blip on our radar. We were overjoyed to be back together again, and I learned what I thought was a valuable lesson about how to ensure her happiness in the future. I would strive to protect her from pain even if I was causing it, holding on to any burdens so she didn't have to, like Mum had explained to me. When you're young, you think your parents are right about everything. It took me far too long to realise she was wrong about this one.

Since leaving college, I knew I had to either go to university or get a job. My mum could only afford to provide for me if she continued receiving benefits from the government, which only happened if I stayed in education. Otherwise, I'd have to pay for myself, and those TV commissioners still insisted on being coy about the development deals they wanted to give me.

Because I'd been evangelising Apple products to all my friends, Steve Jobs had always been a hero of mine, Apple employees got a pretty sweet store discount, their pay was good, and my mum told me I had to, I figured I might as well get a part-time job working for them. If I had to work for someone else, at least I could do something I was passionate about.

The interview at Apple began with a group session in which each of us was asked to share one thing in our lives we were proudest of. The first person talked about his experience refurbishing a dishevelled church and making it presentable for the community who lived nearby. The second talked about giving his time to charity work in a children's hospital and said it had put his life in perspective. I was third and all I had was, 'I do quite well on YouTube.'

It was enough. Before long I was standing in front of my mum clad in a black t-shirt with a lanyard around my neck telling people I could help them.

'I really don't want to do this, Bean,' I said to my mum.

'I know,' she said. 'I'm sorry.'

The problem wasn't that I was averse to hard work. The problem was I was already doing plenty of hard work, and I was working hard enough without having a job too. People used to upload porn to YouTube, but my videos were getting more views than those; more people wanted to watch me chat about going to Australia than see actual sex between two (or more) people — and just like porn, I wouldn't last long on YouTube if I couldn't keep it up.

UPSTAGED

As jobs go, Apple seemed as good as I could get. They encouraged their employees to be positive and proactive. If someone asked us a question we couldn't answer, we wouldn't say 'I don't know,' but rather, 'Let's find out!' and then set about solving the problem. My coworkers at the store were photographers, writers and comedians, and the place buzzed with supportive energy for personal endeavours. One of my colleagues, Greg, took wedding photos to keep himself afloat while trying to make it as a musician, and used that experience to land a job at the store helping people with photo software on the Mac.

'Alex,' Greg said, 'I went on YouTube the other day and you were on the front page. How did that happen?'

I'd seen someone on LiveJournal (a blogging site) write five things about themselves and then 'tag' five other people to do the same. I thought a creative game of tag would be great fun on YouTube (and a great way to send my audience to new people, as Caitlin had done for me), so I made a video called 'Vlog Tag Game'. Like the LiveJournal post, I shared five things about myself and tagged five users to do the same.

Only three of my tagged users made their own videos but it was enough; they each tagged five people and the branches continued to increase. Viewers loved watching where it would go next and were desperate to be tagged themselves. In a week, the concept spread all over YouTube, right up to the most-subscribed vloggers (the most obvious targets for tagging), all of whom started their videos with a version of, 'This is Nerimon's tag game!' and linked to me or the video that tagged them. Over time, a chain of videos developed across YouTube that always led back to me. It was the equivalent of doing a collab video with everyone on the site. In a week, my subscribers tripled.

I infuriated one person so much with this sudden surge of attention that they took the time to create the account 'nerimonisgay', littering my videos and those of my 'tags' with comments.

'He only started the game so he can have sex with you,' he said to a girl called Steph (an interesting charge from someone claiming I was gay).

'I sure as hell hope so!' replied Steph.

Once again YouTube featured my video on the front page, which is where Greg saw it. Overall my vlog tag video got half a million views and the *Evening Standard* featured me on a list of 'London's top ten video stars' — a remarkable achievement for someone who lived in Essex.

When I explained to him what had happened, Greg doubled down on his efforts to get a shout-out for his channel, where he uploaded videos showcasing his music. That evening I checked out his channel and found that Greg was making badly-filmed webcam videos, hunching over his guitar as he sang his heart out on his original songs. His work was raw, authentic and powerful, and he had just four subscribers. I couldn't believe so few people had discovered him. A few thousand people were watching me make self-referential tosh while someone with actual talent was going unrecognised.

Greg ran up to me beaming the next day, saying he owed me free drinks forever. I had made a fifty-second video telling my audience to watch and subscribe, and Greg gained a thousand subscribers overnight. My audience filled his videos with comments like 'Nerimon recommended me. I love your work.'

Off the back of his new YouTube audience, Greg was later able to quit the Apple Store to pursue his career as a musician full-time. He got a manager, moved to New York, signed with Warner Music, had a number one single in the Netherlands and wrote the winner's song for American Idol in 2012. It became the most successful American Idol song of all time, selling five million copies and earning him one of those big gold discs. And all I'd done was take less than a minute out of my life to tell some people to check him out.

One winter afternoon, Charlie came into the Apple Store effusing about a YouTube channel I'd never heard of called 'vlogbrothers'. I pulled up their newest video and saw a thirty-year-old man called John talking into the camera at a rapid pace. 'Good morning Hank, it's Tuesday,' said John. Why was he calling his audience 'Hank'? He seemed odd. What did Charlie see in this guy?

The vlogbrothers channel, I later learned, was a collaborative project between two brothers, John and Hank, who made video messages back and forth every weekday for the whole of 2007. Theirs was the first 'collab channel' on YouTube. The goal of the project, which they called Brotherhood 2.0, was to foster a more genuine brotherhood between the two by ceasing all text-based communication for a year — no emails, texts or Facebook messages — and conversing instead through daily vlogs. They built an audience by exhibiting their natural passions for knowledge, particularly science and literature; Hank was an environmental tech blogger and John was an author of two young adult books. Charlie, I think, felt an affinity with Hank's goofiness, hyper-verbal songwriting and love of science. I became more inspired by John, who seemed more charming, with a deadpan sense of humour and an intense passion for his art.

John and Hank called their viewers 'Nerdfighters', not in the sense of fighting nerds, but fighting for nerds (as in 'freedom fighters'). They encouraged viewers to 'imagine people complexly' and their rallying cry was 'Don't forget to be awesome,' most commonly stated as "DFTBA!" The vlogbrothers blew up when Hank, in anticipation of the final *Harry Potter* book being released, wrote and uploaded the song 'Accio Deathly Hallows'. The silver claw of destiny closed around his video; 'Accio Deathly Hallows' was featured on the front page of YouTube, plucking John and Hank from online obscurity and dumping them into the public hurricane of veneration and bile.

Five teenage girls were inspired by the vlogbrothers to start a collab channel of their own called 'fiveawesomegirls'. Like John and Hank, they were fans of *Harry Potter* and a related movement called 'wizard rock' made up of bands with names like Harry and the Potters, The Butterbeer Experience, and Oliver Wood and the Remembralls who wrote and performed songs about the stories. Charlie and I couldn't resist starting the fiveawesomeguys channel a few weeks later, joining forces with two Americans — Alan and Todd — and a northern boy, 'JohnnyDurham19'. (I'm ashamed to say it took me about a year to realise his name wasn't Johnny Durham. I thought it was just a cool name, like Johnny Knoxville. I later learned Johnny Knoxville isn't his real name either and my mind felt like a tsunami had happened to it.)

I was spending more and more time with Charlie; I was the Bert to his Ernie. He crashed on my bedroom floor when he stayed at mine, making a cocoon from my spare duvet. I would watch him playing my old Playstation games for hours while I ate pizza and chatted to our friends online.

I visited Charlie at his home in Bath, too, and I loved it. Anywhere that isn't near London is like Narnia to me. I would say things like, "Wow, Charlie, you have McDonalds here," pointing like I was at Legoland, and then ask what time the sun set or worry whether or not I had a phone signal.

I was at Charlie's when we filmed our first videos for fiveawesomeguys and it was the first time either of us filmed a video in front of someone else. We sat opposite each other with our laptops open and webcams on, trying to contain our self-consciousness. I loved Charlie, but don't think I'd have got on with his on-camera persona, who was more like a peppy school teacher, the sort of person I'd expect to find wearing a propeller beanie hat. I don't think he'd have got on with 'Nerimon' either, who I played up as a snobby and sarcastic character.

Our online personas weren't false, but they were only one facet of our real selves. The real Charlie was quieter and more mischievous; when I asked him if Bath had a bus service, he almost had me convinced they ride around the town on rented tricycles until I saw his bashful smile. When I was due to have my hair cut short, we concocted an elaborate ruse for Charlie to 'reveal' on fiveawesomeguys that I was wearing a wig and implore me to show my 'real' hair in my next video. I'd already filmed a bunch of videos in advance with my absurd mop of long hair, so for about a month I uploaded up-to-date videos to fiveawesomeguys and pre-recorded videos to nerimon, claiming I was 'still wearing the wig on the main channel because they don't know the truth'.

Our audience suspected foul play, but as the weeks went on, they lost all sense of reality. The comments sections read like we'd locked our subscribers in a dark room and set it on fire. Nobody could figure out if we were telling the truth or not. I even had a colleague at Apple say to me, 'You had that long hair at work. I can't believe you were wearing the wig even then.'

YouTube became like the video games Charlie and I played together, where the 'high score' was our subscriber numbers. I had ten thousand subscribers now and Charlie had droves more, and when our group of online friends referenced each other in videos, or made stuff with us, the collective number of viewers would rack up. (I think this is where they got the idea for the Avengers movies.)

I was having much more fun than most of my peers, who did all the mourning and none of the organising. When YouTube removed their 'Broadcast Yourself' slogan from the site, several YouTubers took to their cameras to blast the audacity, whinging that the site had changed and was becoming business-minded and selling out and wouldn't be the same now. They demanded YouTube fill them in on future changes, or at least listen to the 'community'. I understood why people felt marginalised, but the site is bound to be business-minded. It's a business. I didn't expect anything I hadn't worked hard for.

YouTube's expanding universe was — like everything else — a lot bigger in America. In the US, Google had been running what they called the Partner Program for the last six months, allowing hand-picked users to run ads on their videos and make money from the revenue. One of the most successful partners in America was Tay Zonday, who wrote and performed the song 'Chocolate Rain', a covert commentary on racism that got about fourteen million hits. 'Chocolate Rain' was so successful that Dr Pepper made a drink around it — Cherry Chocolate Rain — and got Tay to promote it in commercials. (Tay's video was more successful than the drink ended up being.)

I was in the bath when I took a phone call from Jamie, the editor of YouTube — a title that sounds like it was invented for a sketch show character with spidery hands typing on a keyboard stomach and a big screen face like a deformed Teletubby — asking if I wanted to become a YouTube partner. This silly thing I'd been enjoying in my spare time would now be a silly thing that earned me money in my spare time. I was in.

Jamie wanted me to speak to the press about the program's expansion into the UK, but I was instructed not to reveal how much I would earn. This was an easy request to comply with because to this day I still don't understand how much I earn. I only know it varies based on how much the advertiser spends, which means certain ads will be more or less valuable and there is no fixed rate, none of which stopped a journalist at the *Guardian* from begging me, 'Go on, tell us!' while I splashed around telling him no like a good boy (because I was still in the bath). So it was that, amongst a flurry of press attention, I officially became the first person in the country to make money from YouTube videos.

The media's growing interest in YouTube led the BBC to commission a head-to-head interactive variety show called Upstaged, described with every buzzword I know; 'innovative', 'multi-platform' and 'an entertainment event' complete with 'red button content' and 'airing on BBC Three'. For the show, two giant glass boxes were built next to each other in Bristol with a stage inside each one. You auditioned online to enter one of the boxes and do your thing (whatever that was) for eight hours, while someone else in the other box did theirs. People could watch the livestream of either box and vote online (or via the remote control's red button) on which act they wanted back the next day. You could also vote in real life by pressing a big button in front of the box, which I assume no-one did.

Some bright spark had decided we YouTubers were ideal for this sort of thing; a bunch of us received messages from the producers encouraging us to apply. 'It's like having your own studio where you can broadcast what you want to the nation live on the internet,' they said, which was to say, exactly what we were doing already, but we had to go to Bristol.

The show offered a ten grand cash prize for the winner but it was clear we were being baited into a popularity contest, pitting our audiences against each other and providing huge ratings for the show in the process. The only winner would be whichever executive at the BBC got a bonus for thinking of something so bloody modern. We all rolled our eyes, seeing right through it (insert your glass box joke here). The allure of being on a TV show held no interest when we could be the star of our own show on the internet — and make money doing it, thanks to the new partnership program.

The only person who disagreed was community enthusiast Myles, who had something more interesting in mind. Instead of competing against each other, Myles proposed we combine our audiences to compete as one group, win the ten grand, use some of the money to throw our audience a huge gathering to thank them for supporting us and split the rest between us for our trouble. A month later, me and eight of my YouTube friends rocked up to Bristol and entered the box together, having teamed up as the 'YouStage Vloggers' — the equivalent of a supergroup — to take on the show itself. Being on a reality show was of little interest; overthrowing one was much more fun. (We entered the show on Valentine's Day, leaving Laura alone in London. I saw an advert in a shop window in Bristol that said 'This Valentine's Day, spoil the one you love,' and I thought, *I have spoiled it; I won't be there.*)

In addition to the idea of applying jointly, Myles had spotted a weakness in the BBC's voting system: instead of voting only once a day, as you'd expect, each person could cast a new vote every three minutes. We were in the box for eight hours, carrying out the equivalent of a telethon for a party our audience could attend with us for free, not to mention chatting with them every night on our webcams to discuss what worked and what didn't. They watched us live by the thousands and voted every three minutes without fail, surging our numbers ahead of the other contestants. *Upstaged* turned out to be the perfect name for the project because that's what happened to it every moment we were involved. We destroyed this show.

The BBC alleged they could do nothing about this, praising it for being part of the 'high-risk viral multimedia democracy millennial' nature of *Upstaged*; they had no control and the audience would decide everything. This wasn't quite true since the BBC were in charge of editing highlights footage every day, allowing them to push for other acts to win by showing them at their best (and us at our worst). This was clearest in the final, when we were pitted against acoustic singer-songwriter 'Don1977', your textbook reality show contestant: he shut his eyes and clenched his fists during every moment of tension, cried every time he got through to the next day, jabbered that he couldn't believe he'd got this far and said he would give the winnings to his mum. The production team made use of the daily recap episodes on

BBC Three (which condensed the eight-hour broadcasts into ten-minute highlights reels) to sell him as the deserving choice, selecting all the shots of us looking like bumbling, untalented twerps — which is not to say we *weren't* bumbling, untalented twerps, just that the show's editors were happy to emphasise it.

Scott Mills (a DJ for BBC Radio 1) had been roped in to present the finale live in front of the two boxes, doing his best to pretend it wasn't abundantly clear who the savvy online audience would declare the winner. During a piece to camera, Scott read his lines off an autocue, which I wouldn't have known if my friend Jazza, standing next to him in the audience, hadn't lip-synced every word of Scott's speech, both of them staring down the lens as their mouths moved in eerie unison.

On the *Upstaged* website the following morning, the BBC concluded the show with grace and impartiality: 'Don1977 went head-to-head with Youstage Vloggers... and Youstage won! It just goes to show, it really is all about who you know.' No further seasons of Upstaged were ever commissioned.

I got out of the box with my share of £10,000 and discovered two things: Jessica Alba had played my five-fact tag game, and I had been fired from the Apple Store.

When I was called in to speak with the managers, they played several of my YouTube videos back to me, highlighting my open discontent with customers who had a penchant for taking iPhone cases out of their packaging, jamming their phones into them, moaning, 'These don't fit mine,' and leaving the whole mess in a pile on the shelf for me to reassemble.

'People go, "Well, it's their job to clean it up",' I moaned in my vlog. 'You don't get that with other professions. I don't start a fire and then ring 999 saying, "You'll be pleased to hear I got some work for ya".' The managers paused here and asked me what I had to say for myself. Viewed through their eyes it looked a lot less funny (and a lot less like a valid point). Talking about my work at the store for any reason violated the agreement I'd signed when I got the job; I thought that meant exposing inside secrets, not exposing frustrating customers, but the line was made clear.

'We don't want people to avoid the store because they think they might be made fun of on the internet,' my manager told me.

Well they won't be if they put the cases back in their packaging, I thought it best not to reply.

A friend once told me one of the biggest hindrances of my generation is that we've been raised by parents who love us. The result is we are wilful and entitled, with little tolerance for doing anything we don't like because we don't develop a real understanding of what it means to suffer. After spending a few days pratting around in a glass box in Bristol ruining a songwriter's dreams, I was happy to lose my job and didn't intend to get another one.

Recalcitrant as ever, I asked my mum if she could see any way to support me while I pursued my own aims. I'm lucky my mum loves me enough to find a way to make me happy. We're more alike than I thought — like me, she decided she would get it done and worry about how to do it later.

'Alright,' she said. 'If you work at it, I can give you a year.'

A NEW GENRE OF MUSIC

For my nineteenth birthday, I organised a YouTube gathering in London and called it 'Nerifest'. Hundreds of strangers chanted Happy Birthday at me in the middle of Leicester Square. I discovered at Nerifest that vloggers had become more image-conscious than I ever imagined possible. People now introduced themselves by handing me business cards for their YouTube channels. They'd started customising the thumbnails of their videos to pull viewers in, made sure never to swear (or beeped out their swearing) to appeal to a family-friendly audience, and ended their vlogs by telling their audiences, 'Don't forget to comment and subscribe.' YouTube used to have ranking lists showing the most-viewed, subscribed and commented videos each day, week and month, broken down by country and genre (comedy, music, politics, and so on). While the site was growing, people found new videos to watch by clicking on those lists and seeing what was doing well, so it made sense people wanted to get on them. Even so, I found their implicit suggestion that I'd simply 'forgotten' to engage with them to be arrogant and calculated.

By contrast, a trend of naked vlogging had also gone 'round the site. People would film themselves nude (shoulders up, tasteful) to illustrate the openness of the medium. For my newest video I planned to sit naked, in frame, with my bits out and everything, knowing it would violate the Terms of Service and my account would get deleted, because I thought it would be funny. It would be a five-second video of me saying, 'I didn't know how naked you had to be so I wanted to make sure I did it right. Bye.' I would live on in infamy, particularly with those lucky — or unlucky — few who got to see the video while it was (ahem) still up, and go out on a glorious high, never making a video again and being remembered, literally, as the original YouTube dick. I couldn't bring myself to do it in the end but I considered it in a lot of depth. I wasn't printing business cards, is the point I'm trying to make. In any case, these 'career' YouTubers were rejected by the vast majority of viewers. When one friend needed help affording a laptop to continue making vlogs for her subscribers, she set up a donation button for people to contribute and mostly received comments telling her to get a job.

At the same time, YouTube was beginning to attract mainstream interest here and there in 'the real world'. In early 2007 Barack Obama announced his intent to run for the United States presidency in a YouTube video. Over the next two years his race against John McCain for the presidency played out all over YouTube, and the Guardian called Obama 'the first YouTube politician'. When CNN collaborated with YouTube for a presidential debate involving questions submitted from the public, Vanity Fair declared the whole thing 'the YouTube election'.

My main exposure to the election came from a guy called Michael Gregory who autotuned political debates for his YouTube series *Auto-Tune the News*. Michael's channel, The Gregory Brothers, had only three hundred subscribers, far less then he deserved, and I sent him a message saying I loved his work, sharing it with my audience in the hope I could provide the same boost I'd given Greg from the Apple Store.

YouTube exposure also helped John when his community of Nerdfighters banded together to get his third book, *Paper Towns*, onto the *New York Times* Bestseller List. It was the first of his books to do so and led to a signing tour of Barnes & Noble stores across America, where John would read from his book and answer questions while his brother Hank would play songs from his self-recorded album *So Jokes*. On the day his previous book, *An Abundance of Katherines*, was released, John said he went to a Barnes & Noble and they didn't have it.

With his signing tour announced, Charlie and I had advance knowledge of where John would be, and the Partner Program gave us an income with which to be spontaneous.

'We should go, mate,' I said to Charlie as his mum shaved our heads. (This was Charlie's idea; we both clipped our locks off and our audience donated a collective five thousand pounds to Cancer Research UK.)

'I don't wanna spend that much,' said Charlie.

'I'll pay for your flight,' I shrugged. Charlie winced at the struggle to be decisive.

'When is it?'

'This weekend.'

'Oh,' said Charlie. 'I'm supposed to be meeting the Queen this weekend.'

There was a short silence.

'She's going to Google HQ in London for a visit,' Charlie explained, seeing my shock at his nonchalance. 'They invited me to shake her hand, or whatever. I'd rather meet John.'

'Yeah, but... you sure, mate?'

'I mean sure, she's the Queen,' Charlie said, 'but what's she ever done?'

Two days later, we were in Manhattan.

By this point, Charlie and I had both signed up to a new platform called Twitter. (Their CEO defined the word 'twitter' as 'a short burst of inconsequential information', the most apt description of it I've ever heard.) Twitter lets you share 140-character bulletins called 'tweets' and was the first to make use of the evolving technology we carried in our pockets — they made it so tweets could be sent and received by text message. Tweets were even limited to 140 characters as that was the maximum amount you could send in a text message at the time. Even people with old Nokias could tweet. It was like sending a text to all your contacts at once, friends and strangers alike.

Twitter eschewed the mutual 'I add you, you add me' dynamic of Facebook in favour of one person 'following' another with no need for acknowledgement or permission, including some pioneering celebrities. If I followed Barack Obama (who, with around 50,000 followers, was the most popular user on the site), his personal updates would pop up as text messages on my phone as if we knew each other. What's more, you could tweet at anyone with an account, even if they didn't have the foggiest idea who you were. We could text Obama back. (Not all celebrities were so forward-thinking; Charlie and I joined one year before Twitter's most famous and notorious user, realDonaldTrump.)

That summer, Apple released a 3G-capable iPhone and opened an App Store for people to make and distribute their own apps; people downloaded apps for Twitter in droves and began reading tweets and replies in an unending stream of chatter. A world of conversation began living in our pockets wherever we went. 'Trending topics' showed the most popular discussion points of the day. Replies were collected in a single timeline. Social networks were becoming the first place for people to get (or make) news stories and I noticed the terminology started to change — people began to refer to social networks as 'social media'.

Charlie and I tweeted during our New York trip, but we were careful to make our messages ambiguous enough to keep the internet from knowing where we were, fearful of spoiling our surprise to John and Hank. We even fiddled with the settings to make sure our tweets weren't tagged with our location. Still, when two girls recognised Charlie in Toys "R" Us, they shared the photo on Twitter and people started speculating that we might be in town.

We walked into Barnes & Noble that evening and approached the waiting crowd to look for empty seats, but it was packed. Everyone looked at us, whispering to each other, and Charlie and I sat down feeling as though we had gone to a zoo and somehow became an attraction. Someone shouted "Nerimon!" and when I glanced in their direction, at least ten other pairs of eyes were looking back at me. Word made it backstage that we were there and Liane (from the fiveawesomegirls) appeared at our side. 'Hank and John wanna see you,' she said.

'Oh my god!' said John when we walked through the door, his face exploding with joy. Before I could say anything, I was scooped off my feet by Hank, who had run up to us like a puppy to give us each a hug. We took photos together; they looked even more excited to be standing there than we did. John was overjoyed knowing we'd travelled so far on short notice just for his book, and became ecstatic to learn he was higher in Charlie's esteem than the Queen of England.

'Can I sign those?' said John, pointing to the pile of his books I had with me.

'Of course!' I grinned, passing the stack over to him. 'You know I wanna write one day too.'

'Do you have a favourite?'

'*An Abundance of Katherines*,' I said, pointing to his second book.

John smiled, scribbled in the hardcover and handed it back to me. He'd written 'To Alex — a fellow author'. I looked up at him, delighted, as he continued to return each book with a different personalised message, thanking me for being there and urging me not to forget to be awesome.

Moments later, John and Hank emerged to start the signing and John cried, 'I can't believe Charlie and Nerimon came all the way from England!' to whoops and claps from the crowd. This broke some kind of barrier between us and the rest of the audience; they felt more comfortable looking and we felt more comfortable being looked at, now that our overlords had allowed it. While John's signing queue got underway (and Hank got to work selling copies of his album), people started asking Charlie and me to sign copies of *Paper Towns*. Charlie refused, saying he couldn't sign someone else's book; I grabbed a Sharpie and took to the task with relish.

After that, people asked us for photos or to record their voicemail messages for them. I signed a glove, a camera and the back of a phone. Our crowd became so large that the organiser at Barnes & Noble improvised a separate signing table next to John and Hank and moved us behind it. People queued to meet John, finished up at his line and joined ours. It became the *Paper Towns* Book Launch and Alex and Charlie Signing Experience 2008.

'Hey, who are you?' one kid said to me on his way out the store.

'I'm no-one!' I beamed. The kid walked out, confused.

I wanted to follow John across America on the whole tour, meeting the Nerdfighters and lapping up the energy at every show. It was my second trip to New York and I loved every minute. It seemed Charlie did too; when we got home, he made a video about the trip called 'Best Friends', about how he had a best friend for the first time in his life.

Charlie had also uploaded a song called 'Blink' about his favourite *Doctor Who* episode of the same name. It got me thinking. The Nerdfighters shared a love of the 'wizard rock' bands who sang about *Harry Potter*; I'd thought of doing the same but I didn't want to be just another *Harry Potter* band. Charlie's song gave me the idea to start a band of our own doing songs about *Doctor Who*, ensuring we could be the start of something new. Not ever doing things by halves, I then made a video saying with my usual humility that I had 'just invented a new genre of music' and was creating the founding band of a new musical concept called Time Lord Rock, or 'Trock'. That's right: a new musical concept. Things are much easier to achieve, I've found, when you don't realise they're impossible.

Along with Charlie (who jumped on board as soon as I told him the idea), we also recruited our friend Liam, the kid I'd called my kindred spirit back in Glasgow. We figured his striking resemblance to a young David Tennant would be a useful ingredient in our band; we neither knew nor cared whether he had any musical capability. Liam shared the news with a friend of his we all knew as Ginger Chris, who seemed offended.

'Why didn't you ask me to be in the band?' said Ginger Chris.

'I didn't know you liked *Doctor Who*,' I said.

'I love it!'

'Oh, okay,' I said. 'Yeah, be in it then.'

Together, we called ourselves Chameleon Circuit. (The rest of the band were not on board with my first suggestion, Guitardis.)

Along with my announcement video I wrote and debuted a song, set to the *Doctor Who* theme music, called 'An Awful Lot of Running'. Within hours, new MySpace pages were springing up from other users making their own Trock bands, debuting new songs they'd recorded on their laptops minutes earlier. On the back of this, I emailed the media office for *WIRED* and got them interested enough to write an article online the very next day. It outlined Trock and described me as being 'at the vanguard of the movement'.

As we pressed on with redefining music as we know it, John continued his book tour across the United States with Hank sharing songs from his album at every stop. Like his videos, *So Jokes* was fast-paced and colloquial, with spoken tracks introducing songs or divulging their meaning. Hank made the CD exclusive to the tour, but saw a huge demand from the Nerdfighters across the rest of the world who couldn't attend the signings but wanted to own the album (and to obtain that most coveted prize, a signed copy). Hank had no idea how to get his CD out on such a large scale and saw this wasn't just a problem for him but for lots of online creators with growing audiences. There needed to be an easier way for artists to get CDs to people without spending all their time buried in envelopes and shipping labels. So, partnering with Alan (one of our fiveawesomeguys), Hank established a new distribution label for YouTube musicians. He called it DFTBA Records.

The label was brought into existence to distribute Hank's album but he and Alan also planned to 'sign' other artists, offer advances, order products, handle shipping, pay royalties and do all the other things a traditional label did. I emailed Hank, and Chameleon Circuit became the first act signed to his label. It wasn't bad for a two-day-old band; now we just had the small matter of making the actual music. We turned to our network of friends from gatherings and found a grime artist called NSG. Although he volunteered to make our album for free, we told him we would split the profits with him equally as though he were a fifth member of the band (which he might as well be; I'd only heard half the band sing).

NSG promised to make the album sound 'current' and 'credible', playing me a Kooks song as a reference for the tracks we were working on. The four of us — even Ginger Chris, who I'd never met — travelled from our homes across the country to NSG's home studio in Hackney. Chris played us two songs he had written on the ukulele and we shared a collective grin, relieved he could both sing and write songs (very useful skills to have in a band). Mhairi, still a close friend of mine, came to stay with us for one of the sessions and sing on one of the songs. We set up a webcam to livestream our work every day so our audiences could watch the album take shape.

Through these livestreams I met a girl called Penny. She stood out to me because she was witty and she teased me, and I was becoming increasingly fond of people who made it clear they didn't take me seriously amongst the sea of more ardent subscribers. Penny, like Charlie, made fun of how I saw the world and didn't seem impressed to be around me, which I valued a great deal. I arranged for Penny to come to our recording sessions and she fit right in, singing on tracks and making us laugh. We made plans to see each other again.

When I got home, I had an email waiting from NSG:

> Hey dude can I ask a favour before we move on
> with the Trock Project. I was wondering if you
> could upload my music video to your nerimon
> youtube page man and link it to my youtube page.
> Its a good music video and I appreciate all the help

I could get man! Feel free to put ad revenue on it man, get a bit of cash coming in...

I really appreciate you doing this man! Your helping me out a lot on this man, Music is my life man and I need all the help that I could get!

thanks a lot dude
NSG

I replied, telling him the email made me uncomfortable, as though he was holding our album hostage, and that, while I adored his music and his work on the album, my channel was not for hire. I said I would be praising and plugging him all over my channel when the album was released ('Every person who buys this is listening to an 11-track advert for your production skills and you're fantastic at what you do') and that I hoped he understood.

He replied:

hey man its just a small favour to ask... these are well thought of really creative videos dude. Besides you will be helping me out man. You helped out someone once man i remember in the past. Besides other peeps have helped me out before...

You can make a lot of difference man.

I again told him no.

A few days later Charlie made the three-hour trip from Bath to record one of our songs with NSG. A couple hours after he was supposed to arrive in Hackney, he knocked on my door in Essex.

'You're back early,' I said.

'Yeah,' said Charlie. He held out a hard drive.

'What's that?'

'Our album.'

I let Charlie in and made him a cup of tea while he told me about his meeting with NSG, who handed him all the files for the half-finished album on a hard drive as soon as he arrived and then sent him away.

'He was very nice about it,' shrugged Charlie.

For several months I took the files to various people in the hope of finishing the album but none of them could emulate NSG's extensive setup of plugins. All the parts had been recorded (apart from one song of Charlie's) but nothing was mixed, instruments needed to be added and vocals were cutting in and out. DFTBA were promised an album and the initial hype over my new genre of music was dwindling.

In a last-ditch effort, our fiveawesome friend Alan — now our record label boss — sent him this email:

Hey NSG,

I was hoping I could ask you a small favor. Alex tells me that he can't get the Logic project files to work correctly on anyone else's computer because of missing soft synths and plug-ins; your set-up is the only one that will work.

There's only one day's work left on the project before we can release their CD.

Can we work something out to get this finished? Can you give access to your computer to someone else for a day so they can finish these tracks for us? Or can you Export all tracks as audio tracks so we can finish mixing without plug-ins and soft synths? (I'm told this is as easy as clicking one button and letting it run while you sleep or shower or whatever)

We'd be happy to pay you for the one day of production time that's left.

I'm begging. It's been months and there's only one day of work left to finish it. It makes very little sense to deny us this whole album based on one day worth of work. Let me know your rate. Or if you'll agree to either of the above scenarios.

Thanks.
Alan

He got a reply fifteen minutes later:

Sorry this doesn't interests me.
thanks
NSG

To make myself feel better, I spent most of my time with Charlie and Penny. The three of us wound each other up, made each other laugh and watched each other's favourite movies together. Even though they lived nowhere near me (or each other), we all met up regularly and crashed at each other's houses. I bought a ukulele (the official instrument of the internet) and bought Penny one too, decorated with an image of Spongebob Squarepants (the official cartoon of the internet — Adventure Time wasn't a thing back then). I made sure not to tell Laura of my growing fondness for her, lest I forget my mum's lesson about happy relationships.

REGENERATING

Not wanting to talk to Laura about Penny, I confided in my online friend Denise (another of the fiveawesomegirls). Denise was graceful, imaginative and adventurous. Like me, she had a crush on a mutual friend of ours, so we tried to advise each other as best we could. We challenged each other to communicate in as many ways as possible — texting, tweeting, 'poking' each other on Facebook, sending each other YouTube and Skype messages, leaving comments on each other's videos and more. Having bonded over our respective crushes through long email and Skype chats, Denise and I developed feelings for each other, and not wanting to leave my future waiting, I booked a ticket to fly to America and meet her in person.

Laura and I had a wonderful thing going and I adored her. I wished over and over again that my desires for other people would go away and that I could be faithful to her without letting myself be strayed by new desires, but I couldn't seem to help them when they arose in me. I felt out of control. We broke up again the day before the flight and, after we met in Washington, I started dating Denise. It didn't feel like a long-distance relationship. She was as close to me as anyone else I knew, thanks to the technology we kept in our pockets.

It was Valentine's Day a week after I returned from Washington. I couldn't spend the day with Denise and it would have been too awkward spending it with Laura, so I invited Penny to London for the day to hang out and have fun. We wandered around the city, sitting on the backs of vacant trucks and trying on novelty sunglasses at market stalls. It felt like we were in our own little bubble outside of reality, where it was Valentine's Day only for us, as though we'd stolen it from the rest of the world. Of course, it partly felt like that because I didn't acknowledge anything outside the bubble. Penny knew I'd broken up with Laura but not that I was involved with Denise. I'd kept that fact from the internet, feeling it would be insensitive to Laura to rub a new relationship in her face on social media so soon after the old one ended, but I also knew the lack of information created a unique window where Penny considered us unattached and free to explore any feelings we might have had. When Penny kissed me on the southbound platform of Camden Town tube station, I was thrilled and kissed her back.

I was eighteen, opportunistic and too excited to think clearly. I knew this might be our only chance to act on our feelings and didn't want to miss it. I didn't want a relationship with Penny, even though I wanted to keep exploring our friendship more intimately. She and I were best friends and I should have treated her better. I ended up telling her I was getting together with Denise, but only after we hung out and acted on our feelings a couple more times. I can't remember her reaction, which just about says it all. In the end, I learned my lesson, but it took many more people getting hurt before I confronted it.

My mum had somehow supported me for another twelve months but my time was up. I'd started making money from YouTube in that time and now I needed some of it to pay the rent. I did some quick maths and discovered living with Denise for two months and paying towards her bills was cheaper than two months living with my mum in Essex, even with what the flight would cost. Without any further thought I booked a flight, packed my suitcase and moved to Seattle (leaving my mother weeping at the airport terminal behind me).

Seattle is cleaner than London. It has frequent outbursts of rain, but between the clouds the sky is a clearer blue. The streets contain many cars and the surrounding concrete slabs support the foot traffic of a city centre but I never felt like I was being rushed anywhere. I breathed fresher air and partook in a constant flow of free water fountains mounted on every inch of the city. I walked into stores and heard people greet me in their optimistic accents; they sounded as though they cared whether I had a good day or not, in contrast to back home where people ask each other if they're alright and never intend to hear the answer.

Denise and I shared a love of music. I was on Denise's sofa when she looked up from her Twitter feed and cried, 'Oh my god, Michael Jackson died!' We spent the afternoon playing his songs on repeat, singing and dancing to the greatest hits of the King of Pop, and I realised for the first time how phenomenal the calibre of his work was. I also fell in love with The Beatles through Denise's influence, a band it turned out I'd loved all my life but never realised the songs I'd loved were theirs. (If the rest of my life can be as full of joy as Paul McCartney is when he shakes his little head on the harmonies of *She Loves You*, I'll have a very happy life indeed.)

Over the summer, Ford approached a hundred American vloggers for a three-month campaign around their new-look Fiesta model. Denise was one of the people selected and got to use the car for free all summer long. A couple months had passed and the two of us were, by this point, in a public relationship. We made use of Twitter to create an interactive road trip, asking our followers to vote for things like which album we should play next in the car or which highway we should take at the next junction. People would tweet us back their opinions and we followed their collective will. We ended up singing full-volume to Lily Allen songs down the freeway, holding snakes at a reptile house and visiting a nutcracker museum in a Bavarian village called Leavenworth.

My days in America were spent making videos, playing Super Smash Bros. on the Nintendo 64 and writing music with Denise for her wizard rock band The Parselmouths (rated 'third best wizard rock band of 2007' by MTV). I helped write and perform some of the tracks for their new album *Spattergroit* and flew to Boston for its launch at a *Harry Potter* convention called LeakyCon. I'd never experienced an event like it: a cross between a concert, a conference and a fancy-dress party, lasting for two full days and nights. with thousands of kids running around all weekend adorned with scarves and wands, taking pictures underneath huge banners of each of the four Hogwarts houses. The vlogbrothers, Hank and John, came to town for LeakyCon and Denise told me the fiveawesomegirls thought of John as their adopted father. (I'd had a Skype call with him before we started seeing each other to make sure he approved of us dating.)

'Oh my god!' Denise said at her phone when we arrived, unleashing a fit of giggles. 'Look at this tweet.' I leaned in. Denise had announced her arrival at the event and John tweeted her (and the world): 'Daddy's here. Where's the party?'

'Daddy's here, where's the party?!' I grinned at him when I saw him.

'I know,' said John, dismayed. 'I judged that poorly. I've already heard a lot about this.'

I hadn't done a gig since my nan watched me in the pub, and this time hundreds of people would be watching. To muster the energy and swagger I needed, I practiced by hunting down live Green Day shows on YouTube, learning from their relentless engagement with the crowd. On the night of the show, I puffed out my chest and pushed back my shoulders, parading around the stage. It turned out doing the gig was as easy as making a YouTube video; just like my videos, I played up a crystallised facet of myself, distilled and projected to the waiting crowd.

After we played our show, we rocked out to The Remus Lupins, led by Shane, the most charismatic man I've ever met. Unlike me, wearing charisma like a mask when I needed it, Shane was a fireball on- and off-stage, playful and charming and full of energy. He knew how to work a crowd and get them singing along to his songs, even when (like me) they'd never heard them before. He ended his show — of *Harry Potter* songs, I'll remind you — by holding his guitar aloft like he was posing for a statue, then setting it on fire, then smashing it to pieces.

For the finale of the night, Harry and the Potters — the founders of wizard rock — tore up the stage, slamming their guitars like punk rockers, jumping up and down and leading a wave of claps and cheers, both dressed as Harry Potter, and the crowd screamed like they'd seen a herald of the end of days. At the end of their last song 'The Weapon', they cut their instruments and led the crowd to join them in singing their final refrain: 'The weapon we have is love.' We repeated it, a cappella, over and over again. I've never had any purer image of online communities than that of people singing that their greatest weapon is love, dressed as magical schoolchildren.

The show had me pumped to get Chameleon Circuit's album finished no matter what. I'd generated a lot of hype about the musical phenomenon that was Trock and, try as I might, I'd grown to accept you can't have a musical phenomenon without actual music. I listened through our patchwork album again. I would have loved it to be honed and fine-tuned but nothing would ever get done if we spent all our time perfecting it first. The album was messy but listenable (with only Charlie's 'Friends of the Ood' unrecorded, bar an acoustic demo), so I told the band we should release the album as it was. This sent shockwaves (or, dare I say, Trockwaves) through the band, most of all in the loss of Ginger Chris, who wasn't willing to stand by as our audience heard unfinished versions of his work.

By the time *Chameleon Circuit* came out (in the middle of 2009), I had over fifty thousand subscribers and Charlie had over a hundred thousand. By this point my YouTube messages were overwhelming in number. Denise's friend Priya, one of the most disciplined people I know, had such a passion for helping people stay organised that she offered to read my messages for me and send me daily digests of the things I needed to respond to.

With the album coming out, I flew to Manhattan, Illinois (they say if you can make it there, you can make it anywhere) to meet Alan for the first time in DFTBA Records' 'office' — his garage. (I was surprised to learn that he and Hank, despite running a record label together, had never been in the same room.) I got to see Chameleon Circuit's physical CDs for the first time and signed over a thousand of them in advance of the launch, packing them up with Alan for shipping. I knew Alan could have done this himself, but I wanted to be as involved as possible in all aspects of the project.

Signing with DFTBA ensured our success was as important to Hank as it was to us, so we got promotional videos about Chameleon Circuit from Hank and John on the vlogbrothers channel. For my part, I did what I do best; I pushed aside all the important things in my life to pursue a single-minded focus on what I wanted. I sent an email to *Doctor Who Magazine* and nabbed an interview by a journalist there called Ben; we got a full page about Chameleon Circuit in the following issue. Prompted by my emails, *WIRED*, *Den of Geek* and *Digital Spy* all wrote about us and reviewed our album, which led to other articles from related sites. My audience played a role, too, without me even having to ask; when the current Doctor, David Tennant, took questions on national radio, an American girl rang in and asked what he thought of Chameleon Circuit and Time Lord Rock. 'Oh, I have heard of this! They're quite good aren't they?' he gushed, and then badgered the radio host into playing our music on-air. 'It's like proper decent music,' he insisted to the resistant DJ.

Even after splitting the profits four ways (and giving Hank and Alan a cut) we each made thousands of pounds from the album — not to mention the money we got from our YouTube videos promoting it. Not bad for a band that didn't care to check whether its members could sing.

Denise and I had a huge fight after LeakyCon. It seemed like I couldn't do anything right. I wrote a song (with the subtlest of titles, 'Impossible Dreams') in an attempt to process my inability to live up to what (I felt) she expected of me. On her part, Denise probably found me stubborn, challenging and uncooperative. If I'd been a better boyfriend I'd be able to tell you.

A short time later I received an email from Laura. We hadn't spoken for months. She was clearing out her bedroom and found a little cartoon she'd drawn of me when we were dating. She thought it would make me smile to see it again, so she took a picture and emailed it over, wished me well and hoped I was having a good time in Seattle. I poured my heart out to her in a sprawling email back, telling her I'd had fun on this adventure but that things weren't working out, that I felt trapped, that none of it was right for me. I was desperate to see her again.

I flew back to England a week later. Charlie and Laura met me at the airport along with my mum, all of them enveloping me in hugs. My mum promised never to charge me rent again, lest I leave for even longer. Laura and I held hands and passed meaningful smiles to each other in the back seat as Mum drove me home.

I knew I had to break up with Denise but while I was in Seattle she'd arranged a study abroad trip to England. I didn't want to keep pretending but I also didn't want to put her through the loneliest summer ever. My plan was to stick it out while she was here and then end things once she was back in America; it was my way of trying to hurt her the least. If you've ever found yourself thinking this way, take some advice from someone who's already made the mistakes on your behalf: it never works out. The true way to hurt someone the least is to give them an authentic image of yourself, not construct one that will be torn down later. You can deceive someone who knows you intimately into thinking everything's fine and you can even deceive yourself, but trust me, the truth always creeps through. Like the the wasp in my school assembly, you can ignore reality by closing your eyes and looking the other way, but you always get stung in the end. And everybody will see it.

Here's how it played out for me: things blew up over a huge email fight one evening in which I hit my limit. We met up the next day on the bank of the River Thames for what I saw as the inevitable end. For Denise, however, it was a total shock. She didn't understand where it had come from or why I didn't want to work things out. A couple weeks later, Priya, my assistant for YouTube messages, figured out I used the same password for my email as I did for my YouTube account, so — in an effort to make sense of things — she and Denise logged into my email inbox and took a look around. They soon discovered all I'd said to Laura while I was in Seattle, and that we'd resumed sleeping together when I got back to England. I found out about this because Gmail sent me a security alert saying I was logged in on multiple devices, complete with GPS locations of each connected machine. I sent a screenshot of the information to Denise and Priya.

'Just sending you this so you don't wonder why I've changed my password,' I said.

'Okay, we read your email,' Denise shot back. 'You were fucking Laura.'

Denise spent the summer blogging to an audience of thousands about her horrible summer in London and how it was my fault. My reputation only remained intact throughout the experience because people felt uncomfortable commenting on private events without the full story. They refrained from judging or condemning me — which would not be the case today.

I hadn't felt any homesickness at leaving, but being back home was a huge culture shock. For all my problems with our relationship, Denise's passion for life was a huge influence on me. She motivated me and expanded my horizons. I had changed for the better, and now I was back in a place that had stayed the same. When I first walked into my room, I was overwhelmed by the sheer amount of stuff in there; the material total of my life to date towered up every wall, threatening to bury me. I had bookcases crammed full of reading material, shelves heaving with DVD box sets and video games, and drawers stuffed with clothes I hadn't needed in months. If my mum had phoned and said, 'The house burned down; make a list of everything you own so we can get it back,' I would have recalled very little of what I'd possessed for the majority of my life. Even the things I liked, I barely used; my copies of *Harry Potter* had been gathering dust for years, hoping for the day I felt like flipping looking through them again before they were banished back to their neglected corner to be subjected to further withering. These books — and almost everything else I owned — could be sold or given to someone who had never enjoyed them before. If they really were my favourite things, it would be a joy to share them with others, not keep them locked up in my castle for me alone to experience when I felt the whim to do so. If I'd wanted to re-read *Harry Potter* while I was in America, I could have borrowed them from a friend, downloaded them, or bought used copies and then resold or donated them. Something had to be done.

I spent the weekend playing Super Mario Galaxy with Charlie, adjusting to the pace of life back home — like a warmup before a big run — and then I took on my items. I spent hours listing everything on eBay and Amazon. Every day I walked to the post office with ten or twenty envelopes full of DVDs, books, CDs and games. In a few weeks I cleared all my shelves and made about a thousand pounds from my stuff.

Once I'd settled back at home, I met up with Ben (the journalist from *Doctor Who Magazine*). He swaggered when he walked, grinning with a glint of mischief as though he was always ready and waiting for someone to dare him to do something — his face had the perpetual light of someone ready to gobble up the maximum amount of enjoyment from every single second of his life. I noticed how trendy he was; he wore black skinny jeans and tight tops, while I looked like I'd bought my outfit from an unpopular jumble sale.

'Where do you get your clothes?'

'Topman,' grinned Ben.

I wanted to optimise my life, and that included my clothes. I'd researched the minimum number of clothes you need in daily life and stumbled across 'Six Items or Less', a philosophy that started as one woman's thirty-day challenge to see if she could rotate the same six items of clothing for a month without anybody noticing. (Sure enough, no-one did.)

Six Items or Less doesn't include underwear or outerwear (coats, accessories, etc.), just basic trousers, jeans, skirts, shirts and tops. With Ben in mind, I went to Topman, bought two skinny jeans and four tight t-shirts and donated all my other clothes to a charity shop. I was liberated. Much like when I dyed my hair blond, I forced myself to become comfortable in my new style by eliminating any other choice. I didn't want a safety net because I didn't want to provide myself with any way out. Even on my laziest day, I would be fashionable by default, whether I cared about it or not.

To avoid owning more than six items, I developed a one-in, one-out system for clothes, so when I saw a top I liked, instead of thinking, *Do I like this?* (which would lead to a purchase) I thought, *Do I like this more than one of the tops I already have?* If so, I bought it and donated one of my existing items, evolving my clothes to only the things I loved most. Everyone has their few favourite outfits, along with several drawers of other clothes — I wear only my favourite things all the time. It's made me tidier, too, because I have less to clean up, helping me appreciate open space and clean work surfaces, which in turn helps me to focus more.

I made a video in my new clothes and told the internet I'd regenerated, just like the Doctor in *Doctor Who*.

THE WORLD IS MINE

I don't know if there's a word for the feeling you get when you realise you can do a thing other people can do, but there probably is (and it's probably German; they seem to have a lot of good ones).

Years before I learned any instruments, I would write original lyrics for songs on my computer and organise them into 'albums', which were just folders with pretentious names: my cousin Danny would help me decide on titles like 'Tainted Tears' and 'The Relationship That Never Was' (presumably by steering me away from even worse choices). Along the way, various friends and family members offered to help by composing melodies or chords for me or even producing the songs on their home computers, but nothing went anywhere. Up until Chameleon Circuit, my career as a musician was conceptual. Now it was real.

The money from Chameleon Circuit's album (paid in monthly instalments from DFTBA) gave me a small budget to realise my first solo album. I grabbed a pencil and paper and drafted a track list of all the songs I'd written over the course of my life that I thought were worth sharing. Since the majority were strained odes to Penny, with me repeating the same sentiments over and over again, I christened the album *Parrot Stories* (also a reference to Tennessee Williams' *A Streetcar*

Named Desire, which Penny had been reading when I wrote several of the songs). I just needed a producer to help me bring the tracks to life.

Like many of my friends, I first came across Tom when he was featured on the front page of YouTube. He was soft-spoken, his hair was styled in a blond sweep across his face, and his laugh was raucous, as though he couldn't contain the volume of his joy. Tom had recorded 'Internet Love Song' on the ukulele, singing into his camera about the hidden agony of talking to people online ('Please don't block me, please don't go offline... We pour our hearts out on the screen one line at a time') and the front-page placement of his song earned Tom half a million views and a sudden gaggle of admirers from across our community.

I met Tom at a gathering in Hyde Park where he endeared a crowd of people by playing a song on his uke about the hidden agony of eating a lobster. (A lot of Tom's songs explored the hidden agony of things.) His esoteric music attracted the attention of Simon Fuller, the former manager of the Spice Girls and creator of *American Idol*, who gave Tom a budget of £5,000 — along with any instruments he might desire — to record an album.

Tom speaks music the way you and I speak English. His fluency in music eclipses anyone I've ever met; I've yet to present Tom with an instrument he can't play. Tom got to work and after six months, having acquired a veritable armoury of toy pianos, xylophones, trombones and a harp, he presented Simon with the album he'd made. He called it *Painfully Mainstream*, complete with an arty boy band-style photo of him on the cover — with a nosebleed. At the core of *Painfully Mainstream* were four songs named after the four seasons, including 'Wintersong', which sounded like a Pink Floyd b-side, and 'Autumnsong', a nine-minute instrumental piano piece Tom improvised in the studio.

According to Tom, Simon listened to the whole album in silence, looked at his assistant, then shook Tom's hand and said, 'Good luck with it all.' In the end, *Painfully Mainstream* found its home with Hank at DFTBA (sans nosebleed, after his mum told him he looked so nice without it).

The two of us nurtured our most disorderly instincts in each other. I gave him the idea to turn the thank-you section of his album into a list of apologies ('Apologies to my mum and dad for raising me, apologies to Oli for engineering the tracks,' and so on). We tried to out-funny each other, building on absurd concepts and laughing until we cried, at which point we cuddled together for afternoon naps, exhausted. We wrote silly songs and sketches together, playing like friends do, except our playing was viewed hundreds of thousands of times by our shared audience and brought in more money and interest to us both. We were manic with desire, both personal and professional; we both wanted the world to see how bright we could shine.

I sat in Tom's room one afternoon with my guitar and played him every track I'd written for *Parrot Stories*. A good producer from the start, he guided me away from two or three weaker songs and tightened the structure of what was left, getting the music to a place where we were ready to record. The studio Tom used to record *Painfully Mainstream* was in a basement in East London, run by a guy called Oli. The only light in the room, other than his computer screen, was a large rubber duck that had been turned into a lamp. Oli fired up an electric heater to keep us warm and told us to ignore the sound of the rats crawling in the walls.

The album cost me £600. I paid for four days of Oli's time (committing a percentage of sales to Tom for his) and we worked over a long weekend, recording three or four songs a day. Tom wanted my music, like my videos, to feel accessible and candid. We ran around the space like children; when Tom found a toy keyboard that played animal sounds, we sampled it for the first track so the album would open with it. We brought Penny in to sing, turning one of the numerous songs I'd written about her into a duet. In between songs we would play games at the pub 'round the corner, giggling and dreaming up ideas for the next song. *Parrot Stories* sounds like our friendship was: naive, affectionate and whimsical. Hank offered to release it through DFTBA.

Charlie's energies remained focused on video; he was putting much more effort into mastering video-editing techniques than the none I was putting in. While I was content to have perfected the jump cut, he was playing with split screen and green screen effects. He pushed himself to learn and implement a new technique on every video he made. I enlisted him to make the music video for 'Holding On', the first song I wanted to share from *Parrot Stories*, and offered him half of whatever money the video made. Charlie agreed. He filmed me from lots of different angles doing different things, and split the screen into four, each quadrant filled with a different me doing something unique. Off the back of his and Tom's superb work, I sold three hundred copies of the album.

When *Parrot Stories* came out I was still selling the last of my old DVDs and video games, so I would burn copies of the album on to blank discs and include a copy free with every item I posted out. With a Sharpie I would write on to the CD explaining what the album was and that I hoped people enjoyed it. I even tried to persuade Alan and Hank to include two copies of the CD inside every physical copy of *Parrot Stories*, so anyone who bought it could give it to a friend. They responded with good, sensible points about value and losing money. I didn't care about that — I just wanted everyone to hear what I'd made.

Parrot Stories and *Painfully Mainstream* came out a month apart. To promote them, Tom and I headed to New York for a launch show; Charlie tagged along, as did our friend and fellow musician Ed. (We barely made the flight after staying up late the night before to watch a documentary Tom had recommended about the font Helvetica.) The four of us led a packed-out gig in a café, all taking turns playing our best work and leading our audience to sing with us. I met a girl, Melissa, who loved my songs so much she'd had some of the lyrics stitched into her jeans.

'Alex, I'm your biggest fan!' said Melissa.

'No way,' I grinned, 'I've always wanted to meet my biggest fan! I found you!'

We were all staying in a room at a nearby hostel, along with a close American friend of Tom's, a short girl with oversized square-rimmed glasses, bushy brown hair, a wide grin and an inquisitive mind. I felt intoxicated by her and — despite knowing of Tom's fondness for her — made out with her at the first opportunity. Tom and I had a huge fight the next morning over it and he spent the remainder of the day standing in the corners of whatever room we were in, facing the wall, struggling to process his anger while I told everyone how childish he was being, belittling his outlandishness as though it were unprovoked and nothing to do with me. Ed tried to talk to Tom about it and keep the peace. Charlie hunched ever further towards his phone.

It was only on the E train to JFK airport at the end of our trip that I realised the atmosphere I'd put my friends in, and — knowing I would be going home to Laura, who I was supposed to be making a fresh start with — burst into tears in Tom's arms and sobbed into his shoulder that I didn't know what to do or why I kept doing this. I said I was sorry, and he said he forgave me. I don't know how much either of us meant it.

'Hey, look,' I pointed, drawing Tom's gaze to a nearby sign. 'Helvetica.'

'That's Verdana,' Tom snarled.

After being in a studio, hearing my songs realised the way they'd always sounded in my head, my work was unfettered. I wrote, recorded and released the whole of my next album in six months, insisting for maximum impact that every track be recorded in order.

'I don't know any album that's ever been done like this,' I gushed.

'I think Bruce Springsteen did it with one of his live albums,' Tom deadpanned. He was unhappy with me for not spending more time crafting the songs, and he was right: the good ones were far better than my first effort but the bad ones were far worse. After hearing one track in the studio, 'Together Tonight', Tom had me throw out all the lyrics and start from scratch. He concocted a new rhythm for the song and, while he and Oli went for lunch, I stayed at the desk and rewrote it (and even renamed it 'The Time Of Your Life' after being advised 'that lyric comes at a more melodic part of the song'). At least that track had room for improvement. Others left Tom so bereft of options he was forced to compensate by making the tracks as unconventional as possible, so a cacophony of crunching drums and oscillating synths accompanied me as I warbled on. Tom even insisted my album cover — a picture of me in black against a bright orange background — was wrong.

'This isn't the right colour for these songs,' he said. 'This album is yellow.'

I had no restrictions, and yet — in my personal life as well as my work — I often had no idea what I was doing. The freedom of not having anyone to tell me what to do came with the uncertainty of... well, of not having anyone to tell me what to do. For better and for worse, nobody could stop me doing whatever I liked. The album reflected this, right down to the title I gave it: *The World Is Mine (I Don't Know Anything)*.

The second album (coming, again, with a music video created by Charlie) sold even more than the first and I gushed with relentless enthusiasm about music in video after video. In the comments, my audience let me know with similar fervour that they subscribed for comedy, that I couldn't sing very well, that they liked it better when I played acoustic stuff, that all I ever did was try to sell things to them, that all I cared about was money and that they were unsubscribing because I'd changed. I didn't understand why my audience didn't respect the artistry and entrepreneurial spirit I was offering them. 'When Walt Disney talked about his new movie, people didn't have a go at *him* for trying to sell stuff,' I lamented, as I compared myself to one of the greatest innovators of all time.

Of all these charges, I most resented being told I was just cashing in. Money didn't matter to me beyond having enough of it. Many of my friends and fellow YouTubers had started selling t-shirts, pin badges, posters and anything else they could print their name or face on; I was only releasing what I was proud of. My work cost me a lot of money and time, and I wasn't forcing them to buy any of it; I made all my music available to listen to for free.

In an attempt to establish some common ground, I decided to mine my back-catalogue for something of the 'early Nerimon' my viewers claimed to miss and stumbled across the silly comedy piece I did about Harry Potter being gay. The video was fine but the editing could be much better and most of my larger audience wouldn't have seen the original, so I deleted and remade it, tightening the jokes and the cuts and adding in some new things, implementing all I'd learned about vlogging over the last three years in the process.

When I uploaded 'Harry Potter Is Gay' this time, it caused a storm of controversy. Too many commenters believed I really had uncovered a secret layer of subtext to the *Harry Potter* books and argued over the authenticity of my findings with others. I had Melissa Anelli (the founder of LeakyCon) on the phone to me saying, while she understood the joke and found it funny, lots of people in her office were bothered or offended by it, assuming I was disparaging gay rights or gay people. I was again accused of having changed — the thing I'd most sought to avoid by making the exact video I'd made in the past. With my subscriber count swelling, there were ever more people to be offended and misunderstood.

My audience, once supportive and excited to be watching my videos, now became demanding and dismissive. The more I shared about my life, the more people could find to criticise, and these weren't the generic insults from my earlier years. People had sharp, precise judgments on my sexuality, my relationships, the way I conducted myself and my career, my hairstyle, my clothing, and what I should or should not do, say or believe. When — for my own mental well-being — I stopped replying to my comments, they didn't like that either, taking it to mean I believed myself above them. They all signed up to a new app for sharing photos with pre-made filters, called Instagram, and were infuriated when I didn't join them. Here's an example of a message I got around that time (to my private email account, no less):

Hey Alex/Nerimon,

I'm a big fan of yours — I love your videos and all of your projects. I bought Chameleon Circuit and I think it's amazing. I also read your diary.

I'm emailing to ask you — wtf?! Your diary is normally very well written and informative and contains your personal insights into situations which are always extremely illuminating.

But...what the hell! You haven't added a single entry about the death of Michael Jackson!! Why?! Instead you've written something trivial and unimportant about some loser who's pretending to be you on Twitter.

What I'm saying is, when you look back at your diary in years to come, you will completely miss the fact that Michael Jackson, one of the most important figures in music within the last century, died prematurely. You will instead remember that some dude was posting as you on a social networking site. Does that not sound like you're getting your priorities mixed up??

I'm not trying to have a go, here. And you'll probably reply (if at all) saying how it's your diary and you can write whatever the hell you like in it. But for the sake of memory! The best diaries include insights into the major events of the day! See Samuel Pepys!

Anyway, bye.
Cath

P.S. You're probably wondering how the hell I got your private email. I can't tell you because the guy who gave it to me will probably lose your trust/ respect/friendship if I do.

P.P.S. Oh and another thing while we're at it. You should start doing some exercise, because although you're a skinny dude now, you'll start putting on weight as you grow older and the sooner you start exercising, the more you can postpone it.

P.P.P.S. stop doing so many less than 3's (<3), they're so annoying and cliche.

I made frustrated videos ranting at my subscribers. My views started to drop.

'YouTube shouldn't be work,' John said at the time. 'YouTube should be what you do instead of work.' It wasn't just the strangers watching my videos who demanded acknowledgement. All of my friends were producing online content too, and I had an ever-growing list of videos, tweets and blogs to keep up with. I needed to disconnect a little, step back and focus on what was important to me. Friendship shouldn't come with required reading.

I unsubscribed from some of my friends' channels and encouraged other people to detach too. I couldn't see how I could make new things if I spent all my time discussing the old ones (and watching other people's). My friends didn't understand; I received angry emails accusing me of turning my back on them.

With my albums, I was finally doing what I wanted to do. YouTube wasn't worth this hassle to me and I believed it had outlasted its value. I decided to delete my channel.

CHARTJACKER

'Delete your channel'. I hovered over the button, then clicked it.

Another box appeared, jamming my signal. YouTube was checking I was sure about this. Deleting my YouTube channel meant I would lose access to all my audience. If I ever started making videos again, I would have to build it up from nothing.

I'd thought I was sure. I always knew my willingness to say whatever I liked, even if my audience didn't like it, would get me into trouble at some point. We all have shelf lives. At least I could leave while some people still valued my work, instead of clinging on until the only one still caring about me was me.

Before confirming, I stopped to send an email to Hank. He and John were my canaries down the mine; they used their channel to sell albums and books and made it clear YouTube was not their main thing without experiencing anything close to this level of backlash from their audience.

Hank took the time to send me a long email back after I sought his advice. He said he and John maintained a three-to-one ratio on all promotional videos: for every vlog they made talking about John's book or Hank's album or some other money-taking endeavour, they aimed to make at least three unrelated ones. This ensured people wouldn't struggle through video after video of things that didn't interest them.

He also told me — with a lot of kindness — to grow a pair and step up to the plate. Audiences criticise, fans especially. The reason I know *Doctor Who* is my favourite show is because it's the one I hate the most. I debate line-by-line acting choices on forums. I judge the value of every single scene. I do it because I love it and I want it to be its best. Real love means honesty.

I could either make good stuff for a big audience and put up with the criticism or I could sit there whining to Hank about it. But if I was going to do this, I needed to do it properly.

Don't mourn, organise.

I began to take my camera everywhere with me. My videos stopped being confined to my bedroom and became about my life outside it. I filmed museums and buskers. I filmed with my friends. I filmed a vlog every day of April, called it 'VEDA', and started a trend of people who joined me.

One afternoon while visiting Charlie in Bath, I wandered into a bookshop and saw the book *Twilight* on sale in WHSmith. I'd just seen the movie adaptation with Penny; when Edward told Bella — a relative stranger — 'I'm very protective of you,' Penny swooned at the same moment I recoiled. Around this time I was trying to make videos targeted to the Nerdfighters, Hank and John's audience, whom I admired for their collective support and kindness. I wanted my audience to be more like that. I knew a significant number of Nerdfighters loved *Twilight*, so I decided to buy the book for a video, figuring they would get a kick out of me reading it and sharing my thoughts. I went in with an open mind — I wanted to judge it on direct experience instead of hearsay — but I ended up with a whole video from my thoughts on the first chapter alone. This book was ridiculous. *This needs to be a whole series*, I thought, and with that, 'Alex Reads *Twilight*' became a regular feature on my channel.

I spoke to my cousin Danny a few weeks later. He was the manager in the Sony Centre in Leicester and one of his co-workers had asked, 'Do you watch much YouTube?'

'Yeah, a bit,' Danny replied. He was a fan of Red vs Blue, a comedy series featuring clips of Halo games with the voices dubbed over (which became the longest running episodic web series of all time).

'Nice,' the co-worker said. 'You seen that 'Alex Reads *Twilight*'?'

The *Twilight* readings were getting hundreds of thousands of views and reaching far beyond my normal audience, even more than I'd intended. When I first started making videos, my audience was made up of guys the same age as me; now my audience were younger, and female. My comments split into two factions vying for dominance — people who wanted me to read books forever, and people who missed 'the old me', dismissing the *Twilight* videos as lazy and low-brow. I cared about what people thought of my work, but I couldn't appease so many extreme and diverse opinions at the same time; I stuck to my guns, making sure to follow Hank's advice to make at least three other videos between each reading so people wouldn't get too frustrated if they weren't into them.

People started recognising me. They would see me on the Tube and ask if I was Alex Day, and as I confirmed I was, I would feel the eyes of the carriage on me, trying to figure out why I mattered. One guy walked past me on a flight of stairs, pointed at me, cheered '*Twilight*', high-fived me and carried on walking. Just off Oxford Street, a girl came up to me and squealed when I said hello. 'Oh my god,' she cried, 'you sound just like your videos!' These encounters always descended into awkward stares after the pleasantries; I think people were unsure how to leave when they couldn't pause me or minimise me from view once they were finished.

My profile wasn't the only one being raised. 'You free to get lunch with me on my birthday?' Charlie asked me one day.

''Course, mate.'

'I'm inviting my friend Stephen too.'

'Okay, fine,' I said, all the while thinking, *Who the hell is this 'Stephen' character I've never heard of until now?*

'He's pretty busy,' said Charlie, 'but he's gonna make time for me. I'm glad you'll get to meet him.'

'Sure,' I said, furious that someone else was this high in Charlie's esteem and that he'd never once mentioned him before.

There was a short silence.

'It's Stephen Fry,' said Charlie.

'Oh. Okay.' This was the level we were at; I was so close with Charlie that it somehow made more sense for him to be having lunch with Stephen Fry than for him to have befriended some other random Stephen without my knowledge. So Charlie and I went for lunch with Stephen Fry, who had subscribed to Charlie's YouTube channel and followed him on Twitter.

Soon after that, I took my mum to see *Wicked* and the girl who sat down next to me started freaking out. She told me she loved my videos and asked for a photo.

'Sorry,' she said, 'it's just I've never met anyone famous before.'

'Sorry,' I replied, 'you still haven't.' My mum roared with laughter. On the Tube back home she said, 'I can't believe you said that to that poor girl!'

I once watched an interview with Lady Gaga at Google headquarters just before *Born This Way* came out. This was peak Gaga: her second single, 'Poker Face', had sold ten million copies, making it the biggest-selling single of the year worldwide; her music video for 'Bad Romance' was, for a time, the most-viewed YouTube video ever and Gaga herself was the first person to pass a billion total views across the site. The interviewer asked her to share the moment in her career she realised she was an international superstar.

Gaga looked at the interviewer, adjusted her steampunk goggles, frowned, and replied, 'I still don't feel like one.'

Everyone in the room laughed.

It was starting to feel okay to say I made money in online video without people thinking I was a porn star, but media attempts to work with YouTubers still left a lot to be desired. HBO commissioned a web series with big American vloggers called *Hooking Up*, a dire scripted soap opera that failed (in part) because talking into a camera isn't the same as being an actor. We watch vloggers because we like who they really are; having them play fictional people misunderstands the appeal about as much as it's possible to do. (HBO have since gone in the opposite direction and produced a show about a world without internet, the critically-acclaimed *Game of Thrones*.)

Opportunities came to me more and more, and with the internet in my pocket I could respond wherever I was. While sitting on the toilet I'd get an email inviting me to the Consumer Electronics Show, or go to Amsterdam to run a vlogging workshop for the European Cultural Foundation. I'd reply saying yes, then wipe my arse.

'He is a rising talent whose fan base is mainly American teen viewers,' the *Romford Recorder* wrote when they covered me a second time. 'They can't get enough of his vlogs that are part rant, part confessional and part wry observation. So why his success?

'"Probably because I'm relatable," Alex said.'

An even bigger newspaper, the *News Of The World*, invited me to a conference to help them connect more with young people in a digital age (probably because I was relatable).

'I want you to write a biography for our press pack,' said their PR woman. 'How old are you?'

'Nineteen.'

'Oh! So it won't be a very lengthy biography,' she snarked. 'Don't worry about good English. We have people who can clean it up for you, so you don't have to be concerned with grammar, punctuation, things like that.' (I thought I might have hit on why they were struggling to connect with young people.)

In the UK, the biggest attempt (aside from *Upstaged*) to integrate the online world with traditional media was BBC Three's *Lily Allen And Friends* (the 'friends' being strangers who signed up to be in the show). They would talk about people who were famous 'on the internet' as though it were a distant moon. It wasn't renewed. Then again, neither was *Firefly*, so I shouldn't be uncharitable. I knew these shows were the best traditional media could do, but when I got a TV offer of my own and the producer started the conversation by slagging off *Lily Allen and Friends*, it put me in a good frame of mind for the potential of our working relationship.

'Now, as a production company, we're obviously interested in making money,' the guy on the phone said.

'As an unemployed teenager, I'm obviously also interested in making money,' I said.

'What a pleasing coincidence,' he replied.

The pitch was pretty open and I steered the producer towards doing something involving a Guinness World Record. I was about as obsessed with earning one as I was with getting my own Wikipedia page, these feeling like broad enough yardsticks to measure one's impact on the world no matter what field you end up in. With music on my mind (as it often was), we devised a show called Chartjackers. Together with Charlie, JohnnyDurham19 and a fellow YouTuber named Jimmy, we would use the internet to crowdsource a number one single from start to finish and release it for the charity Children in Need. It would be the highest-charting single ever by an unsigned act.

The project ran for ten weeks and included lyrics compiled from YouTube comments, musicians taken from online auditions and a music video mashup of our subscribers singing the song. The accompanying TV show aired on BBC Two every week and showcased our progress over the previous seven days. To prevent it being footage of us staring at computer screens for ten weeks, the producers arranged various stunts, press opportunities and interviews with celebrities. The mascot of Children in Need is Pudsey, a giant yellow teddy bear 'boy' (taller than I am) with one eye covered in a bandage, and the moment I accepted my life was weird was the moment I found myself sharing a cab through Hyde Park with him.

I turned these circumstances into chances to rebel against the system that put me there. I tried to get Pudsey to break character for the entirety of my time with him (unsuccessfully, I must say; Pudsey's a professional). When a live gig for the single was arranged, it ended with me encouraging Johnny to crowdsurf and baiting the crowd to chant 'Crowdsurf, crowdsurf!' I ignored the producer's protests of health and safety, yelling that if he just did it, no-one would have time to stop him. At first, I could hear Charlie begging the crowd, 'Don't do it!' but then, when Johnny relented to my demands and fell on the waiting audience, his plea of 'Put him down now, please, oh my god!' was all but drowned out by the triumphant cheers of the crowd.

When Capital FM refused to play our crowdsourced song, I protested outside their office in Leicester Square with signs and a megaphone, encouraging passersby to join me as I played the track through a boombox and, on a mad impulse, marched into the lobby of the building (where I was stopped by security and told to leave).

The BBC arranged for us to attend the red carpet of a Disney premiere, where I spied a huge platform for VIPs to have their photos taken by a flurry of paparazzi and pestered Disney's press woman to let us up there. 'Can we go on the big platform where Jim Carrey is and get our photo taken?'

'No,' she said, unamused.

'Okay, what if I just go up there and then you just pretend you didn't know anything about it?'

I learned, to my dismay, that being at a film premiere doesn't earn you automatic respect. I approached the cinema entrance and was gawped at by hundreds of people on either side of me, squinting at me to figure out why they had no idea who I was. As I walked inside, someone yelled out, 'Alright, skinny jeans!', meaning I not only failed to be recognised as I walked the red carpet but was also heckled. I then had to leave early and discovered the only way off a red carpet once you're on it is to go back in the other direction, swimming upstream against a river of *X Factor* finalists and *Big Brother* contestants. There's no dignity in being the only person at an international film premiere going the wrong way.

The Chartjackers song was called 'I've Got Nothing', a title you'll agree is perfect if you ever hear it. Nonetheless, the song ended up at number 36 in the UK charts. The internet created a Top 40 single, we got to be on TV for a few months, and I interviewed Dappy from N-Dubz, so it was all good fun in my book. My biggest highlight of the whole experience came at the charity's annual gala, when I noticed a giant novelty cookie in the shape of Pudsey the Bear. It had been donated by a bakery but now its left ear was missing. My mouth dropped in horror as I saw Ariel, one of the performers of our song, stumbling around the room chomping on it while sipping free champagne.

Ariel had a huge crush on Charlie so, as you'd expect, he was terrified of her. She was developing real feelings for him and told me they had a real connection and that they'd chatted on the phone for hours, which didn't sound to me like Charlie at all. I asked him about it and *he* told me she'd phoned him up and talked and talked at him, leaving the poor boy too overwhelmed to hang up and too polite to tell her the harsh truth.

The whole thing culminated in him having to — for all intents and purposes — break up with her, telling her with his typical gentleness that he wasn't interested, an event she found quite distressing, having exaggerated their bond so much in her mind. Charlie later wrote a beautiful song called 'This Is Me' reflecting on the dichotomy that can occur between your reality and those of other people: "Are you unaware," he sang, "that the me you care for isn't really me at all?"

Charlie was spending far too much money on train tickets in and out of London to attend meetings and see friends; it would be cheaper for him to get a place in the city. I had a goal of moving to London by the time I turned 21 so I started making plans with Charlie for us to live together. We initially planned for Tom to join us too, but as we spent more time with him it became clear the arrangement wouldn't work. Charlie and I were able to sit in silence playing video games in our own worlds for hours at a time; Tom and I both had dominating egos that led to frequent clashes.

I took Tom out one evening to a Chinese buffet in Leicester Square and broke the news that I thought it in the best interest of our friendship that we not live together. He took it in good grace, agreeing we would get on better if we weren't in each other's space all the time.

About a month later, I got a phone call from Charlie. 'Did you tell Tom we weren't living together?'

'Yes, of course,' I said. 'We had a Chinese in Leicester Square. Why?'

'I'm at a party,' said Charlie, 'and Tom's here, and he just came over, hugged me and said he can't wait for us all to live together.'

So, much like Charlie had to do with Ariel, I had to sit with Tom and explain that his reality had travelled far from mine. This time 'round Tom didn't take it well at all.

'I just wish I'd been given more of a warning,' he sighed.

'Tom,' I lamented, 'remember when we went for Chinese in Leicester Square?'

'Yes,' said Tom, 'of course. Why?'

Helping him recollect the details of that evening, I managed to get him to remember I had already told him this news once before. I found a flat for Charlie and myself in East London (giving him the en suite master bedroom in exchange for him being decisive about the move) and Tom moved a short bus ride away into a house-share with Ed.

Five days later was my 21st birthday and a giant cardboard cut-out of Amy Pond — the new companion from *Doctor Who* — was delivered to my door.

'Charlie,' I said, 'someone's sent me a giant cardboard cut-out of Amy Pond.'

'Happy birthday,' smiled Charlie.

THE NEW MODEL

When I first released *Parrot Stories*, Tom introduced me to a friend of his named Jonathan. Jonathan was a pop star in the sixties; he's now in his sixties and lives a busy and contented life off the royalties of various projects, including the overseeing of the BRIT Awards, the discovery and development of Genesis and the initial studio recording of the worldwide smash 'Who Let The Dogs Out?'. He owns the publishing rights to ABBA's back catalogue and recently got a huge royalty cheque from Marvel Studios after 10cc's 'I'm Not In Love', to which he owns the rights, was featured in *Guardians of the Galaxy*.

Having lived far longer without the internet than with it, Jonathan thinks Tom and I have been rendered superficial by our lifelong exposure to screens. He says people our age are ten years younger than we should be in terms of our emotions, indulging in video games and toys for years after previous generations would be married with kids. I think Facebook in particular encourages this behaviour, nagging us to interact with each other as though we are incompetent without sufficient guidance: *You haven't posted in 11 days. Your friends haven't heard from you in a while. Comment. Write something. Create an event for your Page. Wish Natalie a Happy Birthday.* The ease with which we can react to things online doesn't help. *Like. Dislike. Unsubscribe. Angry face.*

Tom first met Jonathan after approaching him online for music advice. I met him in a restaurant in West London, where he swaggered in wearing a Cannes Film Festival cap and a crooked grin. He started talking before he'd sat down and was still talking as he left in his Rolls Royce, his flighty mind jumping from anecdote to anecdote about songs that should have been hits, things he'd said to John Lennon, bad business decisions that would have been better had he been in charge of them and more. It was impossible for me not to warm to his eccentric, boisterous personality; I raved about him to my mum and told Charlie they should meet too.

'Tom's already told me about him,' said Charlie. 'My mum won't let me meet him.'

'Why not?'

And then Charlie told me Jonathan had spent three and a half years in prison for charges of child sex abuse.

'What's this?' I asked Mum. She was picking me up from the train station to drive me back to her house.

'Heart FM.'

'Why aren't you playing Capital?' I asked. We'd listened to Capital FM since I was a boy.

'I'm boycotting them.'

'Why?'

'Because they wouldn't play your Chartjackers song and I thought it was really not nice. You were doing a good thing for charity and what does it hurt them just to play it? Didn't like their reasoning at all, so no, that's it. No thank you. Not playing them again.'

'Well whoever this is,' I indicated, 'they didn't play it either.'

'Yes, but they didn't turn it down.'

'What a bean!'

'Why am I a bean?'

'You're always a bean,' I grinned.

We drove on in silence for a while.

'Bean, had you heard of Jonathan before I brought him up to you?'

There was a short silence. 'Yes, I had.'

'So why didn't you mention anything?'

'It did make me pause,' she said, 'when I first heard you mention him. You think "Oh my god," you know. But you met him and made him sound like a decent person, so I decided to do some research. I went on to Google and put his name in. I read all about his trial, and what he was accused of, and how he had been treated. I came to the conclusion it was actually really unfair what happened to him.'

What Mum had discovered was that Jonathan's accusations were split across three trials. The first was thrown out of court and in the second he was found not guilty. In the last one, despite five people accusing him of sexual abuse, Jonathan presented evidence showing he was elsewhere for all the dates of his alleged crimes. He had an alibi for every charge.

The prosecutors responded by changing the dates. If I hadn't read it (and heard about it from Jonathan himself) I wouldn't have thought it possible, but the prosecutors convinced the judge to allow the change, saying the specific dates were less important than whether he was generally guilty. I understand, from their perspective, that a specific date could easily be forgotten and might not be the most important detail in the scheme of things; on the other hand, this is exactly the kind of thing that must be scrutinised before proceeding with a criminal trial. When there's no proof sex has ever taken place (as is so often the case in these matters), the details surrounding the charge are everything.

In this case, changing the dates left Jonathan's defence obsolete and gave him no time to form a new one (the defence having already rested). As it was, his alleged crimes occurred twenty years before he was arrested, meaning evidence for either side was long gone (along with everyone's clear memories of exact dates and times). It was a miracle he tracked down proof of his original whereabouts in the first place.

Jonathan hoped the jury would object to the date changing, but what we call a 'jury of your peers' in Jonathan's case was made up of twelve members of the public who all knew his celebrity profile and had spent several months exposed to tabloid headlines like 'Evil Lust Of Pop Beast' before the trial began. You'd have been hard-pressed to find an unbiased juror in the whole of the country. Jonathan half-joked that a jury of *his* peers would best be comprised of Elton John, Rod Stewart and other famous pop stars from the sixties.

'It's one person's word against another,' said Jonathan later. 'It can be the result of delusion or tweaking, or because there's twenty grand in it for somebody — or it can be a combination of these things.'

'But someone wouldn't do it just for money, would they?' I asked him. Jonathan flashed his crooked smile.

In the UK, there is a government body whose role is to grant tens of thousands of pounds to people who have been abused. I went on their website. 'Calculate your compensation here,' it says, and you can fill in different types of abuse and get an instant quote for how much money you'd be awarded if it happened to you — and you can fill this in as many times as you like, trying out different traumas until you find one that's the most valuable.

The site tells me Jonathan's accusers would have received at least £11,000 upon his conviction, and that's in addition to what the press would probably pay for a salacious tell-all story on a bonafide celebrity. Jonathan's original accuser only went to the police, in fact, after he failed to sell the story to the press. This man's story never even made it to trial, but it was reported in the media after the fact, prompting a deluge of people to come forward for their own motivations (whatever they might have been).

After Jonathan was convicted, one of the accusers was quoted in the media saying, 'I said he'd done stuff he hadn't done, but I thought everyone was doing that.' I couldn't believe someone would admit to sending an innocent man to prison just to profit from it. 'He felt guilty, but lied so he could get cash,' the report said. 'He sold his story twice — for £45,000 the first time, then £5,000 from another tabloid when he was released. With the £45,000 he bought a maisonette.'

When Jonathan was released, he went on a mission to prove his innocence. He managed to track down evidence proving he was in another *country* during the second set of dates for which he'd been charged, meaning he had an alibi for every incident of abuse alleged to have occurred. He has since been invited to speak at a government inquiry to discuss his treatment at the hands of the media and police, neither of which recognise the dubious nature of his conviction or the evidence he's presented. His conviction has since been called one of 'the ten greatest miscarriages of justice in British history' by the investigative journalist Bob Woffinden in his book *The Nicholas Cases*.

Of course, despite the availability of these facts, people tend to stop at what they've already read or heard. The jury of my mum and me, however, concluded we had nothing to fear from this pompous, ridiculous man, and even Charlie's mum came around in the end. Jonathan got to know Charlie, Tom and me only as acquaintances, to give advice and learn about new technologies and the way the industry was moving. He denounced the 'old model' of the record labels and was keen to discover what the 'new model' of breaking and releasing tracks would be in the internet age.

'This is a new form of art,' Jonathan kept saying to us about YouTube. 'Imagine being Michelangelo, but before he could design the Sistine Chapel ceiling, he first had to invent paint. You're the ones who are figuring out all the rules, and you'll make all the mistakes. You won't be remembered. You'll be the ones who mess up and pave the way for the next generation to learn from your mistakes — and *they* will be huge.' Ignoring his dismissiveness of my entire life, I played Jonathan my first two albums with enthusiasm. He dismissed them as tuneless nonsense.

'What about this one, 'No More'?' I said, directing him to track three of *Parrot Stories*. It was my audience's favourite.

"No More' no more! What a fucking bore,' he said. '"No more" is right! There's no tune!'

'What do you mean?' I objected, convinced I was singing *something* on the CD.

'Play the song on a piano and you'll see there's no melody.'

'Okay, but the album —'

'Oh, albums! I was there when albums were invented, you know.' (He often said things like this.) 'I remember the first album coming out. Record label people thought 'Here's a good way to make ten times more money on the same songs!' It was just a sales trick. Albums are superficial. I get you want to write an *al-bum*, because your self-delusion is that you want to be an *ar-tiste*, and *ar-tistes* make *al-bums*. It's all bollocks. The biggest albums in the world — *Thriller*. *Rumours*. The Eagles' greatest hits. What do they have in common? Hits! Don't write albums! Write hits!'

'What makes a hit?' I asked.

'Well, that is the question,' said Jonathan. 'If I knew that I wouldn't be sitting here talking to you, dear; I'd be on a private island somewhere having my dick sucked by a string of beautiful women — and men — all of whom were over the age of consent, *your honour*!'

A real hit, says Jonathan, is a piece of work that sells several million copies globally, continues to be consumed decades into the future and tends to turn its creator into a lifelong worldwide star. My quintessential example is 'Baby One More Time', but there are many others; according to Jonathan, Rachmaninov's Piano Concerto No. 2 is a hit, as are the *Harry Potter* books and the works of David Hockney.

In 2009, Jonathan spotted a a gap in the market for a sweet, young male singer, and thought Tom fit the bill (after insisting he shave, to look as fresh-faced and teen-friendly as possible). Jonathan suggested he release a cover of David Bowie's *The Prettiest Star*, a track that was never recognised the way he felt it should have been. Jonathan got nothing out of doing this except the joy of breaking hits; as he kept reminding us, 'The amount of money you'll make from this would barely put petrol in the Rolls.'

Tom recorded the song and released it on April Fool's Day, saying in a video he wanted to 'play a prank on the music industry' by getting the song to number one. Thousands of people pledged to buy the track and if they had, it would have worked, but nobody did, the song flopped and Tom never mentioned it again. *Perhaps Jonathan was wrong*, I thought, until Justin Bieber released his single 'Baby' nine months later. It became the biggest-selling single in US history and the most-viewed music video on YouTube of all time, and Jonathan's gap in the market was filled.

'Oh well,' shrugged Jonathan. 'Another adventure.'

A year later, Jonathan spied another gap in the market for a new kind of boy band, and thought he might know just the boys.

Here's the email he sent us:

> The concept came because I don't feel, from what I've heard, that any of your solo stuff is good enough to gain mass popularity. However, the four of you all have individual strengths.

> Both Tommy and Charlie are quite good looking, gaining fans amongst the teen girl and gay communities.

> Tommy is becoming a very good producer.

> Charlie is becoming a very good video maker/ editor.

> Alex has the passion, need and enthusiasm to be the engine for the group — promoting and exposing it.

> Ed has the more mellow and grounded attitude to hold it together.

So — the four of you together could break big AS LONG as the songs are very very strong, neither obvious "covers" nor flops. I'm happy to suggest songs — Tommy can then choose those he likes best and can produce them. The point is to use the advantages of the four of you to create a solid foundation of popularity which will both bring in funding and — as it is a COLLECTIVE, not a boy band — give increased chances of success for four individual careers.

The task was to generate a hit machine to support our separate ventures, modernising great songs that were unfamiliar to our audience. We only had to record and break the singles and do a few selected gigs. The hits would bring us acclaim and fortune and we could do whatever we liked outside of it. A prominent acting company in Elizabethan times, the Admiral's Men, seemed to embody the spirit of the collective Jonathan had in mind. They were a group of creative people who wrote their own plays, but also performed their work and those of others as a group and were recognised on their own merits as well as through the collective. In the spirit of the Admiral's Men, Ed bestowed on us the name 'Sons of Admirals'.

Jonathan kept impressing upon us that this was the perfect time for a new male group to dominate the pop world. If he was right, we would be huge stars. All we had to do was keep the band together long enough to get there.

I loved the idea from the start, thinking it would be great fun and would lead me closer to the unbridled mainstream success and freedom I desired. I even gave us Spice Girls-inspired nicknames: Nerdy, Quirky, Rocky and Cocky (guess which one I was).

Tom, meanwhile, had dyed his hair bright blue and just finished work on an EP he released for free called *Geometry*. The tracks, called things like 'Fibonacci', 'Two Right Angles', and 'Sohcahtoa', were made by processing mathematical formulas through an audio workstation and recording whatever sounds were generated. As I understand it, he just hit go, left it running, came back when it was done and released it. When I told Tom I'd listened to it, he responded with a grin, 'You've heard more of it than me!' As he became ever more experimental, the idea of being in a huge mainstream band seemed to him like a great way to subvert the system from within.

Ed wanted to be a #SeriousMusician. Of the four of us, Ed was the only one who shut his eyes and bit his lip when he played his guitar. He wanted the recognition that came from mass appeal and the kudos that came from covering the deep cuts of credible musicians.

Charlie wasn't interested at all and only agreed to get involved in the first place because I asked him to as a favour to me. We couldn't do it without his video-making skill or his popularity, both of which eclipsed us all. I made it clear, though, that the project was designed to be low-commitment, allowing him to get far more out of it than he put in.

Our new group was therefore composed of: me, wanting to be a mass-appeal pop star but on my own terms; Tom, who wanted to be intellectual and provocative; Ed, who wanted to be credible and sincere; and Charlie, who wanted to make videos about science for the internet. Sons of Admirals was like asking Bruno Mars, Amanda Palmer, Thom Yorke and David Attenborough to form a band, and all of it was to be overseen by a sixty-six year old man who once got Margaret Thatcher to appear on national television singing 'How Much Is That Doggie in the Window?'

Jonathan said we might be the first group he'd ever heard of to break up before we even formed.

In accordance with the outline in his initial email, Jonathan would pick the songs. Tom would arrange and produce the track in Oli's little studio in East London. Charlie would film and edit a music video for the track. I would promote it by reaching out to everyone who's ever worked in any job anywhere to tell them Sons of Admirals had a song out. Ed would act as the glue, keeping us from killing each other long enough to reap the rewards of our collective marketability before nestling ourselves back into our own projects.

For the first track, Jonathan suggested 'Here Comes My Baby' by Cat Stevens. We got to work in the studio, smashed the song out in a day (with Charlie turning up in the last hour to record the chorus and go home) and sent it to Jonathan the same evening.

'Absolute smash,' he replied, 'global; 14 million worldwide. Well done.'

Charlie made the music video and we put it up on his YouTube channel, by which point I'd already begun the hype, emailing newspaper tech correspondents in advance of the song's release. Traditional music people dismissed what we were doing but I suspected tech people would cover the story due to the disruptive way we were doing it.

'If you wanted a great example of how a new generation of musicians are building their fanbase online... you should take a look at Sons of Admirals,' wrote the *Guardian* the afternoon of the video's release. The next day, 'Here Comes My Baby' was featured in the 'Song of the Week' section of Steve Wright's show on BBC Radio 2. An hour later, my inbox was filled with emails from record label reps, management companies and radio pluggers, and by the end of the week I was in the offices of Warner Music, being congratulated on my shrewdness at being able to generate a hurricane of interest from nothing. We'd been a band for two weeks.

'Don't think this is hyperbole,' one A&R guy said to me, 'but you guys remind me of the Beatles.'

'I'll tell the internet you said that!' I grinned, noting his sudden nervousness.

'You now have a hit,' said Jonathan, 'and everyone is starting to notice.' To help us build on our momentum he set up a meeting for us with the founder of Modest Management, Richard Griffiths, a manager of several prominent pop acts (the biggest at the time being Olly Murs). Having heard 'Here Comes My Baby', Richard asked us to bring other songs we'd recorded. We didn't have any. Thinking that might not be the best thing to admit at a management meeting, I burned a few tracks from my albums on a CD and presented them to him, watching him listen to the first ten seconds of each before skipping to the next while Tom and Ed (Charlie wasn't there) muttered between themselves, disavowing my song choices. When he asked us who our musical inspirations were, I said Green Day and Tom snorted.

'What?' I snapped, shooting him a look.

'I don't really get this,' said Richard, ignoring our spat. 'Are you solo acts, or are you a band?'

'Both,' said Ed.

'To make it in this industry,' said Richard, 'you need five things: talent, luck, money, vision and drive. You have got the talent. Luck is there or not there and money will come. But the vision and the drive... what do you want to be, and how badly do you actually want it?'

'We want to be a collective,' I said, 'and maintain our own individual careers.'

'Well I wish you the best of luck with it,' he said, and we knew we were done.

We had a much more promising meeting with a boisterous American called Stan, who appealed to be our manager. He had no management experience but said if we got to number one in the UK charts we could dye his hair any colour we wanted. He told us, among other things, that he was trying to get us a meeting with Steve Jobs because of how disruptive we were being.

'I am like the genie,' Stan raved to us. 'You just say whatever you want and I'll make it happen!'

'I wanna meet Taylor Swift,' I said without hesitating.

'Great,' he grinned, unfazed, 'I'll text her dad right now!'

Stan's passion for our project had us convinced he was the right person for the job; conviction was more important to us than experience. We signed a short-term management agreement, valid only for the first single, to test things out and agreed to set up our own record label (Admirals Records) to distribute our work. Stan began paying for all our meals and taxis across the city.

Within days, Stan got us a one-single deal with Universal Records for 'Here Comes My Baby'. I was in Zambia at the time; I'd been flown over to make some videos for a charity there (much to the disapproval of Jonathan, who said I shouldn't be doing anything except breaking the single). I was woken at six in the morning by the sound of a muddy bucket of warm water thudding on the ground outside my door. I crawled out of my mosquito net, climbed into the bucket to wash myself, got dried and dressed, took my laptop to the village's designated Wi-Fi area, found out I had a record deal and then celebrated by dancing with a bunch of African schoolchildren. The other Admirals and I wanted to have as much fun as we could, including (much to Jonathan's chagrin) recording the theme song to a kids' cartoon called *Arthur* as the B-side to the Cat Stevens track. (When we next spoke to Stan, he said he'd reached out to the people who make *Arthur* to persuade them to change their theme to our version.)

I resumed my duties as the band's engine when I got home, writing personal letters to my favourite radio DJs and encouraging thousands of our subscribers to do the same. I went to the BBC's Radio 1 building and 'bumped into' DJ Scott Mills, who didn't remember me from *Upstaged* or *Chartjackers*, meaning I had the privilege of making a new first impression.

'How do you get a track played on the radio?' I asked him, feigning innocence, while he was on a cigarette break. 'I'm in a band and we have CDs but I've heard it's nothing to do with DJs anymore and the producers have all the power.' Then, seeing his face change, 'Oh, I didn't mean to undermine you!'

'Well, no, producers don't have all the power,' Scott replied, indignant.

'Sorry!' I said. 'I just thought the producers decided everything that was played and the DJs had to play them.'

'Well... hey, give me your CD,' he said, eager to reclaim his sense of self-worth.

'Sure, I think I have one in here somewhere,' I said with a smile, rummaging around my bag.

I recounted the story to Jonathan with glee. 'You're a good boy; you do work hard even though I have a go at you,' he said.

Requests for interviews started coming in from regional radio stations. Tom, Ed and I took a taxi to Norwich to play our song, then a taxi to Birmingham, then a plane to Edinburgh. 'Here Comes My Baby' ended up playlisted at about thirty radio stations around the country and Stan booked us a live session at the headquarters of *The Sun* to promote it. The gig would go live on their website and be covered in the paper. Forgoing the usual lineup of instruments, Tom planned to add sounds on the fly with a Game Boy rigged up to the speaker and insisted I learn how to play the dulcimer.

The *Sun* gig came with an interview, prompting Tom to argue we were unprepared for the dangers of tabloid journalism. 'We have to rehearse the whole interview!' he exclaimed.

'Why?'

'If you say the wrong thing they'll pounce on you!' he said. 'I'll prove it.'

Tom took on the role of the interviewer: 'What's your favourite music in the charts at the moment?'

'Well, I don't like much music in the charts at the moment—'

'Oh, so you think you're better than the music in the charts?' Tom interrupted.

'Well, yeah,' I said. 'That's why I'm in this band, so I can put better music into the world—'

'See, you can't say that!' said Tom.

'Why not?'

'Because then *The Sun* publish "Arrogant Sons of Admirals Think They're Bigger Than Pop Music!"'

'No they won't,' I exclaimed, 'because if they ran with that headline, everyone would say, "Who are Sons of Admirals?" and nobody would buy *The Sun* that day!'

Ed was doing a terrible job of being the glue. Living with Tom influenced the two of them to agree on issues while Charlie and I disagreed. We formed two opposing fronts. When Stan suggested we make and sell a calendar, Ed thought it a great idea because it would show how serious and credible we were; Tom agreed because he wanted each month to be more surreal and unmarketable than the last. In contrast, I hated the idea because I found it pretentious, and Charlie agreed because he'd started to hate every aspect of Sons of Admirals by that point.

When we agreed to the gig at *The Sun*, Charlie told us he didn't want to do it — or anything else regarding the group from now on — and brought this up to Stan in a meeting. I knew I couldn't convince him (and moreover I didn't want to; our infighting had sucked all the fun out of the project, and I'd already mentally punched out), but with the song only a week away from release, Stan begged Charlie to keep marketing the track with us. 'It's only one more week,' said Stan.

'Look, I can help you promote the song,' Charlie said with a beaten sigh, 'but I'm telling you it will make me really unhappy.'

'Okay,' said Stan. 'That's very big of you. Thank you Charlie.'

Charlie was morose all the way home, stunned that Stan was content with his unhappiness. He did the gig, and when it was uploaded to *The Sun*'s website, our audience went in droves to watch it and their servers crashed. Jonathan saw it too. He was furious when he saw how miserable Charlie was.

'This is *real* child abuse,' Jonathan said. 'It has to stop.'

Our next meeting was scheduled on the day 'Here Comes My Baby' was released. The agreement was that we wouldn't do any more gigs, focusing on our online activities to appease Charlie, who didn't need any involvement beyond an afternoon recording the new song and a music video to promote it. We toasted the song and our work so far and began to discuss how we might break the track in America, as well as plans for our second single: either the Fleetwood Mac track 'I Don't Wanna Know' or an obscure sixties song called 'Lady Godiva'. Then Stan revealed something we had overlooked. It turned out

Admiral Records — our own label — had paid for everything, not Stan. All of the meals, taxi rides and flights had been paid out of our pockets. Admirals Records was £20,000 in debt.

When we objected, Stan said this was standard practice and that he had sunk thousands of pounds of his own money into the project too. He wanted us to break America partly so he could make it back and was frustrated when the four of us refused to sign any definite management agreement or spend a single penny more until the accounts were balanced.

Without a clear way forward, Stan started cooking up an even bigger plan. He hired another guy, Dave, who declared himself 'a specialist in getting deals'. Together they concocted a scheme to get us a record deal with music mogul Simon Fuller (the guy who briefly involved himself in Tom's solo album). The idea was to persuade Simon to pay us money every month which we would use to continue making creative projects in whatever form we liked. In exchange, we would be 'ring-fenced' so Simon got first refusal on the development of any idea we wanted to pursue.

It sounded ideal, even to Charlie, and we were overjoyed to get a message saying Simon wanted to meet us and would fly us out to LA as soon as possible. With that, Charlie and I put ourselves on alert. We stopped making plans. We stopped buying food. We just ticked over in our flat, waiting to be whisked away to Los Angeles at a moment's notice. A whole week passed before Charlie gave in and suggested we let normal life resume.

I asked Stan about the delay and I ran into a problem. Dave had been telling Simon's people he was our manager, which seemed to hurt Stan on a personal level; they'd got into a huge row over it. Dave argued he had been hired as Stan's representative to get this deal and that Stan would mess it up if he took charge, but Stan suspected Dave was trying to oust him as manager by being the only middleman between us and Simon Fuller. For days we watched petty emails fly between our two managers as each questioned the other's motives. They had as much discord between them as... well, as Sons of

Admirals did, so in that way I suppose they were the perfect people to represent us.

Everything culminated in a meeting in West London 'round the corner from Simon Fuller's offices, just before we were scheduled to meet with Simon's 'people'. Stan arrived first and expressed his sadness over the way things had worked out. He worried Dave would exclude him from the meeting and asked for our support. We didn't know what was best at this point. We were exhausted by the whole thing.

Dave turned up next and shook hands with Stan, and they both said they cared about our futures most of all and should put their differences aside. We all sat 'round the table talking about the meeting and how to present ourselves, and when everyone was ready, we stood up to go to Simon's office.

When Stan stood up, Dave said, 'You're not coming.'

'Yes I am!' said Stan. He looked at us. Everyone sat back down.

The four of us watched as Dave insisted Stan would ruin the deal, Stan insisted he had the right as our manager to be there, and Dave brandished his iPhone at us, having drafted an email saying the meeting was cancelled.

'If you're going to be like this I'll do it, I'll cancel the meeting,' he warned, his thumb hovering over the screen.

'I'm not being like anything!' Stan argued.

'I'll cancel it!' said Dave.

'Come on—' I started.

'This is ridiculous,' said Stan.

'Right, I've cancelled it,' said Dave, putting his phone back into his pocket and staring us down, satisfied.

'Right,' said Tom, getting to his feet. 'Well, I've been to Simon's office before, and I know where it is, so *we're* going.'

Ed, Charlie and I stood up with Tom, and the four of us walked out the door.

The meeting with Simon's people went well. We chatted with excitement about our ideas and what we wanted to achieve together, and it seemed like it might all happen. At least for the rest of that afternoon. The problem was Simon's staff had no idea why they'd received an email five minutes earlier saying the meeting was cancelled or why some other guy called Stan kept telling them to speak to him from now on. They saw the brewing power struggle and stepped as far as they could in the other direction. We never heard from them again. In the end, I didn't even meet Taylor Swift.

The last time the four of us met as Sons of Admirals, Jonathan presented us with neon hoodies emblazoned with a slogan he thought fit each of our personalities: for Tom, to try and resolve our squabbles, 'Real Friendship Means Honesty'; for Ed, 'Glue Doesn't Always Stick'; for Charlie, 'I'm Scared Of Everything'; and for me, who tires of everything the moment it's not easy, 'Bored Now!'

At last our lives went back to normal — or at least normal by our standards: *Sugar* published their list of 'Top 50 Hottest Lads of 2010' and Charlie scored 29th, higher than Justin Bieber. 'Not as high as Johnny Depp though,' said Charlie.

'He was higher than you?'

'One higher. *One higher than me.*'

That summer, a teen girl called Rebecca Black uploaded a music video for a song called 'Friday'. It went viral. *The Independent* called it 'the worst pop song of all time' and BBC News went even further, calling it the 'worst song ever'. It got to #60 in the UK Charts. 'Here Comes My Baby' ended up at #61.

A few months later, I got a text from Jonathan: 'Turn on ITV — this should have been you!'

The X Factor was on. I was watching a five-piece boy band bounce around the stage in front of a screaming crowd. Simon Cowell was on his feet, leading the audience in a standing ovation. They didn't win the show, but were later signed by Richard Griffiths — the guy we met at Modest Management — and a year later their first album debuted in

America straight at #1, breaking the record for a British debut previously held by The Beatles.

Jonathan's gap in the market was filled by One Direction.

'Oh well,' said Jonathan. 'Another adventure.'

VIP

In 2009, my friends Jazza and Liam organised a huge gathering in Hyde Park called Summer in the City. Ukuleles were played, shirts were signed and at one point we sat in a huge circle playing Pass the Parcel. I caught up with friends and made new ones. In the evening we packed out a nearby bar and Greg, my old friend from the Apple Store, played a show for us (while Denise wept at stage left, freshly heartbroken, and everyone pretended not to notice).

The event was a huge success and the boys got to work organising a follow-up. I arrived at Summer in the City the following year and, about two seconds after I stepped onto the grass, was mobbed by people who formed a tight circle around me and cut me off from the rest of the event. Some asked me who I was dating, how Sons of Admirals was going or what it was like living with Charlie. Some would lean in, take a photo with me and then walk off without saying anything. Others would monopolise the conversation to tell me about their YouTube videos or engage me in lengthy debates about the casting of the lead role in *Doctor Who*. I went to gatherings to work on projects with people and soak up the creative energy, but people weren't interested in filming each other anymore. Instead, clumps of humanity honed in on one vlogger, then another, taking photos and offering up merch for signatures before drifting off on a new trajectory. The event was a galaxy with planets in orbit around different stars. Overwhelmed by what I was now realising was a public appearance, I finished up my conversations and headed home.

Charlie and I lived in a ground floor flat with an outdoor terrace. Beyond the terrace was a row of small hedges, and beyond that, a public walkway. While I ate meals, I would face the terrace and watch people pass by (as well as streaming twenty-minute comedy shows on my laptop, since I could never be too stimulated). A few days after Summer in the City, I sat down with a sandwich and an episode of *How I Met Your Mother*, brought the sandwich to my lips, looked up, and saw a boy at the window, behind the hedges, wearing a Sons of Admirals t-shirt, filming me.

The sandwich dangled at my lips as I stared at him, unmoving. The boy wasn't looking at me. He kept his eyes fixed on the back of his camera, which he kept pointed toward where I was sitting.

Like that we stayed for a few seconds, neither of us sure what to do next.

Then the boy — still staring at the camera — lowered himself down, inch by inch, until he'd disappeared behind the hedge row. It was almost funny, like when someone pretends there's an elevator behind a sofa. Not quite knowing what to do, I settled for a tweet.

'Can you please not come to where I live and film me through the window? This isn't Where's Wally. That's not how you meet me and Charlie.'

While Penny and other friends tweeted at us in sympathy and horror, the first reply I got from a member of my audience said, 'well then how are we supposed to meet you?'

I then had to go into Charlie's room and tell him someone was watching and filming me through the window. The rest of the day was a write-off; we spent it hugging our legs on the sofa, staring into our screens and peering out from behind our curtains as if under siege.

A few weeks later a guy I didn't recognise knocked on the door.

'Hey,' he grinned. 'You're Alex Day, right?'

'Uh, yeah.'

'Oh man, I really love your videos. You're such an inspiration.'

'Cheers.'

I noticed the guy was leaning to one side, concealing something in his right hand behind our door frame.

'Is Charlie around?' he said.

'Yeah. He's busy.'

'Oh right.'

There was a short silence.

'Okay, well it is so cool to meet you.'

'Sure,' I said, shutting the door as he walked away with my life.

I saw this tweet later in the day: 'Great to meet you earlier! My mate dared me to play Mario Kart Wii with you guys... I had it with me but chickened out of asking. Gutted!'

Summer in the City had been about as English as a gathering of internet people could get: we met in a park belonging to the Queen and bothered each other in the rain. America, as always, displayed more pizazz when their 'gathering' took place in a hotel in Los Angeles, lasted three and a half days and attracted over a thousand people.

I flew to LA for the event. The airport security officer took my passport in his blue-gloved hand and peered down at it.

'Hey,' he said, 'you're Alex Day!'

'I am,' I said, making sure to sound assertive in case this was a security test.

'What brings you here?'

'I'm just here for a conference in the city.'

'Oh, you're here for VidCon?' grinned the security officer.

VidCon was organised by Hank and John, who by this point were the established godfathers of our community. It offered panels, talks, Q&As, meet and greets, a ball pit, an open mic and a karaoke room. I wanted to feel as relaxed as possible to compensate for my experience at Summer in the City, developing a preference for walking around the hotel with no name tag and no shoes on. While waiting one morning in the lobby's Starbucks queue, a girl screamed in excitement at my presence and I nearly dropped my change. I hadn't intended to elicit that level of energy at that time of the morning: I was bleary-eyed, with scruffy hair, unbrushed teeth and worn socks, crunching down a granola bar.

'Can I have a picture with you?'

'Of course,' I said. When the girl thanked me and walked off, two others had appeared in her place. After I signed their CDs, four more appeared. My audience seemed to be undergoing mitosis. Once I'd bought my drink, I told the crowd (more of whom were now there for me than for their morning coffee fix) that I needed to head back upstairs, and was delighted to find them cordial, polite and understanding. Nobody monopolised my time and everybody was respectful. A few of them asked me for hugs and I hugged my way down the line as I made my way to the door, grinning. It was a good way to start my day.

Hank had invited me to play a fifteen-minute gig at VidCon. I'd spent weeks rehearsing my set, using Queen's performance at Live Aid as a model for packing lots of music and energy into a short show. I came up with loads of little tricks for each song like throwing confetti into the crowd, leading the room in chants and getting people jumping along. I wanted one big moment that people would remember in each track, and enough great memories to send thousands of those kids to the merch stand to pick up my CD. Every movement I made was rehearsed to the second.

I was also aware Denise would be in attendance — if not in the crowd, she'd at least be somewhere on the premises. I knew I'd be playing at VidCon when I recorded my second album, and it was on my mind that she might end up hearing me sing, so I wanted to write something to get across what I would have said to her if I'd had the chance: that I knew I'd fucked up, that I missed our friendship, that I hoped we could rebuild one, and most of all that I hoped she was having a great evening. That song became 'The Time Of Your Life' (the one I reworked in the studio with Tom's guidance) and I ended up emailing it to her before the event. Once the ice was broken, we started to talk again, and she sent me a song *she'd* written ('Delete You', which had a bit more venom than mine).

On the night of the show I wore an Edward Cullen t-shirt, showed off a temporary tattoo of the Dark Mark on my forearm and bounded across the stage for my fifteen minutes, doing everything I'd planned to the second and eating up the crowd's energy. I ended my set by duetting a song from the musical episode of *Buffy the Vampire Slayer* with Hank and then jumping into the crowd, who surfed me away. When I landed, I found John waiting for me with his wife and newborn son.

'I have never seen anyone swagger around on a stage like that,' said John, grinning. He told me he'd arrived at the back of the hall when I started and found himself getting pulled in with every song until he ended up at the side of the stage. After that I joined the crowd and watched the rest of the show from the floor. Once Charlie, Tom and Hank had all performed, a dance party started with Ed as the DJ. He played what he called 'the trifecta': 'Mrs Nerimon', 'The Time Of Your Life' and 'Delete You' all in a row, with Denise and me taking turns on stage lip-syncing to our songs. Hank made his way into the crowd and threw me onto his shoulders during 'Don't Stop Believing'. We danced as equals — the organisers, the performers, and the attendees — and then I queued up in the karaoke room to warble my way through 'Sk8er Boi' by Avril Lavigne before crashing in my bed.

Hank asked me to perform at VidCon the following year, but I didn't see the point. I hadn't worked on any new songs and would just be repeating my set from the year before. 'How about if Chameleon Circuit performs instead?' I suggested.

Two years had passed since our first *Doctor Who*-inspired album and we'd been working on a follow-up. Charlie was keen for us to produce 'a really good album', by which he meant one that got finished before we released it. Ginger Chris had 'regenerated' into Ed, who wrote half the songs for the new CD (which we called *Still Got Legs*, after Matt Smith's first words in the show), and we flew our friend Michael over from America to produce it in what we were calling Flipchart Studios, which was how we described our living room with a flip chart in it.

Michael was fascinated by the internet and its potential for grand social experiments. He worked with a friend of his, Dan Brown (no relation), on a project called Dan 3.0. The idea was to run a YouTube channel where Dan's audience would dictate the choices he made with his life, from what clothes to wear to where he would go and what he would do from day to day, like my old 'Pet Guinea Pig' idea on steroids. (It lasted about as long as my attempt.) Technology seemed to fit naturally in Michael's life: he used an app called Foursquare to show his audience and friends online where he was at any given time, and uploaded unedited videos direct from his phone several times a day to a YouTube channel called WhatImDoingRightNow. I would often be thrown off-guard hearing Michael declare, 'It's great here!', only to turn and see he was talking to the internet, not me. Even Michael's sleep seemed oriented around the internet; he seemed to sleep in 36-hour cycles, meaning no matter when he woke up, different parts of the world would be there with him.

Michael and I decided on a three-month timetable to make the album, more than enough time to ensure we would launch it alongside the new season of *Doctor Who* in April. The publicity of a new season would help as I used my engine skills to drive the hype of the new CD. As he flew in, Michael thus asked for entry into the UK for three months. The border office wrote 'Leave to stay for six months' in his passport.

What I hadn't factored in is that Michael is from California and is the most Californian man I've ever met. He speaks softly, he breathes slowly and he's always smiling. Every word Michael uses is chosen with care. I've never seen Michael panic. I've also never seen him rush. With his time doubled from three months to six, Michael only produced one song in the time I expected him to make the whole album. Around the time the whole thing was due, he took off to France on holiday with Charlie. (I would have suspected he fled the country in fear of my wrath, but that would rely on Michael being capable of feeling anything but contentment.)

Charlie came back to our flat a week later. Michael didn't. He'd been turned away at the French border and the plane left without him. It turned out Michael's six months weren't continuous; he could only stay for up to three months at a time. The immigration officers at the French border said he'd outstayed his welcome and wouldn't let him through without a valid ticket back to America. This album was going even worse than the last one: the tracks didn't exist and our producer had been imprisoned in Europe. I started to regret naming our band after the one part of the TARDIS that famously doesn't work. (The chameleon circuit is supposed to camouflage the Doctor's time machine to blend in with its surroundings, but got stuck looking like a 1950s police box in the very first episode due to both malfunctioning extra-dimensional technology and, even worse, budget constraints.)

'Stuck in France lol', Michael tweeted, and someone in Paris replied, offering him a place to stay. For two days, Michael lived with a French family who knew him from the internet while he got himself organised. He bought a return ticket to California and headed back to the border, clutching his passport and a printout of his ticket as he waited in the queue.

'Next.'

Michael walked up. 'Hello,' he said in the silkiest American voice anyone has ever heard. The border agent grunted back, glanced somewhere near Michael's face, and peered down at his passport.

'You have a denial of entry,' the agent said, his eyes tightening. Michael tried to explain what happened but it was no good; because his passport had already been denied once at the border, his card had been marked. The border officer concluded he must pose 'a significant risk to the United Kingdom' and wouldn't let him back to London to finish recording an album of *Doctor Who* songs.

I wasn't sure how I could help, but decided a petition might be a good start. I didn't think the government would change their mind based on some silly online signatures but, if I generated enough energy around the story, I hoped to attract some kind of help. In any case, nobody else was doing anything, and it was better than that. The petition — 'Bring Michael Aranda Back To The UK' — was shared through our collective Facebook, Twitter and YouTube accounts and I jumped on the Eurostar to Paris to visit Michael and film his plight.

The petition got 50,000 signatures overnight and, the next morning I woke up to a message in my YouTube inbox: 'We saw your video and we want to help!' It was from Red Bull. They wanted to get involved and help us complete our album. (Red Bull, I later learned, have a strong history of working with and promoting musicians.) They couldn't bring Michael to us, they said, but they could bring us to Michael; they offered to pay for a month's rent in a house in France to finish the album, and paid for our flights so the whole band could get there.

Red Bull were giving us wings.

A week later, Charlie, Liam, Ed and I were with Michael in a lofty apartment in the middle of Paris, joined by Ali, a friend he'd made over there, and Penny, who flew out on her own dime to visit us and sing some backing vocals. Michael bashed the whole album out in three weeks and Red Bull helped negotiate his return to England long enough to get his stuff and fly home again. During the few days he was permitted to stay in London, Red Bull threw us an album listening party at Red Bull Studios in London, complete with a Dalek in the corner and a TARDIS for us to emerge from after the album finished playing to answer questions, take photos and sign t-shirts. We made a hundred tickets available for the event. They sold out in two minutes.

Michael flew back to LA and we followed him soon after to rehearse our show for VidCon, which was only a couple weeks away. The whole band crashed on the floor of Michael's house, meaning we had no privacy from each other. This would have been fine, but I'd never spent a lot of time with Ed in close quarters and learned it was like living with the reactionary part of the internet embodied in a living person.

'Who else doesn't care that Amy Winehouse just died?' Ed trumpeted one morning, waking me up from whatever pleasantness my mind was showing itself. Ed reacted like this to all kinds of news, from politics to pop culture: out loud and with a strong opinion. He also read out the YouTube comments he received in real-time, often expressing anger or dismay at what his audience had said. In every memory I have of him from that time, he's cross-legged on the floor or lying on his side in his sleeping bag, gazing into his laptop.

When we rehearsed our show, we would wait 'offstage' (in the laundry room), then run into Michael's garage like fireballs, grabbing our instruments and leaping into action. Ed still wanted to prove himself as a serious artist and it showed.

'The crowd can see you,' he frowned when I stood a little too close to the garage door before the 'show' had started. I glanced at him, unimpressed.

'Hello VidCon!' I yelled to the fake mic later in a break between songs.

'Don't say "hello",' ordered Ed. 'Too formal. Say "hi" or "hey".'

'The crowd can hear you,' I said.

By the time we got to the conference, we were all frustrated with Ed's methods and grateful to have a break. Ed and Liam would be sharing a room, separate from the one I was sharing with Charlie, and Michael was driving to and from the hotel each day. I wandered around the hotel before getting my keys, enjoying the quiet.

'Welcome, Mr. Day,' said the clerk at reception. 'Your roommate has already checked in; you're in one of the penthouses.'

I didn't know until then that Hank had put Charlie and me in a penthouse suite. I opened the door a few minutes later to see a huge lounge area with sofas and a widescreen TV, a kitchen, a massive dining table and chairs, double bedroom, bathroom, separate twin room with its own bathroom, and Ed standing in the middle of the lounge grinning at me.

'This is the life!' he said.

Charlie walked in the door with Liam.

'Hey,' said Charlie. 'Where's your room?'

I gestured around me.

'Oh,' said Charlie. 'I thought it was just me here so I gave the spare room to Ed and Liam.'

'That's my room,' I said, frustrated with Charlie for having so little ego that he gave away half his penthouse.

'Our room was tiny,' said Ed, 'and just had one bed. So one of us had to sleep on the floor. It wouldn't be fair to make Liam sleep on the floor—'

'I was happy to,' interjected Liam.

'—and it's not fair for me to sleep on the floor with Liam in the bed,' finished Ed, cutting across Liam's quiet amiability.

I didn't know how I could face three more days of Ed unfiltered, so I snuck off to talk to Melissa Anelli (the founder of LeakyCon, who was helping Hank organise VidCon) and explained my problem. Melissa went to the penthouse and told Ed and Liam that, because of fire safety, they would have to stay in their designated room and an extra single bed would be sent there straight away.

When she left, Ed said, 'I don't buy that; we can just crash here on the sofa,' slumped on the nearest couch and put his feet up. Charlie, still seeing no need for us to command the space of a whole penthouse, dumped our musical instruments across the dining area for easy access, cluttering the table and chairs with drum stands. Realising it would do little good to bother anyone any further with my own issues, I retired to my twin room with private bathroom and shut the door.

My cousin Danny joined me in my siphoned-off section of the penthouse the next day. He'd flown over to stay for the weekend and help promote Sopio, the card game we'd invented together years before.

'Check it out, mate,' he'd grinned one day during a visit to our flat in London, 'I made some new cards.' He opened a carrier bag and pulled out about five hundred cards, bound with elastic bands and adorned with meticulously hand-drawn stick men in pencil. Every deck had a theme — sports, carnivals, movies — and every card was unique, with hundreds of different effects and game mechanics all designed by Danny in his spare time.

'Holy shit,' I said, admiring the extent of his work. A few days later, my mum phoned me.

'Danny's been fired from the Sony Centre.'

'He did spend a lot of time designing a card game,' I admitted.

'Well, not fired,' she clarified. 'They're closing down the whole store. So he's out of a job.'

'That's great!'

'Alex, how is it great?'

'Now he can work on his own stuff full time and pursue what really matters to him without being distracted,' I said. My favourite thing about having a platform to live my fullest creative life was that I could liberate all the talented people around me as well as myself. Liam, for example, worked in a bar before Chameleon Circuit's first album came out and he was able to quit and live off the royalties. When I collaborated with smaller YouTubers, I relished seeing their subscribers and views go up, giving them an audience of their own. I knew I could do the same for my cousin. So Danny and I chose the best cards from his seven decks to make a new, consolidated pack of cards, got it printed by the manufacturers of Magic: The Gathering and set up a website to sell it by mail order. I knew that, as with music, people needed to experience something to think about buying it, so (not being able to sit down with my audience for several thousand games of Sopio) I interspersed the game throughout my vlogs, filming myself playing it with friends and family and talking about my favourite cards as though everyone knew what it was — but never explaining it. More and more people jammed the comments demanding to understand what the hell I was on about and where they could get the game for themselves.

'I've been saving this for years,' he said when the website went live, pulling out a small bottle of champagne. 'For the day we first sell a deck of Sopio. I just wanna sell one deck, so this thing in our heads can be a real thing people like and pay money for.'

That afternoon, Danny took Charlie and me out to Gourmet Burger Kitchen in Greenwich. I'd uploaded a video explaining Sopio and unveiling the website, and we refreshed our PayPal balance with excitement as we ate. We sold a thousand decks to my audience the day we launched. Danny used the profits to put a deposit on a flat in London.

It didn't cost much to rent a small table in VidCon's trade section to sell Sopio directly. Danny manned the stall for the weekend while I prepared for Chameleon Circuit's gig. The first day of VidCon was an 'industry' day, which to me meant loads of talks about how to optimise your reach on YouTube and what the best tags and thumbnails were and how meaningful and important we all were for the future of everything. Ed went to every talk he could. I spent most of the day in bed. That evening, companies hosted schmoozy get-togethers and gave out drink tokens in an attempt to curry favour with the vloggers. A t-shirt company, District Lines, threw a party and gave out free t-shirts to stumbling attendees saying 'I partied with District Lines'.

Michael, Danny, and I spent the evening in my room playing Sopio. 'We're the only people at VidCon who aren't drunk!' Michael cheered into his phone camera for his latest direct upload.

Security was much tighter than the previous year. VIPs had their own private floor with free snacks and beverages, but they also had guards manning every entrance, and an identifying lanyard we were supposed to wear around our necks. I didn't want to isolate myself and didn't like wearing the lanyard but, try as I might, they wouldn't let me around the hotel without it. I liked having a luxurious private room, but I didn't want a luxurious private convention.

Chameleon Circuit organised a signing event, but when 'too many' people showed up, the higher-ups changed it to a Q&A panel and the last question concerned the growing divide between YouTube creators and their viewers. I was glad to hear someone else had noticed. I looked at the rest of the band, then stepped forward.

'It's weird,' I said. 'I don't feel like I'm special.' I held up the VIP lanyard like a noose. 'I don't like wearing this. I don't like walking around with a big sign around my neck saying "I'm different from you". I want us to be the same — because we *are* the same. It's "Broadcast Yourself", not "Watch Other People Broadcast Themselves". You guys can do anything we've done and there shouldn't be anything dividing us or making you think otherwise.'

The room broke into a round of applause. As it faded, a woman walked on stage and took the microphone.'Okay guys,' she barked, 'that was the last question. Thank you for coming. Chameleon Circuit will be escorted out of the room now and everyone needs to *stay in their seats* while the band leaves.' We were then ushered out of the room and up to the private VIP floor by a flurry of VidCon staff walking on either side of us to hold back the crowd of people I'd just called our equals as they tried to get us to sign things for them.

Ed took to his newfound superiority with more ease than me, soaking up the attention from the suits and lording it around the VIP floor slurring his opinions to the world as he blagged more and more drink tokens and then collapsed, a wreck, in our suite.

Because I had my own private quarters, I left the penthouse the next morning without running into the rest of the band, so I didn't know what had happened the night before. I didn't see anyone until midday, when Chameleon Circuit had our sound check on the main stage. Ed was ruined. He kept staggering offstage to drink water and lean on things. He spoke only in whispers, like the survivor of a horror movie; the only words I heard him say were 'Never again.' He was almost translucent; I've never seen a man look so dead while still being alive.

Ed wasn't our only problem. For some reason the music from the turntable kept cutting in and out, meaning a lot of our backing tracks couldn't be heard and leaving us out of key and out of time with each other. Shane from the Remus Lupins, the most ebullient man on this or any world known, was in the audience listening to us, bouncing up and down on the tips of his toes. I wanted to make him proud.

'How's it sounding?' I called out to him.

'You'll get there!' he grinned back, which is American for 'Not good'.

Michael was peering at the turntable and at us, a rare frown appearing on his face. It might have been his first one ever; I don't think his face knew what to do with it.

'What's going on?' I said, running over.

Michael smiled at me and took a breath. 'I went into the penthouse this morning to get the equipment ready and I noticed something had been spilled on the turntable. It looked like it had dried and been scraped off. I was examining it when Ed walked over. He came up and looked at it like this—' he put his hands on his hips and squinted '—and we stood there in silence for a few seconds. Then I asked him, "Do you know what this is?" and Ed just said, "I think I cleaned up most of it".

My eyes widened.

'So,' smiled Michael, 'I asked him, "What is it?" and Ed said, "I think it's excrement—"' He left it hanging in the air for a moment, before finishing '"—but I'm not sure".'

I never dreamed I'd ever want a friend of mine to be *sure* they defecated on something.

'What's going on?' asked Liam, strolling over. Michael looked at me as if to say, 'You wanna take this one?' I, too, smiled and took a breath.

'Oh my god!' Liam exclaimed when I was done telling him. We all turned as one to look at the ghost of Ed doubled over at stage right.

'Hey,' said Craig, the frontman of another band. 'What's going on with your sound?'

'Well…' smiled Liam, putting his arm round Craig's shoulders and leading him away as he told him the story.

Michael looked at me. 'We've gotta buy another turntable. We can't play with this one.'

'What's going on guys?' said Hank, who chose to appear at that exact moment to see how the headlining band for his three-thousand person convention was doing. It fell to me to lead Hank away and tell him I'm sorry, I know you paid all this money for us to come to LA, but Chameleon Circuit can't play the show tonight because Ed shat the penthouse.

'You could just play with acoustic guitars,' Hank said. 'They love you; they won't care.'

'I wouldn't be comfortable doing it like that.'

'My priority is to get you guys out there no matter what.'

'We've been rehearsing for a month, Hank,' I said. 'Michael can get another turntable today if you don't mind us playing tomorrow night instead. It'll be worth it.' We had a great show. I didn't want to go out there unless we played full-out.

Hank agreed and took us off the bill that night. We were replaced by my old friend Michael Gregory, who headlined with his band, the Gregory Brothers. They had come a long way since autotuning topical news stories, achieving worldwide success by autotuning viral videos into hits like 'Double Rainbow Song' and 'Bed Intruder Song' (the latter of which entered the Billboard Hot 100 and became YouTube's most viewed video in 2010 with over a hundred million views). I would've seen the show, but I got a text from Liam: 'I'm with Michael in the diner 'round the corner. Ed's not here.'

'On my way,' I sent back. Then I texted Charlie. 'CC are in the diner sans Ed.' One by one, the rest of the band gathered at a small restaurant 'round the corner from the hotel. By then, the reality of our lives had sunk in.

'The equipment was on the dining table!' cried Liam. 'How did he do this? I have never dropped a deuce that wasn't in a toilet.'

'That is *so* gross,' said Denise, who'd also joined us; friends of ours were gathering at the diner as the word spread, eager to hear first hand what was fast becoming mythology.

'I knew about this before all of you,' said Danny, somehow proud to have been burdened with this knowledge the longest. 'I walked into the penthouse this morning to get the Sopio stock and Ed was waking up, covered in his own fluids. He said, "Can you smell that?" and I said, "Yeah, it's you!" And then I got the fuck out of there.'

'But I just saw Ed,' said Tom, 'and he didn't mention any of this.' Ed was, it turned out, wandering the lobby, alone and dehydrated, wearing yesterday's jeans and a t-shirt that said 'I partied with District Lines'.

'So who do I owe for the turntable?' he texted me later. The new one cost him a thousand pounds. It is, I hope, the most expensive poo he will ever have.

While my friends kept the party going, I broke off and discovered a grand piano in the basement floor of the hotel. With no-one around, I sat in the middle of VidCon and serenaded the empty space.

That was the last YouTube event I ever went to. I went out on a high: with our new turntable, Chameleon Circuit performed our show the following night to a crowd of over two thousand people. They cheered, whooped, clapped and sang along as we ran around the stage, swapped instruments from song to song, pulled people up on stage with us, crowdsurfed, dressed up in silly hats, broke at one point into Eminem's 'I Need A Doctor', and even staged a regeneration with me shooting yellow confetti over the audience from my outstretched hands.

Halfway through our first song, rushed with adrenalin, I took the VIP lanyard off my neck and threw it into the crowd.

THE IMPOSSIBLE INDUSTRY

Penny had a boyfriend. I hadn't spent any quality time with her for nearly a year. When their relationship came to an end, I was single too, in the midst of one of my brief adjourns from Laura. (We'd had another argument about something inconsequential and decided we weren't right for each other after all.) Penny and I made plans for her to stay at mine that weekend, awash with the sudden lack of restraint that comes from being single. She insinuated we could do anything we wanted.

At some point during our evening together I made a move to kiss her. She stopped me and said she felt a bit weird about it. This surprised me at first, but made sense; she had just broken up with her boyfriend so it was natural she might feel weird about doing something with another guy so soon. I spoke to her more about how she was doing and how they were both coping, thinking if I could help her feel better and more at ease, she'd be more comfortable proceeding with something more intimate.

Later in the evening — assuming she was feeling more relaxed about it all — I went to kiss her again and she rejected me for a second time. I wasn't going to try again after that. She slept on the sofa (to my further disappointment) and went home the next day.

I couldn't understand why someone who was attracted to me would imply they wanted to do something and then not do the something. I thought she was contradicting herself, rather than remembering people are allowed to change their minds. It's obvious to me now that after just ending a two-year relationship, she needed a friend far more than she needed a lover, and I wish I'd recognised that. In any case, Penny emailed me a couple days later to say she'd re-read our emails and could see how she might have led me on, and we moved on from the incident without any unpleasantness.

After that, the two of us spent lots of time together cuddling and watching movies, but nothing more than that was ever mentioned again. Instead of wanting our friendship to be something else, I began to appreciate what it was already. After one such friend-date, I ran into my room with my guitar and a notebook and sat on my bed, scrawling out lyrics. Penny and I had tried to sing together on *Still Got Legs* but found our vocal ranges were completely off from each other, so I started there:

> We sing together out of key
> Although we try, it seems we just can't find our
> harmony We just don't fit each other's frequencies
> That makes you out of reach
> And I am finally accepting that
> About you and me.

I wrote in the chorus about the Valentine's Day we spent together, describing 'the time we stole the whole day' and acknowledging that, even though things would never go any further, what we had was already enough. I emerged about an hour later with a finished song called 'Forever Yours'.

I loved my new song and played it all the time on my guitar, but I had no way to record it. Michael was back in America (and took too long to work for my liking), while Tom was becoming ever more eccentric, accentuating his seaweed-coloured hair with a choker and leather trousers and telling me and Ed to stop writing love songs because the human experience has so much more breadth than that. He released an EP of discordant instrumental tracks, one of which was ten minutes long, another twelve seconds. He wanted to be Max Tundra or Dan Deacon (whereas I wanted to be someone my nan had heard of).

Not knowing how to produce music myself, I hunted down contact addresses (through clever googling) for all the biggest producers, managers and songwriters in the world — Dr. Luke, Max Martin, Troy Carter, Scooter Braun — sending them links to my work and asking if they wanted to work with me.

These blind messages earned me two replies: one from the CEO of Spotify, telling me to keep up the good work; and one from Dan Wilson, the guy who wrote 'Closing Time' and co-wrote the smash 'Someone Like You' with Adele. He liked my stuff, listened to my new songs and gave me some advice to help me shape my work, but he lived in LA and wasn't forthcoming when I asked to fly out and record with him.

In any case, I didn't think 'Forever Yours' was a hit so I didn't bother sending it to Jonathan. Besides, I'd once sent a demo of 'The Time Of Your Life' to him and he replied, in caps, 'NEVER SEND ME AN UNFINISHED SONG AGAIN.'

Soon after Chameleon Circuit's memorable weekend at VidCon, an email arrived from a company called ChannelFlip. They referred to themselves as a multi-channel network. ChannelFlip and others like them had realised they could make vloggers more attractive to advertisers by presenting us as part of a single conglomerate. Instead of saying, 'Would you like to do your advert with Nerimon? He gets 3 million views a month,' they could say, 'Would you like to do your advert with ChannelFlip? We get 50 million views a month.' This would attract more valuable companies, willing to pay more for adverts, which would spread across the channels on the network and earn us more money than we would get on our own (with ChannelFlip keeping a cut for their trouble). They could also secure us brand deals, sponsorships and product placements.

'As an incentive for you to join us,' they said, 'we will guarantee you more money every month than you get right now. Could you tell us your average earnings per month?'

YouTube money goes up and down depending on what views and ads you get, but the previous month happened to have been my best month ever. Along with the release of *Still Got Legs* giving me a boost (and the exposure from being at VidCon) I also finished my 'Alex Reads Twilight' series. People went back and rewatched the whole thing, leading to millions of extra views.

Something else had happened, too: while in LA, Liam and I paid a visit to the local Walmart. I found it hysterical. It was the size of a small village and sold every possible thing ever invented by man or beast. Armed with my camera, we giggled at their gluttonous frozen ready meals, their armoury of easy-access rifles and their penchant for liquid cheese — I'm pretty sure America sells cheese as a solid, a liquid and a gas. I told Charlie I probably hadn't captured any usable footage — 'It was just Liam and me pointing and laughing at stuff' — but for my own amusement, I edited it together and put it online as a memento of the fun day I had with my kindred spirit.

After the video went live, someone linked me to the headline 'Alex And Liam visit their first Walmart' on CBS News. Someone else linked me to E! News. 'Two dudes named Alex and Liam [are here] to check out one of our nation's greatest resources,' said the presenter. 'Here they are exploring Walmart!'

'Alex And Liam Do Walmart' was, somehow, international news. It got a million views in just over a week and remains one of my most viewed videos ever. Off the back of all this, I earned £2500 in one month — way more than ever before.

'Well if you want an average,' I said to ChannelFlip, playing it cool, 'let's just take last month for instance. Last month I earned two and a half grand.'

'Okay,' they said, 'we'll give you three.'

'That seems fair,' I shrugged, and then called my mum, overjoyed. Three grand a month for what I did was obscene, far more than I deserved for working about an hour a week. I spent so little effort on YouTube that I couldn't believe people were still watching me. I uploaded my old terrible documentary *Forging An Identity* and it got a quarter of a million views. When my audience moaned about me selling things, I pushed my work even harder, daring them to challenge me. On my Twitter account one evening, I played a game of seeing how many followers I could lose in one night. I can't remember how many people I put off but I know I ended the evening by tweeting the alphabet one letter at a time.

The latest website to grab hold of my audience's attention was Tumblr. (I really didn't like the growing trend of dropping vowels from ordinary words to make them seem hip. After Flickr, Grindr, Scribd and Tumblr were all established in 2013, WIRED published an article titled 'An Obituary for the Letter E'.) Tumblr is a bit like Twitter for blogs. People can post media of any type (videos, photos, blogs, etc.) to their accounts and others can follow their output. Users can scroll through a 'timeline' of all the latest posts from accounts they follow and reblog the ones they like to their own accounts, thus sharing them with their own followers. You're not restricted by character count and you can follow 'tags' to see all the posts about a particular topic. It's also the most anonymous place I've seen online to express yourself. No profile pictures or names are required, people can ask each other questions without identifying themselves and the design of your page is much more flexible than other sites (though the timeline looks the same for everyone). Tumblr reminded me of the old internet, where explicit posts and marginalised subcultures could meet and express themselves without being censored. It was one of the last wild spaces left online.

A lot of people posted to the 'Alex Day' tag (which anyone could follow) on Tumblr, sharing thoughts on my videos, snippets they'd taken from them and turned into GIFs (short animated clips, pronounced 'jifs') or art they'd drawn inspired by something I'd said or a song I'd written. This was how I found 'fuckyeahalexday', a Tumblr account dedicated to my goings-on, run by someone called Crystal.

It was clear from her posts Crystal was friendly, witty and smart. I messaged her to ask if I could work with her in some way, perhaps by doing a Q&A or a giveaway through her blog. Aside from thinking it would be useful to have a more direct awareness of what my audience did and didn't like, she just seemed cool. I found it natural to befriend people who once described themselves as 'fans'; as soon as we hung out or chatted a bit, we become friends on an equal level.

Crystal and I met up a few times in person and (as with Penny) any sense I might be impressive in any way wore off without much effort. Over time she started to open up to me more and I liked the person I got to know. She was a talented pianist and didn't care what the world thought of her (a trait I find more and more admirable with every passing day). She made fun of my body as often as she scooped me up for long cuddles on the sofa. As Charlie became ever more withdrawn, Crystal was chatty and considerate by contrast.

The only conflict was that I was back with Laura, who Crystal found annoying. This might or might not have had something to do with the fact that Crystal and I — unbeknownst to Laura — had incorporated kissing into our friendship.

'You know Gail?' I said.

'Who?' replied my nan.

'Gail from *Coronation Street*.'

'Oh yeah.'

'I met her the other day. She said thanks for watching.'

My nan grinned at me. 'What?'

'Gail from *Coronation Street*. Said to say thank you for watching.'

'What do you mean she said thanks for watching?'

'You know my housemate Charlie?'

'Yeah.'

'He was invited to the BAFTAs and I went with him. And we met Gail from *Coronation Street*.'

'Right?'

'And I told her you watch it, so she said to tell you thanks for watching.'

My nan grinned at me, then laughed.

'I don't know what you mean, love,' she said, and shut her eyes.

YouTube had been encouraging their partners to treat chatting into a camera with the utmost solemnity. Each of us was assigned a partner manager, someone on the inside to contact if we had issues with our account or wanted advice on how to 'optimise our content'. They sent us a PDF called *The Playbook* advising us on the best titles and descriptions to suit YouTube's algorithm (CAPS AND EXCLAMATIONS WERE POPULAR!!?) and found special events (like the BAFTAs) that would draw attention to our channels. In an attempt to create 'event' moments to get people logging on to the site — like the Discovery Channel's famous 'Shark Week' — they paid vloggers to create videos for a specific event in May under the banner of 'Comedy Week', featuring them on the front page and running TV ads to catch people's interest. They opened a space in London for YouTubers to use for free with a huge green room, a live studio, a make-up room and an editing suite. I went there to hang out with friends, and to make new ones; I took to a girl from Essex called Emma with a stubborn jaw and vibrant purple hair who grinned like she was plotting your doom. Emma had just started making videos, so she wasn't afraid to speak her mind no matter what was on it. I made a video with her, eager to showcase her to my audience and give hers a boost (and because it gave me an excuse to chat shit in a room with her for half a hour, which was great fun).

'I'm having a birthday party,' I messaged her a while later. 'You in?'

'I'll try,' she said, 'but Monday's my video day.'

Emma was, it turned out, the first professional vlogger I'd met. She devised a schedule for her videos, uploading on the same day and time every week (just like television, the thing I thought we strove to conquer). The professional vloggers covered their videos with text boxes instructing people to like or comment. The 'endscreen', an informative card at the end of a video with links to previous ones (and the ever-present 'reminder' to subscribe) soon became a standard across the site. I recoiled. I didn't want to trap people on YouTube watching every video I'd ever made; I wanted them to get a camera and make some of their own or, even better, shut the laptop and go for a walk.

Even Charlie got in on the act, his desire to push his work leading him to buy expensive studio lights for his videos and invest in a new high-end camera with manual focus for maximum artistic options, big, fancy lenses for big, fancy shots, and automatic shutoff to conserve battery life. As a result, he was forever turning the camera back on halfway through filming and stopping to readjust the focus, and it was too heavy to hold so he had to use a tripod to film anything. It took him about fifteen minutes just to set himself up for a video (by which time I'd already filmed one from scratch). The musician Tim Minchin came to our flat once to film a song he'd written with Charlie for the charity Comic Relief, and he said at the start he could only stay about an hour, but ended up staying nearly four while Charlie insisted they get the video perfect, doing take after take after take. After Tim left, Charlie watched the footage back and saw the both of them singing in his bedroom in silence; he'd bought a new external microphone for his camera and forgotten to turn it on. I admired Charlie's pursuit for excellence, but I prescribed to the belief Steve Jobs hollered once at an engineer who spent too much time tinkering with a product instead of just finishing it: 'Real artists ship!'

With no way to produce my music, I threw myself into winding up my audience as often as possible. I was merciless. When I was invited to fly to Pixar's headquarters in San Francisco and interview their CEO, John Lasseter, I told people that *Cars* was a stop-motion movie and pretended I had found the props of the cars they used. At various times, I told them 'knackered' was a British adjective based on the word 'knickers'; called California 'the Sunshine State' (that one really messed with them); held up a *Doctor Who* alien plushie and called it the wrong name; said I was quitting my channel because they were 'a bad audience'; and even pretended I was being cancelled by Fox. I hope you're as amazed as I was that some people believed all of these. The comments section below my videos descended into gang warfare between the enlightened and the believers, some of whom really thought I was now sponsored by Tic-Tac and had to wear exclusively white, green and orange in every video from now on, and would rip their eyes out of their sockets in rage when the next video contained no reference to anything I'd said in the one before. ChannelFlip seemed to share my spirit of having fun with YouTube: they threw extravagant bashes for their vloggers with names like 'the "We Haven't Had a Party in a While" Party' — that particular one took place after hours in Madame Tussauds, the waxwork museum in London, where we ran amok posing with effigies of *actual* famous people.

'Are you pitching anything for Geek Week?' Susi, my ChannelFlip manager, asked me. YouTube were following up Comedy Week with Geek Week and accepting pitches for funding on videos that fit the bill; £5,000-£10,000 were offered for each pitch.

'I was going to,' I told her, 'but I don't need funding. The only thing I could make for them is a Chameleon Circuit music video but the minimum I have to ask for is five grand. I don't need that much.'

'Alex,' said Susi, 'ask for ten.'

'I just said I don't even need five, what would I do with ten?'

'Oh my god,' she said, 'you're the only person who has a problem with this.' She emphasised her next sentence, speaking with care to make sure I understood: 'Alex, whatever you don't spend, you get to keep.'

'What? If they're giving me ten grand shouldn't I have to provide some kind of breakdown or budget for how I'd spend it?'

'Just ask for ten,' said Susi. I loaded up the form, filled in the box telling YouTube my music video idea and asked for the money to make it — and they approved it. I had £10,000 to make a video without any need to explain why. I felt like I should spend it all on the video, but my idea would cost about five hundred quid. The only way I could make it cost more was to — I don't know — hire someone who actually played the Doctor to be in it.

'So the song is called 'Teenage Rebel',' I said. 'The idea is about an introverted kid, bit lonely, who sees an episode of *Doctor Who* for the first time. When he goes back into his bedroom, he looks at his rubbish bin and pretends it's a Dalek, and then we see it moving around and attacking like a Dalek would. Then he looks in the mirror — and it's you! We get to see the reality of his imagining that he's the Doctor, fighting off the monsters in his life.'

'Sounds great!' said Sylvester. 'This is my agent's number; arrange the details with him.' Sylvester McCoy was the seventh actor to play the Doctor (playing the part in the late eighties). I rang Susi and told her I had a Doctor in my music video.

'Brilliant!' she said. 'By the way, we're trying to get the TARDIS for you.'

'No you're not,' I said. 'What do you mean? You can't "get the TARDIS" for me.'

'Yeah, we're talking to the BBC about it.'

'Right. The one in the Doctor Who Experience?' (A *Doctor Who* exhibition in Cardiff had an old TARDIS set; I thought perhaps they could negotiate the use of it after hours.)

'Um, no,' said Susi. 'I can check, but I'm pretty sure it's the real one.'

'You're trying to get me *the* TARDIS? From the actual show?'

'Yeah.'

'Okay. Do check that,' I said. Call me cynical, but I'd once been promised lunch with Taylor Swift.

I should have had more faith in the impossible industry I now worked in; everyone who worked as, or with, vloggers had at some point decided to push themselves to be successful. It was an environment that bred supersized goals and lofty achievements. Susi had been right. ChannelFlip got through to the production team at

Doctor Who and convinced them to do what they had never done before. They hired out the flagship set of their flagship BBC drama to me, a professional nobody, for a music video I wanted to make for my YouTube channel. YouTube helped with the deal, giving the BBC £20,000 to hire the set for the day. The biggest tech company in the world had now spent thirty grand on a three-minute music video for a song about a sci-fi show; a classic Doctor was being put in the modern TARDIS set; and I was the person in charge of it. Which made Susi twitch a little when I told her the TARDIS would only be at the very end of the video.

I knew the TARDIS had to be at the end. The grand reveal of that beautiful set would eclipse anything else I had planned. I couldn't top it. If I wanted people to watch the video all the way to end, the TARDIS shots couldn't be wasted in the first minute or two or it would peak too early. I couldn't even make it the thumbnail; it would spoil the surprise.

'Okay,' Susi said when I told her this. 'Well, it's your video and I won't tell you how to make it, but just bear in mind, we did get the TARDIS, and it did cost £20,000.'

'Yeah, I know, mate.' I guess she thought I was making a standard music video of the band playing instruments in the TARDIS, which would be fun to watch for about ten seconds. It was too generic. 'If it helps,' I said, 'I'm not gonna be in the video either.'

'... you're not?'

'Nah, why would I be? I'm not an actor.' I'd hired my friend Quinn for the day, perfect for the role I had in mind but an unknown as far as YouTube were concerned. 'Anyway, the idea is about a lonely little kid feeling better watching *Doctor Who*. It's well sad if it's a man in his twenties, playing in his bedroom on his own.'

'Okay,' said Susi, taking a breath. 'I might regret asking, but how long are you planning on using the TARDIS in the video?'

'About twenty seconds,' I said. 'Right at the end. Hey, you could think of it like it cost a thousand pounds a second.'

'No, I won't be thinking of it like that,' said Susi.

'Just trust me,' I said. 'It'll work.'

'Okay,' she said. 'Anyway, there's one other thing. The BBC don't want you to use Sylvester in the shoot.'

'Why not?'

'Just makes it a bit too official, the BBC financing a video with a past Doctor in the new TARDIS. Goes beyond just being a fan thing.'

'So what are my options?'

'You can have anyone in the world play the Doctor,' said Susi, 'except someone who already has.'

'Then what am I gonna spend this money on?' I lamented. I somehow heard Susi roll her eyes down the phone.

After the call, I phoned Sylvester's agent to break the news, but I couldn't tell him the truth. In case you don't know your history, *Doctor Who* was cancelled by the BBC back in 1989 due to poor ratings and perceived quality, and remained off air for sixteen years. Sylvester McCoy was the Doctor helming the show when it was cancelled. I couldn't bear to break it to him that the same company had just fired him as the Doctor a second time.

'We've gone in a different direction with the video,' I told his agent (which was true), 'so we won't be using Sylvester now. I'm really sorry.'

'Oh,' said the agent. He sighed, defeated. 'Was it... did you get another former Doctor instead?'

'Oh no,' I reassured him, 'that's not it! We're not going with any Doctors now.'

'Right. Okay!' he said, a noticeable perk to his voice.

The music video went ahead with a different concept and I paid for Quinn's train to Cardiff (on a first-class ticket, because I literally couldn't spend this money any other way) so we could film on set for the day. The TARDIS shots looked beautiful for the last twenty seconds and Susi agreed, once she'd seen the finished video, that it wouldn't have worked any other way. The video was promoted around YouTube on the day it went live, I got to run around the set of my favourite show (I even met a Weeping Angel in the warehouse), I paid everyone involved, and I still kept over eight thousand pounds of the budget.

YouTube never organised another weekly event. Both Geek Week and Comedy Week were perceived as flops by the mainstream media and failed to ignite as much interest in the site as the company had hoped. Either way, I had a huge amount of fun and started looking for my next adventure: Charlie and I began planning a road trip with Michael, eager to spend more time basking in his Californian stillness. We decided it might be a laugh to spend six months driving around America with him, visiting all fifty states. Michael wanted a GPS tracker on us at all times so people around the world could see our location and even take the trip with us in their own cars. Charlie and I were less keen on that bit.

Even though we could more than afford it, Charlie felt uncomfortable spending that much money, so we approached ChannelFlip to find us a sponsor for the project.

'We can't pitch to advertisers without a clear motive for the trip,' Susi told us. 'You need a goal. We have to present a narrative.'

Faced with the task of applying retroactive significance to a pointless road trip, the best we came up with was 'burger road trip: travelling 'round America and eating a burger in every state'.

'Keep thinking,' said Susi.

I was still thinking when I reached for my phone on the morning of October 5th, 2011, starting my day by illuminating my barely-wakened eyes with the harsh opinionated light of Twitter.

The hashtag #RIPSteveJobs was trending.

Every one of my YouTube videos was made on a Mac. All my photographs have been taken with an iPhone. My songs were produced on a Mac Pro, then sold through Apple's iTunes Store. My first job was *in* the Apple Store, and it was Steve Jobs' 2005 commencement address at Stanford University that inspired me to kick off my dreams in the first place. Steve and the company he founded had facilitated my entire life. The man who encouraged me to follow my dreams would achieve no more of his own and, in his wake, I was trying to get a free trip around America (that I could have paid for myself) so I could spend six months eating burgers with my mates.

'Your work is going to fill a large part of your life,' Steve had said in the commencement speech, 'and the only way to be truly satisfied is to do what you believe is great work.'

I didn't want the most significant thing I'd ever done to be the release of an album of songs about *Doctor Who* and I didn't want to be making YouTube videos in my sixties. I wanted real success — the kind I came so close to with Sons of Admirals. For that, I needed Jonathan.

'Music is the thing that makes me the happiest,' I wrote to him.

'Let's talk,' Jonathan said. 'I have an idea.'

DON'T MOURN, ORGANISE

As a kid I loved listening to the radio to see what song would be crowned the Christmas Number One. Getting the prestigious honour means your song is at the top of the UK Charts during the week of Christmas Day, a time when music sales are at their peak. All my favourite pop artists used to get involved, releasing songs to compete for the coveted top spot. In 2003 'Christmas Time (Don't Let The Bells End)' by The Darkness was set to be number one all week but a surprise surge of sales on Saturday left it at #2, beaten by Gary Jules' 'Mad World', and mine is a mad world because after fifteen years I *still* want justice for The Darkness.

It wasn't just me who cared. The Christmas Number One was once a national obsession but, in recent years, the title has been awarded to whomever won *The X Factor* that year. They have an advantage because the winner's first single gets released the week of Christmas. By 2009, *X Factor* winners had been Christmas Number One for six years in a row and, having had enough, a motivated couple launched a Facebook campaign to replace it with Rage Against The Machine's revolutionary anthem 'Killing In The Name Of'. The movement spread across Facebook, gaining momentum and press attention as more and more people saw the opportunity to take the establishment down a peg or two (missing the fact that whoever won *The X Factor* would be signed by Sony, the same label as Rage Against The Machine). In the end, Rage Against The Machine got the number one, gave all their profits to charity and were cut off on national radio in the middle of the afternoon when they started screaming the line 'Fuck you, I won't do what you tell me' at the crescendo of the song.

The race for Christmas Number One is, in short, a pop culture phenomenon, perhaps the most exciting calendar event in pop music apart from Eurovision, and the year Steve Jobs died, Jonathan noticed two small details about it.

First, the charts this year would be announced on December 25th. The Christmas Number One would be revealed on Christmas Day itself.

Second, for the first time in seven years, *The X Factor* would not be a shoo-in for the Christmas Number One because their winner's single would be out the week *before*.

'Because Christmas Day is a Sunday this year, I don't think they realised it threw everything off by a week,' Jonathan said. 'It'll be the first genuine Christmas Number One in ages.'

With those two things in mind, Jonathan spied another of his gaps in the market.

'The Christmas Number One is up for grabs,' he said. 'You should go for it.'

We both knew we wouldn't get anywhere near the top of the charts. Jonathan's plan was pure marketing hyperbole; the buzz around being a Christmas Number One contender, and making it look like I might have a chance, would drive sales and publicity, leading to radio stations picking up my song and breaking me as an artist across the world. 'If you set your goals ridiculously high and it's a failure,' James Cameron once said, 'you will fail above everyone else's success.'

'Of course, you'll have to fucking shave,' said Jonathan. 'Why does your generation never shave? None of you fucking shave and none of you can fucking drive. These are the basic human things that one has to do. Why are you looking at me like that? This is brilliant advice you're getting for free, all as part of the privilege of being my friend. So yes, once you've shaved you might be able to do this. But you have to have a hit. None of the songs you've sent me are hits.'

'Well, I do have this,' I said, playing him 'Forever Yours' and ignoring everything else he said. He listened with his mouth half-open, squinting.

'That might be it!' he said.

I went to visit Crystal two weeks later and sat cross-legged on her floor as I filmed a call to arms. I explained the significance of the Christmas Number One and asked my audience to help me get my song there, explaining that I'd be giving a significant chunk of the money to charity. (I don't like telling people when I give money to charity — donations are far less wholesome if you do them with an audience — but I wanted to make it clear I wasn't trying to exploit my viewers for money.) I invited people to help me with buying and promoting the song in a personal street team, setting up a private email address people could use to contact me.

'I don't want your help unless you really love the song,' I said. 'Please don't get in touch unless you really wanna go the extra mile to help me out with this cos it's gonna take a lot of time and energy.'

I was throwing my YouTube channel on the line. I could alienate my entire audience by focusing so much on my song and this campaign but I believed in Jonathan's power to spot potential. It was time to start taking my career — my real career — seriously. If I alienated them, so be it. I couldn't let anything set me off course from my goal.

'*Doctor Who* are filming in New York,' said Ben. 'They're flying me out to cover it. Come with me! I've never been to New York before and it'll be great fun with you. We can hang out on set and party with the cast in the evenings.'

Ben was inviting me to see the Weeping Angels, one of the Doctor's most iconic foes, fighting Matt Smith in the final episode for his companions Karen Gillan and Arthur Darvill, who would all hit the town at night when filming finished — and I'd be right there with them. At best, I could become friends with the Doctor and his mates. At worst, I could give him Chameleon Circuit's albums.

'I'm sorry, mate,' I said. 'I have to focus on this new project. It needs everything I've got.'

'No,' said Ben. 'What are you talking about? You can't pass this up. It's just a week. You can spare a week.'

'That's how it starts. I can't do it, man.'

'It's *Doctor Who*, on set, afterparties, in New York! You're gonna regret this forever!'

'I'll regret it more if I don't give this everything I've got.' I had to make a music video, find a radio plugger, register the song for the charts, think of ways to get the press interested and plenty more besides. It was the middle of October; I had ten weeks until Christmas Day. Jonathan had impressed upon me how devoted I needed to be to pull this off: 'Every second you find yourself wasting precious seconds by having a wank, stop and do something more to break the track. It is — and always was — almost impossible unless you go that extra hundred miles. It needs every second of energy that you have. Unless of course you don't really want to — or can't.'

Jonathan first suggested I go to a gambling shop and bet on myself to get the Christmas Number One. I asked my older subscribers (or parents of younger ones) to do the same. News stories about the Christmas charts always include the odds on different tracks; I needed odds of my own to make myself more legitimate to the media, and odds come from bets. Betting shops monitor the bets coming in from 'round the country and it only takes two or three from different locations for them to suspect a big trend and give good odds on a song. Sure enough, after about a week, William Hill gave 'Forever Yours' odds of 16 to 1 for the Christmas Number One.

Next, 'Forever Yours' needed to be produced — not for the first time, I was creating a surge of support for music that didn't exist yet. I had no idea how to produce my own music and had no choice but to learn. Figuring it would all work out once I got to the studio and that my best strategy was to relax, I spent the night before the session at a

Halloween party hosted by the TV presenter Jonathan Ross — his daughter Honey watched Charlie's and my videos online and invited us. I went as Doctor Horrible, a mad scientist super-villain played by Neil Patrick Harris.

'Oh, that's *brilliant!*' I heard while standing under a canopy, turning to see Derren Brown dressed as the devil taking a photo of me with a bright grin on his face. 'I know Neil very well!'

'Come on!' said Honey, dragging Derren and me past Stephen Fry and into the photo booth.

'Oh hello, Alex,' Stephen waved.

I crashed on the floor with a bunch of Honey's friends at who-knows-what-time, woke up for the studio still in costume and stumbled to the nearest train station. I didn't have a change of clothes or any idea where to start. Trying to learn from what I'd seen Tom do for my music, I flew between keyboards and microphones and instruments like the mad scientist I was dressed as, trying to actualise the formula for a hit song.

'Charlie,' I asked as though the wrong word would send him falling through a vortex, 'how would you feel about making a music video for me?'

Charlie was hesitant, afraid and overwhelmed, but he said yes. Then he said he didn't think he could do it. Then he said okay. Then he said no. Then he said yes.

We both felt it made sense for the video to go on his channel. It allowed him to showcase something he would be proud of making; would give him new content for his channel; would give him more subscribers as I sent people his way to watch it; and, of course, it would maximise the exposure of the song and our campaign. I needed something as soon as possible so I told him to make something great but not too ambitious. Charlie didn't understand what I meant by 'not too ambitious' and storyboarded a video filmed of us turning into superheroes with machine guns, mowing down a horde of zombies and flying off into the sky.

At the same time the video was being planned, Charlie and I moved house. We had enough money now to buy our own place together and I'd convinced him that a mortgage wasn't the terrifying commitment he thought it was because you could just sell it again. We bought a four-bedroom house in East London 'round the corner from what would become the Olympic Park. Since Charlie likes to spend months on things and I needed the video done in about a week, on top of moving our things into a new place, the project nearly killed him. We settled into our new home on Wednesday, and on Thursday five of our friends (including Penny) slept on the floor, ready to be made up as zombies over the weekend. Charlie had found a guy who did prosthetic latex makeup to work on the shoot for us and hired another to do the various special effects we would need once filming was done. I'd never seen him work so hard.

Charlie uploaded the finished video to his channel and it got a million views in its first week. Yes, half of those views were from people who thought Charlie wrote and sang the song, but it didn't matter to me as long as they supported it. Armed with this 'million in a week' statistic as well as the William Hill odds, I used both as evidence of a growing nationwide movement and sent the story to journalists and TV stations throughout the country. I thought the story would be too good to resist, especially because I was unsigned. Getting the Christmas Number One would make me the highest-charting unsigned artist in history (and would get me the Guinness World Record that eluded me when we released the Chartjackers song).

To get songs on the radio, record labels and independent artists hire radio pluggers to meet with the radio bosses and push for songs to be added to their playlists. I'd met a plugger during Sons of Admirals days and emailed him to ask for his help.

'How much would it cost to work with you?' I asked.

'You can't afford me,' he said.

'Try me,' I shot back in my four-bedroom house.

'Look, go to the Radio 1 building; I'll give you the receptionist's name. She's a nice girl. Tell her I sent you and she'll let you into the building.'

It was all rather clandestine but it worked; the receptionist led me to the pigeonholes where various DJs were given their mail and I left promotional CDs of 'Forever Yours' inside for them to listen to.

I did everything I could, but no-one picked up on my story. Radio 1 started a Christmas mission of their own when Chris Moyles, the breakfast show DJ, campaigned to get 'Dominick The Italian Christmas Donkey' to number one because he thought it'd be funny. Meanwhile, Radio 2's breakfast DJ, Chris Evans, backed the Military Wives Choir, a group of soldiers' wives singing a cover of the song 'Wherever You Are' to their husbands across the sea. (They were also donating their earnings to charity. The Christmas charity track was not a hook unique to me.) The group's progress was the subject of a BBC reality show called *The Choir* — they seemed to be the act to beat.

When I tuned into *The One Show* on television the following evening and saw various novelty groups featured in a piece about Christmas Number One contenders, I was gutted not to have been included, especially because they were instead interviewing a group of men in mole costumes called The Wombles. I knew the show was aware of me as I'd contacted them myself. It's one thing to write to a national television show and get your interview declined; it's quite another when they overlook you in favour of a band of fully-grown man dressed as moles. I thought I'd caught a break when I read an article in a newspaper with the headline 'Unsigned YouTube star in the race for Christmas Number One' but I was aghast to discover it wasn't about me. The story concerned a ten-year-old girl covering a Fleetwood Mac song on YouTube. She had odds of 25 to 1, which weren't even as good as mine.

I couldn't let anything set me back. Jonathan had taught me to plan for success but prepare for failure. To make myself feel more like a musician, I threw out my entire wardrobe for the second time in my life and bought a couple of monochromatic patterned t-shirts, tie-dye skinny jeans, pointed red boots and a shiny gold jacket. Whenever I looked in the mirror I saw a musician. When people said on the street that they liked what I was wearing, I would reply, 'Thanks! I'm a musician.' (To my delight, they would often respond, 'I can see that!') They were now the only clothes I owned so I had to wear them all the time, forcing me to become comfortable in my new skin. In turn, I started feeling more confident and able to achieve my goals. ('As a man changes his own nature, so does the attitude of the world change towards him,' Ghandi said once — and he just wore that little blanket.) I'd read that the key to a strong cartoon character was to make them identifiable in silhouette (think Bart Simpson or Mickey Mouse). I found the same applied to famous musicians like Elvis, Michael Jackson and The Beatles, all of whom are recognisable by their shape and style alone, so I based my look on that. I wasn't just shooting for musical success. I wanted to be iconic.

I woke up early each morning, researched the names of the DJs who decided the national radio playlists, figured out the best way to contact them all, sent a brilliant email to each of them at the perfect time... and then thought, 'Right, that won't work' and started focusing on something else. On the flip chart in our office at home, I wrote a list of a hundred things I could do over the next couple weeks to progress the momentum of the track. I tried to come up with more ideas each day than I had the day before. I read the chart rules on the official website, looking for some kind of loophole I might be able to use — perhaps I could register my house as a shop and report that I'd sold a million copies of my song there or something — and I stumbled across this:

> An unlimited number of digital variants of the featured song may be combined for a chart position. The featured song across all formats of a single need not be identical for their transactions to be combined, but should be substantially the same

— that is, an identical OR extended OR remixed
OR live OR alternative version of the basic song.

Here's what this means in non-legal terms: if you buy 'Forever Yours'
and then buy, say, 'Forever Yours Live', as far as the charts are
concerned, you bought 'Forever Yours' twice. All the individual
versions of a song combine for one single chart place. I might not
have a hundred thousand people who would buy my song, but I did
have some willing to buy the song twice (or more times). I could
inflate my audience by empowering each person to count for more
than one sale.

This felt like the ace up my sleeve. In secret, I started approaching
musicians I knew, asking them to record remixes of the song for me
and assuring them the money for their version of 'Forever Yours'
would go to a charity of their choice. Ed, Tom, Charlie and others all
recorded variants of the song, while I prepared a live piano version,
the instrumental track and the original demo of the song for release.

'This is it,' I raved to Jonathan. 'This is how we'll do it.'

'Stay focused,' he cautioned me. 'It's a good idea but it's just one.
You need to do a hundred things a day because almost none of them
will work!'

On the eve of the song's release, Charlie went to a Christmas party
hosted by ChannelFlip. It probably happened behind the clock face of
Big Ben or something; I wasn't there, needing time to make a separate
video for each version of the song. I was touched, though, when
Charlie told me later that our friends were buzzing about the song and
had all committed, with considerable enthusiasm, to buying the track.
This was a great comfort because I had no idea how it would go. The
best case scenario in my mind was that it would sit just outside the
Top 20 — no mean feat — but I knew it could also sink without trace,
as my previous attempts had done.

I wanted to make the event as fun as possible for my audience, even those that didn't care about the track or the campaign, so I declared that Sunday, December 18th (the song's release date) was an official YouTube holiday called 'Forever Day'. (I like to invent special occasions as well as genres of music.) On the 18th, I made a video revealing my secret weapon: thirteen different variations of the song, including an acoustic version, a rap version, an 8-bit version, a dance remix and more, all for sale at the same time. I asked my audience to buy as many of the tracks as they could afford from iTunes, as well as AmazonMP3 and other outlets if they wanted to be even more helpful. I emailed the few thousand people who signed up to my street team and encouraged them to tweet, share the track on Facebook, bug their friends, print out flyers and anything else they could think of to help.

At midnight, 'Forever Yours' appeared on iTunes and fourteen videos appeared on my channel: the one explaining my strategy plus all thirteen variations of the song.

About five minutes after midnight, three thousand people had unsubscribed from my channel.

About ten minutes after midnight, 'Forever Yours' became the second-highest worldwide trend on Twitter.

At 8am, the song broke the Top 40 on the iTunes chart in the UK — and in Sweden, Canada, New Zealand, Australia and Ireland.

By 9am, we broke the Top 20.

By 2:30pm, 'Forever Yours' was in the top five. Because of all the remixes I'd released, I was also in the Top 20, 30, 40, 50, 60, 70 and 80 all at once.

My YouTube friends tweeted their combined millions of followers to tell them about what was happening. People changed their Twitter and Facebook profile pictures to the 'Forever Yours' single artwork (a pirate flag with a pink skull and a heart for a mouth; I called our movement the Pirates of Love, because we were subversive but well-intended). Penny told me she saw the flag so much she started to believe it was the default Twitter image.

A few people tweeted that they couldn't buy the song because their parents 'didn't trust iTunes' so I gifted the track to their accounts. From there, a hashtag was set up connecting people who couldn't buy the track with people willing to buy it for them.

In that first day, my song and its remixes sold a total of 30,000 copies in the UK. I checked my email; Polydor Records wanted to meet with me.

The official midweek chart was released on Wednesday, announcing I was in the top five without any help from radio, television, press, management or a record label. I turned on the TV that evening to see what the news was and it was me. I got on the Tube and picked up the *Evening Standard* to read what the news was and it was me ('Singer set for monster hit with zombie spoof'). I turned on Radio 1 to listen to some music and it was me; they played 'Forever Yours' on their midweek chart show, where DJ Greg James complimented my song and said the station were receiving texts and tweets 'every minute' with requests to play it.

I was with my family and Laura on Christmas Day and we gathered 'round the radio to listen to the chart show on Radio 1. I wasn't sure where we'd end up. Sales suffered a sharp drop in the latter half of the week, but the DJ got to the top ten and still hadn't played my track yet. Concerned about how the song was doing, some of my subscribers started ringing in to Radio 1 to offer messages of support. How do I know this? The station started playing them. I would hear the track at number eight, then a girl from Nottingham saying, 'I want 'Forever Yours' to be number one. I think Alex is great!', and then the track at number seven. Around the world, we were listening in with cheers and crossed fingers. I checked my Twitter and saw a message from a girl called Marilyn whose brother was in McFly, the band I loved listening to with my nan when I was younger. 'We're all sat 'round the radio rooting for you!', she said. I told my nan and she gave me a big hug.

Due to a last-minute surge of Saturday sales from well-wishers in my audience wanting to make a final push, Coldplay's 'Paradise' landed at number five and we overtook them by just two thousand sales, me and my audience, working together on this crazy song — the song I'd made a month ago — and after 'Paradise' finished playing, the DJ announced 'Forever Yours' at number four, at which point, on Christmas Day, I became the highest-charting unsigned artist in history. The Military Wives Choir took the top spot, with Little Mix (that year's *X Factor* winners) coming in second, 'Dominick The Donkey' third, me at number four and the rest of music below that. I finished ahead of Justin Bieber, One Direction and — perhaps most satisfying of all — the Wombles.

The song played, my family cheered and I went upstairs to film a video about it. My laptop had two emails waiting for me.

'You'll have three #1s next year,' Jonathan wrote. 'You should be very proud. I'm proud of you; you did exactly what you needed to do.'

The other email was from Penny. 'Remember the time when we stole the whole day? And nobody knows it — oh, wait, everyone knows it, they played it on national radio. xxxx'

'Forever Yours' (and its variants) sold 52,000 copies in the UK. It reached number 20 in Ireland and number 79 in Canada. It sold a hundred thousand copies around the world. It raised £30,000 for my chosen charity, WorldVision, who I'd worked with in Zambia. And it gave me a Guinness World Record. But my work wasn't over. The goal was to have a hit, not an impressive week. Through Christmas and into the new year I kept contacting radio producers, appealing for them to consider the song for playlist. I didn't see how they could ignore me anymore, but none of them played the track. Most DJs were away for the holiday and weren't around to pick up on the story; one regional broadcaster told me he couldn't even get into the system to play my song as it was locked out for the rest of the year. I reached out to stations around the world like Australia's Triple J and news outlets like America's *Billboard*, telling them a big song had broken in the UK and trying to convince them to pick up on it, but I got no replies. I even hunted down the person who curates the *Now That's What I Call Music!* compilation CDs to lobby for my song to be included in the next edition, but got a polite message back saying songs had to sell at least 100,000 copies in the UK to qualify.

Our surface-level goal of getting into the charts had worked but the real goal of breaking the track (and me as an artist) worldwide had failed. Without the media to push the song, the music-buying public (who don't listen to charts) didn't hear about it. The momentum crashed to a halt. The week after I charted at #4, the track fell 108 places and set a second world record for being the biggest drop down the charts in the history of recorded music. (When I spoke to the Guinness World Records people I begged them to give me two certificates, one saying I had the highest place and the other saying I had the biggest drop. They refused to acknowledge it and said they couldn't understand why I would want a record for that.)

I saw a friend of mine a few weeks later. 'I heard about your chart success!' he grinned.

'Yeah,' I said, shrugging. 'Number four. It's a start.'

MUPPETS

'You own that,' said Laura. We were in my mum's car, pulling up in front of a three-bedroom house nestled in a cul-de-sac at the end of the road. Laura pointed to it. 'You own that there. In the same way you own that—' she pointed to my bottle of Lucozade '—and those clothes, you also own *that*.' After giving World Vision their share of the money from 'Forever Yours', and reimbursing Stan, our former Sons of Admirals manager, for the few thousand pounds he lost from his own pocket in his attempt to break our song, I used the rest of the money to buy a house in Essex for my mum.

'Everything's good to go,' said the previous owner. 'I've left the fish in the fish pond for you. It was easier than transporting them.'

'Okay, great!' I said as she walked off, then added (realising I had a once-in-a-lifetime opportunity to say it): 'So long — and thanks for all the fish!'

Charlie and I were settling into the house we'd bought together, too. On the day we first moved in, both our next-door neighbour and the students living opposite recognised Charlie from YouTube, which made it harder to maintain my claim that we weren't famous (though I kept on trucking). I had half a million subscribers, while Charlie had over a million. YouTube gave Charlie a huge plaque in honour of the achievement, and I mean *huge:* it was about as big as a widescreen TV and just as heavy. Much like the rest of YouTube, the plaque didn't correspond with reality as we knew it. Charlie kept it propped on the floor against his video lights.

I liked the students opposite us. They often sat outside smoking because they weren't allowed to do so in the house, and I strolled over when I saw them there. I enjoyed saying hi and seeing what they'd been up to. These conversations never went well.

'Have a good Christmas?' I asked.

'Yeah, mostly studying,' one of the girls replied. 'You?'

'Uh, yeah,' I said. 'I got in the charts.'

'What?'

'Yeah. Number four.'

'Huh.'

'Got a Guinness World Record.'

'I got socks,' she said.

'I didn't come over here to brag,' I said. 'Just weird stuff happens to me sometimes.'

'Uh-huh.'

'What you up to this week?'

'Got a dissertation deadline. What you up to?'

My face fell as I realised the answer.

'I'm interviewing Kermit the Frog.'

'Oh, fuck off!'

To promote the new Muppets movie, The Muppets Studio made three custom Muppets in the likeness of people who loved their brand. They made one of Jonathan Ross, one of Charlie and one of me. (I guess we were the answer to the question, 'Who are the UK's three biggest muppets?') Hence my trip to the Savoy Hotel in West London accompanied by a custom-made Muppet-clone of myself to interview Kermit the Frog.

I was put in a waiting room while Kermit — and his 'handler' Steve — prepared for me. I say 'waiting room' but it was more like a walk-in-wardrobe: every visible surface was covered in hundreds of gloves of various lengths and colours, most of them sequinned. The only other person in the room was tending to them, keeping them organised and free of creases. She saw me looking and smiled, 'She travels with them everywhere.'

'What's your job then?'

'Maintenance.'

'Cool.'

'Normally it is,' she said. 'Right now I need the loo, and I can't leave this room unattended.'

'I can watch over things for you,' I said, 'I'll be here a little while anyway.'

'That would be wonderful! You sure?'

'Course,' I shrugged.

'Okay, I won't be long,' she said. 'Thanks for keeping an eye on her.'

'Her?' I said.

As she moved aside to leave, I saw the owner of all those sequinned gloves. It was Miss Piggy. Our eyes met across a table of gloves and I felt something come over me — I don't think the woman had even shut the door before I was on the other side of the room with my hand in Piggy's head.

We stared at each other like Hamlet and Yorick. Neither of us spoke. We just looked into each other's eyes, trying to make sense of it all.

Ross was the A&R guy for Polydor Records. I didn't even know what A&R meant, but he wanted to meet with me, so there I was sitting in his office in West London. I was wearing a geometric-patterned shirt straight out of the Zack Morris catalogue, zebra-striped Versace jeans, spiky black Christian Louboutin shoes and a fake fur coat from a girl's clothing store, which is why it surprised me when Ross turned up fifteen minutes late to the meeting claiming he couldn't find me in the lobby.

'First of all, I have to say congratulations,' said Ross. 'It's amazing, big chart success. Getting to number seven!'

'Thank you,' I said, wondering whether to correct him and then deciding to. 'It was actually number four.' I didn't want to be the dick who corrected praise but it was kind of his job to know the right number; he was the one who called the meeting. (And it *did* set a world record.)

'Yes, of course it was,' he said, unfazed at such an audacious misfire so early in his attempts to endear me to Polydor. 'So.' He leaned back in his chair and looked at me like David Brent. 'What can we do for you?'

There was a short silence.

'Well I don't know,' I said. 'That's why we're here, isn't it? I've just had a song in the charts *without* a record label; perhaps you should tell me what you can do for me?'

'That's a very valid question,' said Ross.

'Thank you,' I said.

'Well first, I should hear some more of your music,' said Ross with an air of general disinterest. 'All I've heard is that one song.'

'It's all online, for free,' I said. 'There's loads of it.'

'Great; thank you!'

'You're welcome,' I frowned. 'Let's start with: what does A&R mean?'

'Ahh,' said Ross, 'it stands for 'artist and repertoire. Looking for new acts and looking after people. My job is to fill the roster.'

'Well then, I feel special,' I said. Ross missed my tone as expected.

'So how did you do this?' he said, looking at me like I was the key to his bonus. 'What's your secret?'

'A lot of people watch my videos,' I shrugged, 'and some of them bought my song.'

'Yeah, yeah,' Ross nodded, leaning forward, 'that's really interesting, yeah. So what I think we can do for you is take everything you've done so far — and expand it.' I was disappointed he didn't stretch his hands apart on the word 'expand' and look at me with amazement at the space he'd made.

'What does that mean?' I said.

'Well,' said Ross, 'let's say you come to us with your next single. We would say, "Right, we can do this, this and this," and we'd really push you forward in your career.' (I'm not paraphrasing. He said, 'We can do this, this and this'.) 'Especially outside of the UK,' he blathered on. 'We can really expand things where you're not getting much reach.'

I didn't want to brag, but felt it relevant to add some context, so I said, 'Well just to let you know, I did end up selling a hundred thousand copies of the song and about half of those sales were outside the UK. We charted in Canada.'

'Well,' said Ross, 'you might as well stay unsigned forever then!'

'Right,' I said. 'What is it you wanted out of this meeting? Did you wanna offer me a deal, or... ?'

'No,' Ross smiled, 'we just wanted to say hello.'

'Brilliant. Hello,' I said, glad to have travelled all the way across town in my most exciting jeans. I'd arranged to meet with someone else that day, too — the A&R guy for Island Records. He'd said he was interested in hearing my next single but cancelled our meeting at the last minute and said, 'You can just play it to my assistant.'

Both Polydor and Island were part of Universal Records and I'd had a huge grin on my face when I walked through the doors of their building and saw pictures of people like Eminem and Rihanna on the wall, various photos and record discs lining a plush waiting area. I'd sat with my eyes gazing to the top of the high ceiling while I waited for Ross, taking in the scale of the building. A short while later I shuffled out of there with my shoulders slumped, burdened not with the knowledge that they didn't want me, but that I didn't want them. The exposure I'd had to the industry made them look arrogant, obstinate and lazy. I wanted to show them a new kind of artist was possible: one that produced their own music and made their own videos, infusing creativity into every aspect of their work, while focusing on music instead of tours and singles instead of albums. But I was so tired of being the one in charge. I didn't want to face more months, let alone years, working every second of the day on my music alone and without reprieve to try and prove to people that it would work. I feared becoming a professional writer of emails who sometimes gets an idea for song. My only ally was Jonathan.

'Wankers,' he said when I told him about my conversation with Ross (who, as a matter of record, no longer works for Polydor). Jonathan was keen for me to release a new single as soon as possible to keep the momentum going. Because I didn't have any more hits, he suggested a cover from the 1960s, 'Lady Godiva', which he'd first earmarked as a potential Sons of Admirals single. It was a song about a girl (the titular Lady) who rode naked on a horse through the town of Coventry, based on an old English legend. It was a fitting track; I had nothing left to do but get back on the horse myself. I would push this song with all the energy I had left and earn the respect of the industry myself.

I jumped into the studio to produce a modern version of the track, but when I asked Charlie to work on the video I saw his head turn a full three-sixty on his neck. The hardship of working non-stop to a deadline seemed to have caused him lasting trauma. 'I'm still recovering from the last one,' were his exact words.

I took to my camera to tell my audience the plan: 'Lady Godiva' would be released on April 1st and would chart on my birthday a week later. Maybe this second attempt would show the industry that there was something in my approach. What I didn't realise was that, while I treated the campaigns to promote my singles as a war on the music business with my audience as the army who would help me upend it, they saw 'Forever Yours' as nothing more than a fun way of proving the power of the internet. The main response I saw in comments was, 'We've already done this. Why are we doing it again?' Even supposed friends of mine wrote things like, 'Let's just say I'll be supporting 'Lady Godiva' 100% less than 'Forever Yours'.'

My main support around this time came from Marilyn, the girl who'd tweeted me at Christmas. We'd arranged to meet up in January to record a song together and I was floored the moment I saw her waiting for me at the train station, grinning at me amidst a tangle of blond hair in a patchwork overcoat and happy-face Doc Marten boots. 'I'm in awe,' she said, her wide eyes taking in the fake fur coat I was wearing.

We both wanted a career in the music industry and had struggled with record labels. She wanted to step out of her brother's shadow and prove herself, but she'd seen projects stalled for no good reason and had no choice but to wait for her time to come.

'You can't ride a horse, can you?' I asked her while we were sat on my sofa.

'Not really. Why?'

'I need someone to ride on a horse naked for my new music video.'

'Okay, if you need someone to ride on a horse naked, you don't just ask, "Can you ride a horse"! That's not the most important part of the request, is it?'

'Fair point!' I said amidst bellyfuls of laughter.

'Even if I could ride a horse, I'm not gonna do it naked for your music video!'

'What's the one thing you most wanna do?' I asked. 'What's your dream job?'

'Not that!'

'Right,' I chuckled, 'well what is it? I'm interested.'

Marilyn smiled. 'If a meteor was coming, and we only had one day left on Earth, I'd be Éponine in *Les Misérables*,' said Marilyn. ' That's how I'd wanna go out.'

'Nice.'

'I played her when I was younger.'

'Éponine?'

'Yeah, I was Young Éponine and now I wanna go back and finish the job.'

'Has anyone ever played the young *and* adult versions before?'

'I don't think so.'

'Mate, you'd be the first ever. That's so cool!' I said. I had no doubt she could do it. With her certain vision and abundance of confidence and energy, she struck me as an obvious star. I felt privileged to have met her right before her inevitable takeover of the world.

'So why are you doing these livestreams?' I asked her. Every week, Marilyn hosted a live show for about an hour, playing songs and taking questions.

'They're fun! Did you watch it?'

'No, I was living my life,' I grinned. 'What are you doing 'em for?'

'My manager thinks they're a good way to connect with people.'

'Sod what he thinks, you should be doing YouTube,' I said. Marilyn had videos on the site but only covers of songs. Her personality wasn't on display.

'I think he knows what he's talking about!'

'YouTube is better for everyone,' I said. 'People can subscribe even if they don't like your music, they get an alert when you have a new one out so they won't miss it if they're not there, you can edit them, they're shorter, you don't have to do it at a certain time, they can be shared and rewatched, you can put more creative energy into it *and* you can make money from them.'

'We'll see,' she said, smirking.

Though we had a lot of affection for each other, we disagreed on a lot of things and bickered all the time. Marilyn recognised she was a role model to a huge young audience and spent a lot of time every day reading comments from her followers on Twitter. She would even search her name to see the things that were said about her, rather than to her. She cared that she was received well and clarified herself whenever she was misunderstood. I saw this like walking up to someone in a pub and interfering with their private chat. We were both right; online there's no difference between something intended for a small audience and something broadcast to the world, so there wasn't much social etiquette in place for it.

In contrast, I had just given away my iPhone because I wanted to be less connected. I texted all my friends, 'Just to let you know, I'm not using this number anymore so delete it from your records!' then turned my phone off, gave it to a mate who needed a new phone and threw my SIM card in the river like I was in the mob. Marilyn and I made all our plans through email instead; technology had advanced enough that I could reach people on their phones without having one of my own. When I went outside, I enjoyed the novelty of not being pulled out of the present moment. I didn't like being so tethered to my audience, and I'd definitely heard enough of their opinions about me over the years. People were always bound to disagree with something I said, did or believed, and I'd accepted the inevitable backlash as par for the course. Even the Dalai Lama has haters, chief among them the state of China, which is more people than hate me, and he seems to do alright.

We also disagreed on relationships. (Me and Marilyn, not the Dalai Lama.)

'My brother's having his wedding photographed by *OK!* magazine,' she said.

'Why does he wanna do that?'

'Why wouldn't he?'

'Isn't it supposed to be the happiest day of their lives? I wouldn't want a photoshoot in the middle of it.'

'All weddings have a photoshoot in the middle of it,' she pointed out. 'And they pay for everything. You get your dream wedding and your honeymoon all for free.'

'My dream wedding doesn't include paparazzi!'

It came down to Marilyn wanting to share her life — including her romantic life — with the public, and me not wanting to share my personal life with strangers. Relationships are hard enough without people you don't know telling you how amazing you are together, especially when you're a teenager bound to make mistakes and get into things that might not last or be right for you. I was burned by my relationship with Denise, which ended in such public heat that we wrote songs about it and sang them at each other on stage at VidCon. I felt there was an important difference between a secret life and a private life, had no problem with the latter, and didn't feel anyone was entitled to know anything just because they liked my professional work.

Having observed all these differences, I concluded the two of us wouldn't work in a relationship at all. I didn't want children, for example, while she did. Those were big obstacles and she recognised them too. Of course by that point we were becoming more intimate and having so much fun in each other's company that we couldn't stand to let each other out of our sight.

If you're wondering where Laura was in all this, imagine how she felt — she had to live through it. I once believed that Laura and I would be perfect if only we'd met five years in the future, giving me time to fuck around and make mistakes, but those five years had passed and here I still was, struggling to commit to her. I'd given up trying to figure out what it was about us that made it so hard for our relationship to work; it wasn't working, that much was clear, and that was all that mattered. (I've since figured it out, by the way. Spoiler alert, it was nothing to do with her.) From the moment I saw Marilyn at the train station, I knew things had run their course with Laura and that it was for good. It took three days for us to break up through in-depth text chats on Skype. I didn't mention Marilyn (who was aware of Laura's importance to me but not that we were together when we met).

'Stay the fuck out of my life from now on,' Laura said in the end. 'If you have an epiphany and realise you know what to do to make this relationship work... just keep it to yourself. I wish you the best of luck with your music. I love you.'

And she blocked me.

After breaking up with Laura, I thought I should be on my own for a while. However, I couldn't deny how I felt about Marilyn or make my feelings go away. I'd welcomed her into the online community I was a part of, sharing her new videos with my subscribers when she began to make them and introducing her to all of my friends. I convinced myself it was pessimistic to dismiss the idea of our relationship before even giving it a try. That was part of the old me, I told myself, that had been so unfair to Laura. The new me — the one that wouldn't hurt the women in my life — had to be kinder and more willing to compromise. After all, Marilyn and I adored each other. She surprised me with breakfast picnics and late-night chats. I was upfront with her about how I'd treated Laura and told her I didn't want to cheat on anyone again. We thought everything would work out through the sheer force of our both wanting it to. Together, we agreed to date and figure it out. I took her agreeing to be my girlfriend as a sign she didn't mind giving up children. I learned later that she took it as a sign I had accepted having them. The seeds we planted at the start didn't bloom for a long time, but the roots took hold early on.

'So,' said Marilyn, 'how naked would I have to be for this video?'

'You'd have a body stocking on,' I explained. 'Like one of these.' I showed her a picture of the laciest and most see-through body stocking I could find.

'I'm not wearing *that*!'

'They have it in your size,' I said, frowning. She scrunched her face up and punched me in the arm.

I'd managed to obtain a horse for the afternoon by contacting a friend of a friend on Facebook. Marilyn and I headed to a farm in Surrey to get the shots of her riding it. She'd bought a flesh-coloured bodysuit to use for the day, though it was the middle of February and freezing.

'Say hello to the horse,' she said as she climbed on top of it.

'No, you're alright.' (I have a lifelong wariness of animals, and so should you: they could do anything and you can't understand or reason with them. We should all be terrified of all animals all the time.)

'Come on, say hello.'

'Nah, I'm good.'

'Alex,' she said through clenched teeth, 'I'm sitting here, looking like I'm naked, for *your* video. Say hello to the freaking horse.'

'If you're not enjoying it, mate, just climb off,' I smiled at her. Her eyes narrowed at me.

At Marilyn's signal, the horse took off and I got fantastic footage as it galloped along, faster and faster. On the unedited footage we filmed, you can hear me say, 'This looks great!' about half a second before Marilyn loses control, bounces off the horse and crashes to the ground on her back, the horse tearing off without her while she lies in the middle of the field, not moving.

I've killed Marilyn.

I ran over (in what I'd decided was my farm outfit: pointed red boots and a t-shirt that looked like a composition notebook) and pulled her up, relieved to see she was not only alive but basically unharmed.

'We got it; you're done,' I said, walking her off the field.

'You're gonna have to make a whole video about how great I am for doing this.'

'I will.'

With my 'unsigned artist in Christmas Number One race' story expended, I had to come up with something new to attract press. I was fortunate when an opportunity arrived from a guy called Warren at Universal Records. His son was a fan of Chameleon Circuit and, having seen the videos I made after my label meetings (with titles like 'Record Labels Are Rubbish'), had encouraged his dad to work with me in some way. Warren got in touch and offered to distribute 'Lady Godiva' to music stores around the country. Ten thousand CDs would be printed, and the best part was it wasn't a full record deal; it was just distribution. They would get 15% of the sales and I would keep control of everything else. This was real progress and unheard of for an unsigned artist; I could plug into the machine while still keeping the lion's share of the profits. This was my hook. Without a record label, I would have CDs in shops all over the country.

We organised a signing tour on the week of release and arranged in advance for my music video to be played on national TV chart shows. I did a variety of phone and online interviews, including one with a radio station in Coventry who kept a coop of chickens and insisted on playing my song to the chickens on-air.

'Alex, your song has gone down brilliantly with the chickens!' the presenter said.

Repeating my previous trick, I arranged a raft of new remixes, including a fantastic a cappella performance from Marilyn and a jungle-drum remix from Jonathan.

'Here you go, Struwwelpeter,' Jonathan said in his email when he sent the track. (Due to his constant demands for me to shave my face, Jonathan had taken to naming me after a German children's story, 'Struwwelpeter', about a boy with enormous hair who doesn't groom himself and is subsequently unpopular.)

'I've had another great idea,' I sent back. 'I've promised my audience that anyone who buys the song, and sends me a receipt to prove it, will get a personalised thank-you video from me.'

'Don't do that!' Jonathan sent back. 'It'll take forever!'

'Already done!' I said. I didn't care. I wanted even the people who didn't like the song to have a good reason to spend a pound on the track and push me closer to my dream. To make sure people everywhere could get a signed CD whether they could make the signing tour or not (and to satisfy my desire to participate in every part of the process of my career), I insisted on visiting the manufacturing plant where the CDs would be printed. My plan was to sign all ten thousand CDs before they reached the stores, but my request caused more of a fuss than I expected. It seemed, to my dismay, that no artist in the history of Universal Records had ever been interested in going there. The idea put everyone in charge on their guard, as though I was about to Guy Fawkes my way to the top of the charts on the burning embers of the biggest record label in the world. I was only allowed in for one afternoon, with a hard hat and a high-visibility jacket over my world-map-patterned clothes, and only managed to sign a couple thousand CDs in that time. Nonetheless, with all this effort made, I felt confident we could replicate our success, get that elusive number one and build a mainstream profile for my work in the music industry. Things did not go to plan.

'Lady Godiva' wasn't the only song released that week. The other contender was 'Call Me Maybe' by Carly Rae Jepsen, which had gone viral on YouTube a couple months earlier thanks to an alternative music video created by Justin Bieber and Selena Gomez. (Justin had tweeted that 'Call Me Maybe' was 'the catchiest song I've ever heard lol'.) Still, I felt confident when I turned up in Edinburgh on the day of the song's release and a thousand people had queued up in and around HMV to buy my CD.

'This is the biggest response we've seen since McFly!' the member of staff said (to Marilyn's delight).

'Well, let's get 'em through the door,' I said.

'There's one problem: we've run out of CDs. We had no idea so many people would show up.'

It wasn't just Edinburgh — branches of HMV across the country were short on CDs. I learned on the spot that, even though we'd ordered ten thousand to be sent to record shops, the record label doesn't send those CDs out unprompted. They just make the CD available in the system. Individual stores still have to order the stock based on what they think will sell, and no-one in the music industry believes you can sell physical CDs unless it's a charity release or an *X Factor* winner. I was keen to disprove that, but it was hard when the CDs weren't on the shelves in the first place. After telling my audience they could walk into their nearest HMV and see my song in a real-life place, I was overwhelmed all week by tweets from disappointed kids around the UK who were turned away or even laughed at by apathetic staff members who told them they 'don't stock singles' and had never heard of me. At my Edinburgh signing, hundreds of kids were being turned away at the door, and I demanded to speak to whomever was responsible.

'We don't have any CDs left,' he tried again.

'So what? I'll sign their train ticket,' I said, as confused by the idea of not meeting them as he was by the idea that I would.

I had thought I would have another hit on my hands, but I shouldn't have — as they say — counted my chickens. Lady Godiva ended the week at #15 in the UK charts. No stations playlisted it the week of release (apart from the chicken one in Coventry), the track tanked out of the charts the following week, and I was left having to make ten thousand videos thanking each individual person who purchased it (which took me about three months). 'Call Me Maybe' got to number one, sold eighteen million copies around the world and became the fifth-biggest selling digital single in the history of music.

I could claim only two small victories. First, when the song was first released fifty years earlier it charted at #16, so I was able to get the song one chart place higher than it had reached before. And second, in Slovenia — where iTunes isn't popular at all — Lady Godiva got to number one on the iTunes chart with just two sales, making me (as I later told my audience, and the media) a two-time Top 5 artist with 'a number one in Europe'. You have to make the best of these things.

The day Lady Godiva charted, I tuned in to watch my music video airing on TV. I had to pay a few hundred pounds to the music channel's chart show to be included, a point I resented and used as further proof of the backwards-thinking of the industry: if you're making a show of music videos in the charts, wouldn't you be desperate to get them all? I was appalled to see half the videos by labels who didn't cough up were just skipped over, with a voiceover saying, 'These songs are at number 23 and 22, and now here's the music video for number 21.' Still, mine was there, and it would give the video even more prominence amongst the no-shows (if anyone even watched a show with that many gaps in it). I tweeted that we were coming up so my audience around the country could tune in for the big moment. Danny and I sat watching the telly as the announcer came on and said, 'This next song just proves you don't need a record label to make it in the music industry. Or any talent.' Then they played my song.

I'd just been insulted on national television — and paid three hundred quid for it.

GHOST

'So,' I asked, 'how much is this Disney World trip gonna be?'

Marilyn has visited Walt Disney World in Florida at least twenty times. Her mum and dad planned to go with her the year we met, but — noting her parents were now of the age where they were keen to skip the thrill rides in favour of a more leisurely vacation — she'd been sending me daily emails since before we started dating to outline the many reasons I should accompany her on the trip. I acquiesced after becoming her boyfriend.

I'd only been to Walt Disney World once, with my dad when I was six (another of the reasons Marilyn insisted I go). Marilyn left it up to me to arrange my own transport from the airport to the hotel, which she regretted when I rolled through the front gates of the Caribbean Beach Resort in a private limousine complete with champagne and multi-coloured flashing lights inside, grinning out the window with one fur-sleeved arm toasting a glass to her.

'Why did you do that?' she shrieked in disbelief as the chauffeur opened the door for me.

'Thought it'd be fun,' I grinned. 'It was.'

'You are ridiculous, Bugsquash,' she said. (Marilyn had taken to calling me by a different nickname every time she spoke to me. She finally settled on 'Bugsquash', which caused her to snort with laughter every time she said it.)

Marilyn carried a wealth of experience, knowing what parks opened at what times and what rides to go on, in what order, to skip the queues and secure good views for the various shows, parades and firework displays on offer every day. In turn I generated a force of mischief for her to contend with, leading her towards paths that were out-of-bounds and challenging what she thought was possible in the place she knew and loved.

'I wanna get a haircut,' I said.

'You can't.'

'Yeah I can,' I pointed. 'There's a barber on Main Street. Look.'

'You can't just get a haircut, Squash!'

'Let's find out!' I said, strolling in. Minutes later my hair was being cut by the woman who does the hair for all the Disney princesses as they stroll around the Magic Kingdom. 'D'you want one?' I asked Marilyn, gesturing in triumph at the scene I'd created.

I'd assumed I wasn't going to Disney. I wasn't sure our romance would last that long. Marilyn brought me a lot of joy but I wasn't sure how we could sustain our differences long-term. (She didn't know any of this — I suppressed things. You don't break up with a wonderful person like Marilyn just because things don't feel like they're working.)

One of the biggest issues for me was the amount of energy she spent on the internet. For months I'd known about the existence of an online gossip forum where anonymous users dished the things they most disliked about various YouTubers. Marilyn had her own thread and I'd done my best to prevent her from discovering it. Once she found out, she spent hours reading the posts and even went as far as to create a secret account of her own to defend herself. She responded to critical tweets and comments with more fervour than the positive ones. Her audience started to realise the best way to get their favourite vlogger's attention was to rag on her or her work.

Marilyn's critics dismissed her success as the result of her connection to her brother, or to me, but while I tried to steer her away from caring so much, she tried to get me to care a little more. I was as concerned about her feverish obsessiveness as she was about my chilly detachment.

Lady Godiva hadn't done anything to earn me the attention I was working for. After being mocked on the chart show, being ignored was a bit of a step up. Either way, the mainstream music industry didn't recognise me as a legitimate musician. The music critic Bob Lefsetz, after being swamped by emails from my audience recommending he check me out, tweeted 'tell your minions they can stop e-mailing me', following up with an email: 'This all means nothing to me. When I feel the groundswell from the outside, then I'm intrigued.'

'I have more YouTube views than One Direction,' I lamented to anyone who would listen. 'Why are they being so dismissive?'

I met with Island Records again — to their credit, they took the meeting at my request — and played their A&R guy a cover of 'This Kiss' by Faith Hill (which I'd recorded with Marilyn). Halfway through the track, he reached over, stopped the song and said, 'Alex, you need to get your fans off their computers and into a club. You're good at the online stuff but not the real-world stuff. There's no proof these kids will walk into a store and buy your record just because they clicked a button on a computer.'

'I've sold over 300,000 songs in the last three years,' I told him.

'We only sign artists who can sell a million in the next three months,' he shrugged.

Opportunities were coming my way but I had to be disciplined about the way I wanted to represent myself. When I got an email from the BRIT Awards inviting me to their star-studded music show to interview the other artists on the red carpet, I told them I was a musician, not a presenter. When Capital FM reached out to ask if I would record a pilot show with a view to becoming a DJ for their station, I grumbled back that I was a musician, not a DJ.

Like me, YouTube and its users were going all-in on their desire to be taken seriously. The new brood of creators I met were professional and ambitious, even if they were lacking in imagination. The newest YouTuber du jour, JacksGap (a guy who filmed videos on his gap year), often made entire videos reading his fan mail aloud. My friends, despite their other interests in life, were also planting their flags ever deeper in the world of online video. Ben, the *Doctor Who Magazine* journalist, started making videos of his own, collaborating with everyone he could find. My YouTube partner manager, Hazel, saw such potential on our side of the fence that she quit her job to become a full-time vlogger herself. People were uploading big-budget animated videos, glossy sketches and short films. YouTube gave Charlie a loan to make five short films for his channel over the next twelve months — he buried himself in screenplay books and angst.

As YouTubers became more preoccupied with call sheets, scripts and lighting rigs, the audience loved them all the more. The growing love for YouTubers started to feel more and more separate from the community I'd signed up for. It was becoming like a teen idol phenomenon.

'It's frustrating,' the animator TomSka told me once. 'I tell them, "No, I'm just a regular person, I fuck up, don't admire me," and they respond, "Oh my god, he's so humble!"' He threw his hands in the air.

In my search for a new angle on my music, I stumbled across Ryan Holiday, the former head of PR for American Apparel, who is now a writer and newspaper columnist. He was about to release his first book, a treatise on media manipulation called *Trust Me, I'm Lying*.

'I have a proposal for you,' I wrote him. 'If you can get press attention to my music, thus raising my profile, I'll use that raised profile to showcase your book. You'll be manipulating the media for me and I'll be a walking testimonial for you.'

'I'll do you one better,' Ryan wrote back. Over the next two days, he published two back-to-back profiles about me on Forbes: 'Tracking

Indie Musician Alex Day's Next Big Move' and 'Is Alex Day the Future of Music?'. Off the back of that, I was invited to deliver a TED talk titled 'The Future of Music' where I recounted the adventure of releasing 'Forever Yours'. I was turning my lack of mainstream interest into a selling point. Labels were outdated, so the story went, and I rebranded myself as the little unsigned artist that could.

Now I had to carry that momentum forward.

'Excuse me, can you shave please?' said Jonathan when he opened his door and saw my stubbled face. I smiled and waited. He stood there for a few seconds, staring me down, blocking the door. 'Don't know why I fucking bother,' he sighed, giving up and moving aside. 'It's not easy having a good time. Even smiling makes my face ache.' (This was a quote from *The Rocky Horror Show*, which — as he often reminded me — he attended on the night of their second ever performance, offering on the spot to fund and produce the soundtrack, which he still earns royalties for. 'All good fun! Another adventure!')

After an hour of Jonathan telling me he invented the modern awards show ('...and that's why George Michael still hates me to this day!'), that he won the Eurovision Song Contest in 1997, and that Jimi Hendrix, David Bowie and John Lennon had each sat in his living room playing their newest songs in the very spot in which I now sat, I managed to take advantage of a pause for breath to wrangle the conversation over to myself.

'We have chart fatigue,' I said. 'My audience is bored of trying to get in the charts.'

'Yes, well, the charts don't matter anymore,' acknowledged Jonathan. 'No-one knows or cares who's number one. In the old days, when I was running *The Tip Sheet*, all the labels would have noticed you and we would have got you a meeting for a huge deal. That's how it went with Chumbawumba,' and another thirty minutes passed.

'They don't like me doing covers,' I said as Jonathan coughed in between anecdotes. 'They like to know I wrote the song.'

'Who cares who wrote the song?' cried Jonathan.

After much debate, we agreed to come up with something new. We would do the opposite of a chart push. I was to release three singles in the same day and it would appease everyone: a cover, a new original song and an unreleased demo from another band Jonathan knew.

'None of them will chart because they're all out on the same day,' said Jonathan. 'But people can support the one they like most and, if one of them takes off, it has all summer to build momentum.'

Along with my cover of 'This Kiss' with Marilyn, I needed a new song of my own. I'd developed a habit of booking studio time without any songs written, motivating me to get something done as I saw the day loom towards me. But this time I had lurched right up to the day before before recording and still had nothing close to a smash hit summer single, though I'd been putting time aside every day to write something great.

'How's your dissertation?' I asked my student neighbour as I left the flat that afternoon.

'Long,' she said. 'Writing every day.'

'Mate, I hear ya. I'm doing this thing right now with my music where I write for half an hour every single day, no matter what.'

'Oh fuck *off!*'

While sat on the Tube, I tried to think of something to start me off. The only thing on my mind was that it was the first day of the year I could go out without my coat on. 'Good morning, sunshine,' I wrote out. 'I hope that you're well.'

By the time the train doors opened, I could hear the entire song in my head. I've never had a song stuck in my head that didn't exist yet. I was fortunate that I only had to wait until the next day to get in the studio, where I tried to extricate it from my brain as though I were remembering a dream. It didn't feel like I was producing it, just listening to it mentally and describing what happened next: 'And then the bass goes "bu-bum, bum, bum, bum,"' I said to the engineer, swinging my shoulders as I mimed a jaunty walk. 'And then a trumpet goes "blam!" and then harmonies come in and go "mm-baa-baa, mm-baa-baa"...'

I didn't know how to play the song on any instrument. I didn't know what the chords were. I just knew what the finished song sounded like. We worked from the start, filling in every layer as I listened to my inner radio and heard each part cut through. When I came out of the studio with 'Good Morning Sunshine', we'd worked up to the end of the second chorus; it played, fully formed, for little over a minute and a half, then stopped at the moment we ran out of time. I got home and played it to Charlie, who listened in silence to my ninety seconds, an inscrutable look on his face. When it cut out, he raised his eyebrows and said, 'Holy shit, mate.'

With two of my three songs in the can (or on their way to being), it was down to Jonathan to supply the third when he introduced me to The Vacancy, a band with a great demo that was never released.

'We heard the track and promoted it like mad. The band got signed, the label insisted on changing their name and recording a bunch of new songs, all of which were shit, and they sank without trace,' Jonathan recounted. 'Labels do this all the time. They sign artists just to stop other labels getting them, then leave them to rot.' The song (which I loved) was called 'She Walks Right Through Me'. It was about a guy who falls in love with a ghost.

Just when I thought it was hard work trying to get one song to be a smash hit, I now had to work on three. Charlie had, after many furrowed brows, agreed to make the video for one of them, leaving me to work on the other two. I was about to start filming 'She Walks Right Through Me' when I touched my face.

'Fuck,' I exclaimed, my eyes wide.

'What?' said my cameraman, Ciaran.

'I've forgotten to shave.' Ciaran had spent nearly an hour setting up the equipment and lighting the room, but I heard Jonathan's voice in my head demolishing me for looking scruffy and I knew he was right. I apologised and told Ciaran I needed to go back home. I ran to the nearest train station and turned up at my door half an hour later,

Charlie was out, and I'd realised in my haste to get back that I'd forgot to pick up my keys. *I have to shave*, I thought, right before I leapt at the wall surrounding the back of my house, hoisted myself up on top, jumped across to the roof, shimmied along the roof tiles, prised open my bedroom window (which I happened to have left open that day) and collapsed through it on to the floor. Then I punched the air, screamed out with joy, strutted to the bathroom and shaved. I was unstoppable.

My three singles all charted on iTunes in the Top 40, and 'Good Morning Sunshine' — the strongest of the lot — was featured on TV shows in America and Australia. It was heard by over ten million people, ended up selling as many copies as 'Forever Yours' and gave me my most-viewed music video with three million views to date. Even with so many people connecting with it, though, I failed to build any long-term traction with my happy song about appreciating and celebrating life. *Perhaps there's no appetite for a song like that*, I thought.

A year later, Pharrell Williams released the song 'Happy', which became the first single to spend an entire year in the UK Charts, rose to number one on three separate occasions and ended its run as both the best-selling single of the 21st century and the most-downloaded song of all time.

I was filming the music video for 'Good Morning Sunshine' on the day I first cheated on Marilyn. Charlie had long since fallen under the weight of his self-inflicted pressure and bailed, leaving it up to me to make all three videos. Marilyn stayed up all night making hand-written signs for the video. Danny, Ben, Hazel and Crystal turned up to feature in it, as did my new friend Freya, a blogger and writer from Essex who I met and clicked with at one of my Lady Godiva signings. I even got my nan to stop by for a few minutes, waving to the camera from her wheelchair as she recovered from a hip replacement.

Eager to get the shoot done on time (and viewing it as the genesis of my status as a global superstar), I was snappy and impatient throughout the day, ushering people to their marks with no tolerance for anything that wasn't being filmed. Crystal and Marilyn were both staying over that evening, by which point I was exhausted from being around people all day and in need of a fortress within which I could hide myself.

'I don't have to stay tonight,' said Marilyn. 'I can go home if you need your space.'

'I would actually really appreciate that,' I said. 'I'm knackered. Thanks.'

'Oh. Okay.'

'What?'

'No, it's fine.'

'What's wrong?'

'I've done so much today,' said Marilyn. 'I've been looking after everyone and serving food and making signs.'

'I know,' I said. 'You suggested this. You just said—'

'Yeah, fine.'

'Well if it's a problem, I don't mind you staying—'

'No, I'll go home, you don't want me here.'

'It's not that—'

'It's okay.'

'This was your idea!'

'Yeah, okay.'

Marilyn left. I spent the evening complaining about it to a sympathetic Crystal, then being intimate with her.

STUPID

I used to have sex with people for a lot of silly reasons that undervalued us both. I once had a challenge with a few girls I knew to see who would be the first to sleep with the entire Zodiac — i.e. twelve people with different star signs. I undertook a crusade to sleep with someone from every Hogwarts house, a goal defined by one of my friends as 'winning the House Cup'. Thus, when a Swedish YouTuber flew over who, in her own words, got into vlogging because the boys were hot and she wanted to bang them, it didn't take much beyond 'She's Swedish; that's new' for me to colour myself interested. She was over for a week and slept with at least three YouTubers on what one friend called 'her UK fuck tour'. Her schedule was so full, she stopped at my place on her way back to Sweden, spending an hour at mine before her flight like I was a layover (which I suppose I was).

'You slept with her?' said Crystal later. I nodded. 'Nice,' she said, high-fiving me. 'She's hot!'

I perceived these further acts of cheating as collateral incidents. Because I was already keeping the truth of my failures from Marilyn (and because I — incorrectly — believed her finding out, rather than the acts themselves, was where the harm lay) I didn't see what difference it made whether I hid one act of unfaithfulness or several. Either I was good or I wasn't. And I wasn't.

It goes without saying that this is pretty dumb, because the relationship you had is over the moment you cheat on someone. Maybe you try to compensate by being even more attentive and loving, or maybe you become anxious and paranoid about them knowing the truth, or maybe your desire to get away with it leaves you controlling and possessive, or maybe you check out and become distant and moody, but there *will* be a shift in your dynamic, and don't think the other party won't notice. We aren't the Jedi we think we are. A tear will appear, and all you do by ignoring it is make it wider. The sooner you stitch it up, the better for everyone.

It's only now I can see that the real person I was trying to spare the truth from was myself. I didn't want to admit how much I was hurting someone I cared about, so I pushed it out and tried not to think about it. By not thinking about it, I didn't think about the consequences of it, which meant I kept doing it. But the more you push it out, the harder it'll push back.

A friend of ours had recently moved into our spare room; his girlfriend, Silvi, visited so often that she became a de facto housemate with him. The evening I slept with the Swedish girl, Silvi knocked on my bedroom door.

'Can we talk?' she said.

'Sure.' I shuffled aside to make space for her. 'What's up?'

'I heard you earlier.'

I realised what she was referring to and avoided her gaze.

'What's going on? Why did you do that?' Silvi said, sitting beside me.

As usual, I burst into tears at the impact of my behaviour. As usual, I said I didn't know why I'd done it or what I was doing. I felt the full wave of shame smash into me, threatening to drown me.

'I'm not gonna tell Marilyn,' said Silvi in the end. 'But if she ever asks me, I won't lie.'

I nodded and said I understood.

A few weeks later, sat at my desk, I flipped open my laptop and loaded YouTube. On the front page, where my subscriptions lived, I saw Charlie had uploaded a new video. He was staring, solemn, in black-and-white. The video was titled 'I'm Scared'.

I turned 'round from my desk to look at him. He was gazing into his computer screen, his back to me.

I grabbed some headphones and pressed play.

'I am not here to entertain you today,' Charlie began. 'I don't have the capacity to do that right now. I am here as one regular human being to another because I am not happy right now. I am not happy with myself and I need to talk to someone about it.'

Charlie elaborated on his struggle to write a short film, his worry about how it would be received by his audience and a general anxiety he felt at how people might (or might not) be talking about him when he wasn't around.

'The simplest answer to me is that I should just stop caring about it so much,' he said, 'but I have no idea how to do that. All I want to do with my life is make and do things that make other people happy. I can't think of a better way to spend my time on this planet, but right now I just have to hope, I guess, that I have the capacity within myself to be that person that I want to be because right now, I just don't know. I am unsure. And that scares me a lot.'

Charlie's upload prompted a deluge of responses from our peer group (many of them uploading in black and white in solidarity), sympathising with the struggle of YouTube video-making and talking in their heaviest voices about the pressure to create.

I chatted a bit to Charlie about the video and his feelings, but I didn't know how to help him. *It's only the internet*, I thought. Easy for me to say; the internet didn't know the real me at all.

'Good news,' Jonathan told me when I stopped by his house that week. 'I have three hits. They could all be smashes. Let's co-write one of them and go for the Christmas Number One again.'

'Go on then,' I said.

'Number one is called 'Don't Break My Offline Heart'. That's good, isn't it? Modern, talks about the new technology and how young people and your generation are interacting these days.' (Jonathan was always keen to separate me from 'young people', emphasising that — six months after my success with 'Forever Yours' at the age of 22 — I was now 'a fucking has-been'.)

'Don't Break My Offline Heart,' I repeated.

'Yes. So that's track one.' This was when I realised Jonathan hadn't written anything beyond the title. His idea of co-writing was giving me the seed and hoping I would grow the tree.

'Track two. You know how much I love trees,' Jonathan said, as if reading my mind. 'I often say they're the best species on Earth. I love them far more than people.'

'So you tell me,' I smiled.

'So the second song is 'Trees Are Better Than People. People Are Worse Than Trees.'

'Bit long.'

'Last one,' Jonathan rolled on, 'is called Stupid Stupid.' He repeated the title with a loud football-stadium slur to his voice: 'STUPID STUPID!'

'Any more to that?'

'Yes,' said Jonathan, puffing his chest. 'The chorus goes: Stupid, stupid! Dur nur nur nur nur, you're stupid, stupid! But I love you. BUM BUM!' He prodded his index finger in the air to emphasise the last two beats.

'That one,' I said, grateful to be given something with more than a title. A hook from a hitmaker was something I could work with.

'All a bit of fun, isn't it, Miss Day?' shrugged Jonathan. 'Another adventure!'

While writing 'Stupid Stupid', I allowed all my most commercial impulses to surface. It was pure bubblegum pop, the kind I'd always loved, with a silly message about embracing people despite their flaws. It helped that the biggest song at the time was Psy's 'Gangnam Style', a fun and absurd track with a ludicrous over-the-top music video that became the first YouTube video ever to pass a billion views. ('Make sure to start your own dance craze,' Jonathan emailed me after seeing Psy's 'horse trot' dance imitated all over the world, as though I could just pick up a dance craze at the store. I really was the Pinky to his Brain.)

I made my video about being too attached to social media and computer screens, depicting a family at Christmas not talking to each other because they were too immersed in their own devices. That all changes when I come in and prance around the room, invoking ever-more cartoonish dance moves and props, reconnecting everyone by talking about how we're stupid (stupid!) but it's okay, because we love each other, the whole thing escalating to the point of me dancing in the middle of the room wearing only a Union Jack mankini. (The mankini was a no-brainer on my part and took mere seconds to conceive: *I'm gonna have to turn this around so I end up looking the stupidest. What would make me look stupid? Union Jack mankini.* That was plan A and there was no plan B. I'll do whatever it takes.)

I involved my whole family in the music video. My nan and grandad grinned at me while I swaggered around in my silly clothes. My mum and aunt did their best 'shocked and appalled' faces watching my own repeated dance move. My two young cousins, who thought I was famous, were sure they were in a real music video that would be on television (not that I was paying to get slagged off again, thank you very much).

My audience hated it. *Hated* it. Despite me writing a song about falling in love with a ghost, being in a band that wrote songs about *Doctor Who*, and wearing ridiculous clothes as part of my standard wardrobe (which had now grown to encompass a *Flintstones*-style caveman shirt), the trend on YouTube was to Take Things Seriously and I insisted on doing the opposite. At one point in the Stupid Stupid video, I wore a top hat and pouted at the camera while playing the riff of my song on a plastic keyboard for children.

A civil war broke out in the comments about whether or not my song — right, the one called 'Stupid Stupid' where I danced about in a mankini — had any musical credibility. It was a win as far as I was concerned, since I believe great art polarises people. (It didn't hurt that my mentor on that front was Jonathan, producer of the song 'Leap Up and Down (Wave Your Knickers in the Air)', which stayed in the UK Chart for 17 weeks in 1971.)

It had been a year since 'Forever Yours' and I had lost the element of surprise, the excitement of the unknown and most of my energy and belief, but I pressed on nonetheless. The big idea this time was to break the Guinness World Record for the most downloads of a song in a single hour, something I wasn't even sure could be measured. But Jonathan — observing that interest in supporting my campaigns always seemed to free-fall after about a day — thought it best to concentrate the effort into sixty minutes, a length of time more accommodating to my inattentive viewers. I only had to get them to care for an hour. The iTunes chart is updated close to real time so the focused push would surge the song to #1 on the iTunes chart where the rest of the world would then see it. Radio, television, and global media interest would follow, with worldwide megastardom not far behind. The path seemed clear.

To push the moment, I planned an hour-long gig that would be livestreamed around the world. I hunted down a free space in East London and four hundred people turned up at short notice. Tom and Marilyn came along for support.

'Got the cameras all set up?' I asked Ciaran.

'Yes, boss,' he nodded.

I emerged onto the stage in a multi-coloured fur coat like a pimp selling Muppet skin, and the show was almost as hectic as I looked. I pulled people on to the stage and threw them back into the arms of the crowd. I encouraged people in the audience to buy the song then and there on their phones. After I had the crowd going, Marilyn and Tom came out to perform some of their own songs, giving me a chance to check my Twitter feed off-stage.

'No sound'

'cant hear anythin'

'this is shit'

'WHY IS THERE NO SOUND'

I returned to the stage, now with a palpable awareness that the event was a disaster, and continued to perform for twenty more minutes as if it wasn't.

'Where are we?' I called out as the show neared its end.

'11,' someone yelled back, referring to the chart place of 'Stupid Stupid'. We needed to crack the top ten to make the front page of iTunes and get additional exposure.

'11,' I repeated. By this point I'd changed into a suit, thinking I needed to look smart for my moment of triumph. Now I just felt like a boy dressed up in man's clothes. I shook my head. 'Just have to think of something else.'

'Stupid Stupid' landed on the UK chart at #25. A recording of the gig was preserved on my YouTube channel, filmed from the only working camera at the far end of the room. If you squinted you could see a tiny speck of a man jumping around the stage trying to attract a global audience to his song, not knowing the sound was so distorted that the show was unwatchable.

By any reasonable measure, this had been a pretty good year. My combined music and merchandise sales made me over £10,000 a month, I'd had three Top 40 hits, sold half a million copies of my tracks on iTunes, garnered plenty of coverage for 'disrupting the music industry', and my nan was proud of me. But I didn't appreciate any of it because I'd submitted my music for Producer of the Year at the Grammy Awards and I wasn't even nominated.

My next musical endeavour was an album, except I didn't call it an album because albums were boring and not the sort of thing the Future of Music would release.

'Call it... a collection,' said Jonathan. 'Then when people say you're a boring artist releasing an album, you can say it's not an album; it's a collection.'

'Nobody else minds albums.'

'Some of your new songs,' Jonathan continued, unperturbed, 'along with some old ones, some demos, some covers, a song you produced for someone else, all on one disc.'

To promote the release, titled *Epigrams and Interludes* (after a chapter in *Beyond Good and Evil*, the Friedrich Nietzsche book I both passed and failed in my college Philosophy course), I planned out a music video for a song called 'I've Got What It Takes' (which I'd written to keep my spirits up). Ciaran and Marilyn got to work filming but I wasn't on set; I was in Bournemouth with Freya, my blogger friend. We texted each other goodnight and sent each other extracts of books we were writing. As we became closer, I didn't think about where I was inevitably leading us. It was as though I was seducing someone by accident — more of that 'blocking out reality' move I kept pulling. In Bournemouth, we spent long afternoons cuddling and watching movies in bed, though Freya had made her boundaries clear.

'Don't bring condoms,' she'd said. 'We shouldn't have sex.'

'But whenever we start doing stuff,' I said, 'you tell me you want to have sex.'

'Yeah, so don't bring condoms and then we won't.'

'Well, which you should I listen to?'

'Don't trust anything *that* Freya says,' said Freya.

I'd been quite specific to Freya about my intent to end things with Marilyn — I knew it was for the best — but grew frustrated by Freya's insistence that I should get on with it, then, if that's what I wanted. I wanted Marilyn, but I knew it wasn't going to last. I kept hurting her, but I cared about her. I knew I liked Freya and would love to give something a try with her, but what that 'something' might be, I had no idea. Freya lost patience and gave up on me while I continued to string everyone along. Although hundreds of thousands of people thought they knew me, I didn't even know myself — and if I didn't know what

I wanted, I had no chance of communicating it to others. Perhaps I was a sex addict, no, I was a love addict, yes, I craved emotional intimacy with everyone I met, no, I was incapable of commitment, right, it just wasn't for me, no, wait, it wasn't for anyone at all, yes, that's it, monogamy was unnatural at a biological level and oh, I was enlightened for being in touch with my primal instincts...

Epigrams and Interludes came out in March 2013. The album — sorry, collection — debuted at #8 on iTunes and sold seven thousand copies. I released half the album online for free in a partnership with a torrent site, where it was downloaded a million times. The following week, it sank out of the charts and, for all practical purposes, died.

On the day of the album release, Crystal tweeted a joke at Marilyn's expense. It was a silly joke. She didn't mean any harm. Marilyn didn't see it that way.

'...wow,' Marilyn tweeted back. 'I actually didn't think you'd EVER be that bitchy. xxx' (Marilyn insisted on kisses at the end of every message as part of her directive to be kind even when she was angry. Crystal assumed she was being passive-aggressive.)

'Haha um do you have something you wanna talk about via email or smthn because like. What,' said Crystal.

'I feel like I should have some popcorn right now,' jay30 (a bystander) tweeted them both.

Marilyn strove to live a heartfelt life. She assumed any problem anyone had with her was the result of some wrong information that she then sought to correct for them — or, if not, that the people themselves were problematic and not worth her time. So I got a phone call from Marilyn recounting how mean my best friend had been to her on Twitter and that she'd sent Crystal an email telling her she was 'horrible and offensive and inconsiderate and not worth my time'. Crystal then emailed me about it, the exchange having brought her to tears. Taking Crystal's side, I burst at Marilyn that she was 'being mental' and that I couldn't be in this anymore. I met up with her that evening and she couldn't understand why I didn't want to work things out.

'It's just not right,' I kept saying, because I didn't have the guts to tell her how I really felt and what I'd really done.

Between sobs, Marilyn said, 'I'm sorry I was such a bad girlfriend to you.'

It only took her a week. Determined to understand what had happened, Marilyn spoke to everyone I'd ever breathed near to ask them why I didn't want her anymore. Nobody had an answer for her (and if they did, they weren't telling) until, running out of options, she bumped into Silvi at a bar with some friends and thought it might be worth asking her if she had any thoughts.

An hour later, I was enjoying an evening with an Australian friend of mine — the two of us stepping around the subject of sex, which we'd both acknowledged was inevitable — when my iPad beeped at me and I saw four words pop up on my screen.

'You cheated on me.'

'Um, one sec,' I said, taking the tablet and typing the only reply I could at this point: *Yes. I'm sorry. Now you understand why I had to be alone.*

'You alright?' said the Australian.

'Have you ever cheated on anyone?' I asked. She frowned at me. 'I cheated on my ex-girlfriend,' I continued, 'and she just found out.'

'Okay,' she said, standing up, 'I'm gonna go.'

'No, you don't have to—'

'It's fine,' she said. 'Call me again when you're not gonna have a mental breakdown.'

Another beep from the iPad.

'I'm coming over.'

I saw my friend out and slumped down in front of my door. I stared out at the road and waited.

PINKY PROMISE

I watched Marilyn stride down the street towards me. I didn't say anything when she reached my door. She glanced at me with the devil's disgust, marched on past me into the living room and rooted herself on the sofa. I followed her in and sat opposite, unable to meet her gaze.

'I was in a pub,' she said, after a hateful pause. She emphasised each word, taking long pauses so each fact of her misery could penetrate me to its fullest extent. 'With Ed, and TomSka, and Hazel — all our friends. I broke down in front of everyone. David was there and he had to pick me up off the floor. They all watched me sob in his arms. And then, Alex, they said they couldn't believe I'd stuck it out with you for so long. You know they warned me about you when we first got together?' She looked around the room. 'I've come over here so many times,' she said with a dark smile on her face, 'and you ignored me. You sit at your desk, emailing DJs, while I'm sat here, reading a book, waiting for you to pay attention to me. There was never an 'us'. There was just 'me' and 'you'.

'They all stood up and clapped,' she said. 'All your friends got up and applauded me for staying with you as long as I did.'

I knew cheating on Marilyn would hurt her. I'd expected my role was to be an airbag for her pain, withstanding the force of her impact against me until she stormed into the night, carrying with her a perpetual disgust for my general existence and leaving me ashamed but otherwise unmarked. I hadn't considered all the other civilians caught in the blast radius: my housemates, who knew something was going on and thus inherited an unwanted culpability of their own; my friends, who watched with increasing discomfort as I flirted with women when Marilyn wasn't around, unsure of how (or whether) to get involved; and the girls themselves, many of whom lost the chance to make an informed decision about me because I'd obscured my relationship from view. And most of all, here was Marilyn, sitting broken in front of me, and it was all on me. I had done that.

I told myself all along that I was acting out of compassion and courtesy — pleasing Marilyn by dating her, pleasing other girls by sleeping with them, and pleasing Marilyn further by not telling her about it. I'd been so arrogant, sometimes getting with people because I didn't want my unavailability to *disappoint them*, as if I was hot shit and they'd be devastated not to grab a slice of this. If physical intimacy with someone is a ten-step process — like climbing a staircase — I found it natural to engage in steps one to eight with almost anyone I met, befriending them, spending time with them one on one, opening up to them about my hopes and troubles, and so on. I skipped along the parade of life, constantly opening myself up to emotional closeness that should have been reserved for the girl I'd claimed was my partner, and by the time I was on step nine, I was in too deep. I'd got too close to them to only *now* reveal that I was unavailable. The easiest thing for me to do (always for me to do) was go through with it. But it was all done with kindness, right? I was a kind person. I was sure of it.

But Marilyn shattered that image. I saw myself, for the first time, the way everyone else did. I wasn't acting out of kindness. I was acting out of fear. I wasn't a sex addict. I wasn't incapable of monogamy. I was just a fucking dick.

'Look at me,' said Marilyn. 'You never fought for me. Fight for me. For *once*.'

I snapped up, fixing my hardest glare at her. We stared through each other.

'The worst thing,' she said, sighing, 'is I just want to tell you that we can get through it and that everything will be alright.'

My gaze broke. I heard my mum's voice say, 'What are you crying for?' and ran into the hard wall of stoicism that she had ingrained in me. I knew I needed to feel the full impact of my actions so I pushed myself against that wall, forced myself to knock it down, and it burst like a boil as reality flooded in. I drowned in tears and snot, my mouth set in a distorted stream of spit, my throat crammed full of heaving moans. I buckled into myself in front of her, overwhelmed by the weight I'd pulled down on myself. I forced myself to keep crying until my reserves were depleted and nothing more would come. My eyes stung with salt and shame.

Marilyn killed me with kindness. She was far braver than me that night. Her mix of compassionate understanding and surgically precise barbs had lobotomised me. The choice was easy after that. I never wanted to make *myself* feel like this again, let alone others. The benefit of accepting you're the cause of all your problems is that you alone can solve them without waiting on anyone else.

We sat together in the aftermath of my disassembly.

She took a breath. 'Was there anyone else?'

My stomach lurched towards the floor. *She only knows about the Swedish girl.* I stared forward with wide, scared eyes as the impact of what I had to do crushed against me. I looked up at her. She looked so hopeful.

'No,' I said. 'No one else.'

'Are you being honest with me? I need to know.'

'Yeah.'

'It was just her?'

'Yeah.'

We were quiet for some time. I watched as conflicted thoughts and emotions made their way across her face one after another. After a while, she sat up and looked at me.

'Okay,' she said. 'We can make this work.'

'No,' I protested, 'we can't—'

'You don't get to decide this!' she barked at me. 'You've been in charge of everything this whole time. You've taken away my right to choose for this entire relationship. You don't get to take this away from me as well.'

'Okay,' I said.

'I'm not gonna be with anyone else while we figure this out.'

'Neither will I,' I said, knowing for the first time in my life that I meant it. She held up her pinky finger and I linked hers with mine.

I had learned a lot already, but not enough to realise that, by withholding the rest of the pain from her, I was still withholding her right to choose. People will always choose the truth over being spared the pain. I still didn't get that — and it would take a lot worse than that night for it to sink in.

Seeking Marilyn's forgiveness was an exercise in humility. Every few days I would receive a text saying, 'I just can't understand why you did this,' and my attempts to make amends would be derailed. I poured myself into songs like 'Keep Me Up', which used the language of fragile packaging to describe my inner emotional state ('Keep me up, and handle me with care'). I would apologise over and over again, in every possible way I could think of. I apologised with such regularity that she accused me at times of being insincere, as though I were offering an automatic 'sorry'.

The day after Marilyn tore me down, I composed several emails to my friends apologising for ever making their lives uncomfortable. I even emailed casual acquaintances like TomSka, Hazel and Ben. (What replies I received were sheepish, saying it was none of their business anyway.) I emailed Danny and told him I needed his support to make better choices from now on. I sent the same to Crystal, adding that she should have been more supportive of my relationship with

Marilyn. She countered that she was my best friend and I should have been more supportive of *her*. Crystal found Marilyn false and two-faced, while Marilyn found Crystal mean and vindictive. I didn't ever want Marilyn to feel pain again, so came down hard on her side, and Crystal and I became a lot more distant when I did so.

I emailed Charlie, too, and said I felt we were growing apart and needed to confront that. He would often sit in the living room, playing New Super Mario Bros. on his DS with his headphones plugged in and his hood over his head, not acknowledging me as I came and went. He wasn't selfish or unkind — just a bit thoughtless, unaware of his surroundings. It bothered me more and more that he never made me tea when he made his own. I decided it was time to fly the nest and sell my half of the house to him. He decided we might as well sell the whole thing and move to smaller places. I needed a fresh start in every possible sense.

I threw all my clothes away, switching my wardrobe for brown baggy trousers and muted t-shirts. 'Right now in my life, I'm feeling a little bit less ostentatious,' I explained in a video. 'I've started wanting things that are a bit plainer and more grounded.' I wanted to shave my head again — and was more tempted after a YouTuber with short hair talked about how easy it is to manage, saying, 'You'll never go back' — but my motion was overturned by the combined veto power of Marilyn and my mum, who thought it wouldn't suit me.

In contrast to my new stolid lifestyle, Marilyn pressed on with all guns blazing. A short while after all this happened she landed a prestigious acting agent.

'What's your dream role?' they asked her.

'Éponine in *Les Misérables*.'

'Then let's start there,' they smiled.

That summer, she progressed through a series of auditions, each time telling me she was happy to have got that far and that it would be great practice for trying again the following year. She didn't want to believe she could get the part — hope would render her complacent, and make any possible failure all the more painful — and refused to let herself accept the possibility until the call from her agent came through to confirm the role was hers. A few months later I sat in the Queen's Theatre in London and wept as I watched her first performance, seeing her stride on to the stage she first graced as a child and achieving her life dream in the process (and also because *Les Misérables*, translated into English as 'the miserable ones', lives up to its name). It was euphoric watching someone I loved reach their ultimate goal while having thousands of people applaud and cheer her while she did it. She was achieving everything I always knew she would.

Hundreds of her fans were at stage door that night along with Marilyn's friends and family. She posed for pictures, signed programs, received presents and accepted congratulatory comments for what felt like hours, beaming at everyone from within her shock of blond hair.

I gave up my quest for status that evening. I wanted to spend the rest of my life with a low profile, functioning mainly as her boyfriend. I wanted to tell people, when they asked what I did for a living, 'I'm Marilyn's boyfriend.' I wanted to help her step ever further into the limelight and then stand in the shade beside her and clap.

'I want to write a book,' I told Susi at ChannelFlip. 'About the London Underground.'

'Okay,' said Susi. 'We can set you up with an agent we know.'

One meeting later, Ivan agreed to become my book agent, provided I finish my book — a meandering look at the past and present of the London Underground — by the end of the year (a deadline I stipulated to him, rather than the other way 'round, to motivate myself to get the work done). To give myself uninterrupted time to write, I filmed loads of videos in one day and used a new YouTube feature to schedule them for upload. It meant I could have three months away from the internet to work on my book without anyone noticing. 'I like your new video,' friends would sometimes say, to which I would reply, 'And which video was that, again?'

I'd moved 'round the corner from my house with Charlie to a space I'd fallen in love with the moment I saw it. The space was a thousand square feet of laminate wooden floors with underfloor heating, subtle integrated cupboards in space-station-white, a frosted glass shower and a deep bath accented by soft blue LED lights, an open-plan kitchen and living area with exposed brick walls, and arched windows stretching from floor to ceiling. It was £1625 a month and I thought it was worth every penny.

'Don't you get lonely?' Marilyn asked, peering at the cavernous ceiling over our heads.

'No,' I said, 'There's nobody else around! I love it!' I led her to the washing machine, which I'd half-filled with dirty clothes. 'Look,' I effused, 'when you live alone, the washing machine *is* the laundry basket!'

I'd installed a grand piano in one corner of the flat and meditation cushions in another. I got into meditation after my friend Chris recommended I read a book on mindfulness, *Peace Is Every Step* by the Buddhist teacher Thich Nhat Hanh. Being Marilyn's partner would require the mental fortitude to help her through any crisis.

'I'm thinking of going on a silent retreat,' I told Marilyn.

'Ooh, I'd love to do that!' said Marilyn. 'Let's go together.'

'Okay,' I sighed, knowing this meant we would never go, because when Marilyn had a holiday, she went to Walt Disney World. We'd been twice in the last year. When I said I didn't want to go a third time and asked if she had considered New York, she booked a trip to the Magic Kingdom with a friend from the theatre instead.

'David and his girlfriend broke up,' Marilyn told me, and I lost my appetite for the rest of the day. David and Marilyn had always maintained a spirited chemistry, and — despite the hypocrisy of it — I'd been threatened by their close friendship. I once told Silvi I was 'just waiting for David and Marilyn to realise they're in love'.

Most of my days were spent in a Starbucks across the road from the Queen's Theatre, where I wrote my book while Marilyn conveyed the sorrow of 19th century Paris. I met her after the show one evening and she suggested we head 'round the corner to a pub where many of our friends had congregated to celebrate Chris's birthday. I wasn't too enthusiastic (still feeling ashamed at the mess my behaviour had caused in their lives) but we had been invited, and David was texting Marilyn to ask if she'd be showing up, so we strolled over.

Soon after she arrived with me, David walked out like he'd seen a ghost. Me being there seemed to have thrown out whatever plan he had. Marilyn followed him to talk and came back after a few minutes.

'He's leaving,' she told me. 'I'm gonna go with him. Make sure he gets home okay.'

'But…' I looked over at him. 'But you pinky promised.'

Marilyn looked up at me and held out her pinky again. I took it in mine.

'Okay.'

'I love you.'

'I love you too.'

I didn't get any sleep that night. Although she indicated nothing was going to happen, it did nothing to quell my suspicions. I rolled into a ball, heaving, throwing the covers to either side of me as I launched myself this way and that, playing every nightmare scenario over in my mind — all the while choking on the delicious irony of the distress I'd caused Marilyn.

It was the first of October, giving me three months to finish my book, but I didn't do anything the next day. I didn't even get out of bed till 6pm the following evening. Marilyn was performing two shows that day; there didn't seem to be a point doing anything other than waiting to hear from her. We had a tense exchange after she finished her show, and then I realised I was going off the rails. I phoned my mum. She drove to London that night and took me back to our home in Essex.

October of 2013 looked like this:

Every morning I would wake up around eight with my mum serving me a mug of tea and some toast. At nine or ten, I would start writing. By two in the afternoon I would stop, having written two or three thousand words of my book. My mum would come upstairs to find me playing Pokémon X on my DS and ask how things were going.

'Done for the day,' I'd say. 'Three thousand words.'

'Wonderful! You must be thrilled,' she'd beam.

'It's all shit,' I'd scowl. 'I'm writing shit. I wrote three thousand shit words.' Due to my end-of-year draft deadline, I wasn't stopping to edit or even read back what I was writing for some semblance of quality control. I just poured my book out of me every morning and caught Pokémon for the rest of the day. My mum made dinner for me in the evening — I would come downstairs for that — and we would watch a film, after which I'd go to bed and start the whole thing over again. I restored the same life I had ten years earlier, ridden with angst and purpose, writing books and playing games in my bedroom.

I needed to let Marilyn go. I thought we would never get back together, but that I would never be allowed to stop trying. She was in too much pain to take me back but too much in love to leave. I decided I wouldn't text her unless she messaged me first, I would be polite but give her space, and she would be free to move on with David (or someone with whom she *didn't* have a relationship I'd invented in my head). This plan worked for about half a day — as I said before, you can't hide the truth for long.

'I can feel you distancing from me,' she texted.

'I want you to be happy,' I sent back. 'I want to be happy.'

'I haven't made any decisions yet,' she said. 'Keep fighting for me.'

Okay. If I'm gonna fight, I'm gonna fight.

That evening, I came up with a plan to make all of her environments magical. I spent about three hundred pounds on a huge bouquet of two dozen red roses to be delivered to the stage door of *Les Misérables*, accompanied by a note which read only 'forever yours xxx'. For her 21st birthday, I went to her house while she was at work and hung twenty-one lanterns in her room in the style of the Disney movie *Tangled*. When she came to my flat a few nights later, I sat us down for a gourmet dinner of sweets, served at a candlelit table with a Disney playlist of romantic songs playing in the background. I even tried to hire a skywriter to put a message for her in the sky above Walt Disney World, but it would have cost several thousand pounds more than my budget could accommodate. I applied my 'do everything because nothing will work' mentality and thought of every possible thing I could do to regain favour in her eyes. I bought a phone so Marilyn could stay in touch with me. I even convinced myself I'd be happy to have children with her if that was what she wanted. We both loved the name 'August', although I thought it suited a girl and she thought it right for a boy (short for Augustus), so we decided that, when the time came, we would see what gender it came out as and let fate decide which of us was right. We even decided on two sets of middle names. Marilyn would write letters to August from my flat, sealing them to be given when the child was old enough.

My closest friends hated Marilyn. They saw me blowing them off to put her first at every opportunity and assumed she was making me do it (or that, at the very least, that she was raking over the coals on purpose). It didn't help that almost all of them had argued with her on Twitter at some point, and they were all friends with Crystal, with whom things had become particularly strained. I burst into tears during one conversation with Crystal when she told me I'd been a bad friend to her. I burst into tears over a lot of things around this time. I went to *Les Misérables* about ten times and cried every time I saw it. I cried at Richard Curtis movies. I met up with David to talk about Marilyn and burst into tears while he sat opposite me nibbling on a slice of millionaire shortbread, looking uncomfortable.

'I don't care about winning anymore,' I said to him. 'I care more about being peaceful than being right.'

He told Marilyn it was clear how much I'd changed for the better.

With my YouTube channel running on autopilot, it grew to the cusp of one million subscribers. I had made good enough stuff that a million people had been convinced to hear more of it. I couldn't picture that many people, filling multiple stadiums or rallies, with me standing on a stage in front of them chatting rubbish about Twilight. The first thing I did when I noticed my proximity to the million milestone was upload a video called 'If You Love Me, Unsubscribe', telling everyone I didn't deserve the audience I had, that I put no effort into this and that I shouldn't have this much power.

In the meantime, I thought again about deleting my channel, or at least not making any new stuff. After all, if my book went well, I wouldn't need it anymore. But I knew the one thing I still enjoyed about making videos was sharing the more interesting details of my life with an audience of people who were interested in what I was up to. If I didn't bother with gimmicks and just made honest stuff, I'd be happy. I decided, for the first time, to share myself unfiltered.

'I tend not to be honest with you in my videos,' I said in my next video, 'which is something I'd like to change.' I explained I'd had 'a really shit year' and promised to elaborate in a later video, thanking people for being here in the meantime. I called it 'Hello, I'm Alex Day'.

I finished my book draft on schedule and celebrated by going on holiday with Marilyn (to Walt Disney World). I dedicated the book to John, for believing in my ability to write all those years ago when I first met him at his own book launch in New York, and he acknowledged me as a fellow writer. A month later, my agent Ivan got me a deal and a huge advance with Penguin Random House, the world's largest publishers. No other YouTuber had ever been published or written a book. I was, at last, legitimate.

I uploaded 'Hello, I'm Alex Day' on December 2nd, 2013, just after I hit a million subscribers.

Marilyn and I got back together four days later.

EXIT STRATEGY

Mike was a YouTuber and songwriter with music released through DFTBA Records. I met him at VidCon when he was twenty-one and found him ambitious, charming and sweet. That was all I knew about Mike until the FBI arrested him.

Mike was arrested for 'encouraging minors to send him explicit photos and to send videos of themselves masturbating'. The charges covered six girls from the ages of fourteen to seventeen. When asked by one of the girls if he'd kept the images she sent him, he'd said he hadn't because 'that's like 5 years in prison and sex offender registration'. Mike pleaded guilty, and was given that exact sentence.

Hank learned about Mike's arrest the same way the rest of us did: through an online blog. He and John released a joint post on Tumblr letting people know his music had been removed from DFTBA 'partly because we don't want to make any money from this sort of publicity and partly because we didn't feel it appropriate to continue our business relationship given the situation.' They added, 'it's also very important never to blame victims in situations of sexual abuse and assault.'

People took to their blogs to share anecdotes of their own encounters with Mike. His ex-girlfriend wrote an unflinching post detailing their relationship, ending with: 'He is an abuser. He abused me, he abused many other people, and he's done irreparable damage in many people's lives.' Mike, silenced by first his lawyers and then his incarceration, was unable to respond.

Around the time Mike was charged with his crimes, I found out something about Ed (my shit-the-bed bandmate) when his then-girlfriend wrote a post on Tumblr titled 'THE BREAK UP':

> So it turns out the Ed has been cheating on [me]
> So that's done
> thats all
> I would appreciate it if I got no further comments
> about it

Included was a link to the other girl's Tumblr page, leading to an influx of hateful messages from people accusing her of indiscriminate home-wrecking. The original post got about twenty 'notes', units of attention as measured by Tumblr (every comment, like or reblog corresponds to one note), so it wasn't high on anyone's radar.

In response, the other girl posted an exchange of messages she'd had with Ed that day over Twitter's private message system in which she recounted a sexual experience they'd had together and said she hadn't wanted it to happen.

'I know I didn't get massively "ARGH NO WHAT WHY STOP",' she told him, 'and I get that if I did, maybe you would've stopped. But I'm a bit of a wimp, and I felt like I owed you or something.'

Ed replied saying he was 'really ashamed and sorry', that she didn't owe him anything, and that 'as hollow as it might sound I promise from now on not to put you or any person in a situation like that again.'

Ed's ex-girlfriend shared this second post and added to it (emphasis hers): 'Ed not only cheated on me but was **abusing** her... this is a **warning** for any girl who might meet him at SITC or any other event. Please be careful, he has abusive tendencies and we don't want this to happen to anyone else.'

This post got over a thousand notes, and the mob — grown in number — redirected themselves to Ed. I counted my blessings that my mistakes had happened in private, not under the withering glare of the online spotlight. Ed said nothing for 24 hours, then spoke up:

> I am deeply sorry to everyone involved and to those whose trust I have broken or who are disappointed in me. I will be making every effort to address and change my behaviour. As far as the near future is concerned, I will no longer be attending Summer in the City, and will be taking a break from social media and youtube.

> In light of these allegations a person has taken it upon themselves to release information about my family, and the address of my family home. Please, I urge you not to spread this information or drag my family into this. They are aware of what I have done, and they do not deserve to be harassed.

And then Ed disappeared.

'This is the year,' said Susi in January. '2014 is the year YouTubers go mainstream.'

I didn't know what was going to happen in 2014, but if things went to plan, at least I would be going mainstream when my book was published in the summer. Working with a publishing house was far less restrictive on my creativity than I expected. The only thing they insisted on was that I change the title: mine, 'The Underground Storyteller', sounded 'too fictional', and despite how much I argued that nobody would be confused as long as my book was in the nonfiction section of the store, the editor instead pushed for 'You, Me & The Tube'.

'It's great,' she explained, 'because your audience is from YouTube, and it's You, Me & The Tube... You-meandthe-Tube. YouTube. It's like YouTube.'

I was chatting to a Canadian girl called Kerri at the time (a long-time commenter of my videos who seemed cool and who I'd since befriended on Facebook) and when I told her their title, she said, 'It sounds like a sex fetish book.'

We also disagreed about the cover. 'You have to be on the front,' my editor said. 'It's important.'

'But no-one knows who I am,' I retaliated.

'But that's how you intrigue people. They'll see it and think, "Ooh, he's on the cover of a book, who's he?"'

'I have *never* bought a book that way,' I protested.

'We want to establish your profile.'

'But I don't want a profile,' I argued, 'it's not about me. It's a book about the London Underground!'

Nonetheless, things were on track. The book was set to be published in June.

At the end of January, I woke up to find a long Tumblr post written by Crystal in which she outlined the abuse she had suffered for the past year at the hands of anonymous fans of Marilyn, who bombarded her with hateful messages after their spat on Twitter. Crystal's post made it clear she didn't consider me her friend anymore. She said, 'Throughout these interactions, he's either remained strictly impartial (which I understand) or taken her side (which I don't)... when I asked if I could meet up with him to talk about this, he said it was nothing to do with him and he didn't see the point. He's basically been a pretty shitty friend.'

Crystal was right — my allegiances were clear. I had decided I was with Marilyn and would always take her side. Having spent so long trying, without success, to get her to ignore people's opinions of her, I now simply embraced that part of her personality. I wasn't going to tell her how to engage with people, especially ones she didn't care about anyway.

On February 2nd, I got an email from Crystal. 'You constantly made me feel like shit throughout 2-3 years of friendship,' she wrote, 'and even went so far as to berate me several times because you thought I should be the better person even though it wasn't me initiating any of the conflicts we had... [and] you consistently made me feel like if I wasn't any use to you, then you didn't want me around.'

Crystal and I called each other best friends for a long time. It seemed to me that, for at least the first couple of years, we were both having a lot of fun. I knew a rift had formed between us but I thought we were on track to mend it. A few months earlier we had met up to celebrate her birthday and had wandered around Windsor holding hands, just being friends and enjoying each other's company.

Crystal then said the last few times we hooked up (while I was with Marilyn) were 'pretty strongly initiated' by me. I remember asking her multiple times if she was enjoying herself and her saying things to the effect of, 'Yeah, it's great!' — but now she said I just lay next to her until she 'gave in'.

Reluctance isn't a turn-on for me. I would never want to put pressure on someone to be intimate with me, yet that was the charge. Since my memory of it seemed so different from her recounting, all I could do was apologise. She didn't accept it.

Two weeks later was Valentines Day and I made a further commitment to Marilyn by telling the online world about our relationship. It was more important to her that our audience know about us than it was to me to keep them in the dark. We had been in each other's lives for two years, and with Crystal's accusations still fresh in my mind, it felt like the right time to come clean about my past behaviour:

In all of the past relationships that I've had, I would treat the person I was with a bit like an accessory to my own life. The way I can best explain this is, if you imagine I'm running down a path, and someone you like is also running down a path, instead of seeing them and being like, 'Oh man, why don't we jump into the middle and make a path together', I would stay on my path and encourage her to come and run alongside me. I wouldn't deviate from the path I was already on. I was like, 'Oh this is great! This is just like my regular life but now I have this girl here! This is awesome!' But if she — or any of the people I've dated, or even friends of mine — if they did things that put me off them, or were inconvenient or put me out, I was very bad at ever putting myself out for other people or making any sort of sacrifices. I would just drop that person and be like, 'This is annoying, I wanna stay on my path'.

So I spent basically the rest of last year trying to be better because I realised as well — all my friends thought of me this way. They all just knew I was a bit shit and I didn't want that. I didn't want people to think of me in that way.If you realise that you've done a bad thing or that you're kind of a bad person, or a misguided person in any way, then it's up to you to do something about it. It's never too late to do that thing about it, but no-one else can do it for you. There's always the opportunity for second chances and redemption, I guess, in life, but it'll only happen if you make it happen.

A month later, I went to Canada to visit my cousin Dean. (I asked my friend Kerri if she lived nearby — it would have been nice to meet her for lunch — but she was in a different part of the country, it turned out.) I came back from my trip and flew into a new storm on Tumblr about Steve, another of my YouTube friends. Now it was *his* ex-girlfriend writing some damning statements about him online, saying they'd begun an uncomfortable relationship when she was fifteen.

> let's start with weird skype sex? there was so much of it and i hated it i litearlly told him i did not like it and i never partook in it but he just wouldn't stop sending me fucking vile shit and like talking about his boner and asking me for nudes and oh my god

> the first time it wasn't even in a bed i can't even figure out why it was on the floor and it fucking hurt and was really horrible and unpleasant ugh like we'd go out to the mall or something and come home and he'd start making out with me and slipping his hand down my pants oh my god this is making my heart beat so fast i feel horrible

> i was sick with like a flu/strep throat and we took a walk down to the park at night and like sat down on a bench and he started fucking around and touching me and i ended up.......GOD nvm like outside at night kill me

> i'd say it was really painful and i ended up really sore and bruised for like days like literally everything hurt so bad and i told him that and it didn't really matter i didnt stop anything

> he'd like sob and cut himself in front of me he
> threatened weird suicidal shit a lot like i'd just have
> to sit there and watch him freak out cos i was doing
> something wrong apparently when i left my dad's
> and i skyped him to tell him his immediate reaction
> was like 'wow you haven't talked to me in a while
> you've been so busy..' like yeah i was at the police
> station filing reports and in family court trying to
> resolve my own bullshit

> i uh

> my stomach hurts

> we began our relationship when i was 15 and he
> was 22, but we did not [physically] have sex (skype
> sex and idk nudes and whatever aside) until a
> month after my 16th birthday... in missouri, where
> i live and where everything took place, the legal age
> of consent is 17. it's great that he lived in england
> and that the age of consent there is 16, but it's
> completely irrelevant

For a couple weeks, there was no response from Steve. In his absence, the internet brought down its sword of judgment with swiftness and venom.

'What he did is disgusting and awful,' said a friend of ours, adding that he deserved to be ostracised and that, 'It's never the victims' fault.'

'NO blaming the victim,' added Melissa Anelli. 'This is how we get into these messes. This is how victims are afraid to come forward and this is how abusers are convinced of their own immunity.'

'He is vile, psychologically abusive, and a rapist.'

'[Steve] was my friend. I looked up to him,' wrote Hank, already past-tensing their relationship. 'I am furious.' He added that, 'Sexual relationships need to be equitable and they can't be when people are in dramatically different life stages or when one person enters the relationship as a fan of another.'

After a couple weeks, Steve spoke up in a series of tweets:

> have I made a mistake waiting so long before saying anything? People are taking my silence as an admission of guilt which sucks

> I just don't know what to do, this whole situation's so surreal you know?

> MAN this talking to people after a bad thing happens is REALLY HARD this is why people said don't do it I guess

> I just couldn't keep not saying anything, and twitter's always been a place for me to write how I'm feeling.

> it seems weirdly disingenuous to lock you out of this particular psyche-wracking

> thing is, talking to these tens of thousands of people was getting too stressful for me anyway, I was gradually leaving it all behind

> this kinda feels like the boss level of public interaction before I can gracefully bail

> I'm gonna say this and then rapidly delete all of these because I don't know what I'm doing and it's scary ok here we go

a lot of accusations have been made at me, some of which are so plainly transparent that I'm amazed they gained traction

I guess when john and hank had to step in because I wouldn't it legitimised a lot of what was said, which sucked

but like… yeah I dunno what I can say here, now. I just wanted to check in and say hi I guess.

aite I'm taking off, stay cool guys. xx

He deleted his account, took down most of his YouTube videos and never appeared in public again.

I didn't know what to think. I didn't blame her, but I also didn't condemn him. I had no idea what the truth of their lives was, had no experience of their relationship and wasn't about to draw thorough conclusions after reading a blog post and some tweets. I knew if it had happened to me that there would be huge differences between (for example) Crystal's version of past events and mine, given the tone of her recent emails. I couldn't imagine how you'd resolve that without the whole thing descending into a painful slanging match. I felt uncomfortable even admitting to the internet that I was in a relationship, let alone confronting ugly remarks about the nature of it in a spectated forum. That's why I thought judgment was the court's job, not mine. But there was no court case. It was done.

'*Office?*'

'Sure,' said Marilyn. 'Back in a bit!'

I was sat on Marilyn's bed with Netflix open. While I waited for her to make tea, I loaded up the next episode of the American version of *The Office* and, in the same moment, my email pinged. It was from Alan at DFTBA.

The subject line was blank. The email contained only a link and the words 'is this true?'

I clicked it and read: 'I was coerced into having sexual contact with Alex Day.'

CRYSTAL CLEAR

I was coerced into having sexual contact with Alex Day.

I met him when I was 17 and a fan of his videos, and after talking online for less than a month he invited me to stay over at his place. I was initially adamant that nothing would happen between us and he initially agreed, but continually expressed a disregard for that further into our interactions.

Once we were sleeping in the same room (as what I thought of as "just friends") and he woke me up by kissing me and touching me sexually.

I'm going to repeat that: I was asleep, I had fallen asleep stating my desire to have no sexual contact with him, and he woke me up by violating those wishes. I know for a fact I'm not the only girl he's done this with.

It already had thousands of views and comments.

I felt like I'd swallowed a football. My whole body was shaking. I replied to Alan — John and Hank had been copied into the exchange as well — and said no, it's not true, I felt sick, what should I do?

'Look, if it's not true, it's not true,' John emailed back.

'Ready?' said Marilyn, carrying two cups of tea into the room. I mumbled, 'Look,' and turned the screen to her. Marilyn read the post in silence, reaching for my hand.

'It's not true,' I told her. She held me. Then she retreated into her phone to read all the things they were saying about me.

I read the post again. The writer was anonymous but it was obvious to me who was behind it.

'He cheated on his girlfriends with me multiple times,' they wrote. 'I wanted to please him because he talked a lot about how as soon as someone in his life did something he didn't like, he would cut them out completely.'

I'd only had conversations like that with Crystal. Either this was Crystal or it was someone writing about us on her behalf.

'He managed to convince me that this was a mutual thing,' the post went on. 'In hindsight, it definitely wasn't.'

I don't know how long I sat there, staring at the wall. I knew the kind of person I was and the bad things I had done and sexually assaulting someone wasn't one of them. I didn't remember ever waking up Crystal by touching her sexually. That seems like the sort of thing I would remember. In any case, we made out for months before anything further happened between us. She was making it sound as though I just pounced on my platonic friend and sexually abused her. And she knew *for a fact* I'd done it to others?

I didn't know what to do. I'd been taught — and I agree — that you don't blame a victim. Crystal *was* a victim of my manipulative behaviour, and she wasn't to blame for what I did. But I wasn't to blame for what I didn't do.

With no idea how to defend myself, I resigned to ignoring it and letting it die. Acknowledging it would only validate it and attract more attention its way. I had to bury it and move on.

Marilyn couldn't.

For hours, my girlfriend stared at her screens as though she were in shock, hanging over the precipice of the internet's most hateful centre with no harness to protect her. I could shut it out, but I couldn't shut her out.

Either way, it didn't matter. Hours later, I read another post. This one was anonymous too.

'I was also coerced into sex by Alex Day. He wasn't physically abusive with me, but beyond a doubt he was emotionally manipulative. He made me feel like I was special. He told me he was single. I didn't find out for months after that he wasn't and had also been doing the same thing to other girls.'

I knew, based on the dates and anecdotes she provided, that this was legit. It was a girl called Ellie. I'd started falling for her back when I was trying to end things with Marilyn the first time 'round. We went on a couple dates, then reality reminded me it was still there and I had to break things off. I never told her I was with Marilyn; she'd since found out after contacting Freya, who revealed the truth. (Freya — and Penny — were now good friends with Crystal.)

Ellie continued:

> After a couple of weeks I demanded him to meet me to explain himself. He obliged. He was really repentant, and explained that he had been selfish and thoughtless with his relationships his whole life, and was only just coming to realise how destructive that was. He was changing. I asked if it was just me, he said yes… I always suspected he was lying about it only being me, a manipulation with positive intentions, he didn't want to cause any more harm than he already had.

That was true — we had met up for her to confront me — but I didn't know how to tell Marilyn that. She was reading all these posts with me, unable to speak.

A third anonymous post appeared that evening: 'Alex Day is a sexual predator who targets underage people'. That was one hell of a headline. Fortunately, I knew the girl who'd written this too, and it confirmed for me that it was all bullshit. I'd spoken to her on Twitter and met her at an event for my card game — when I saw she'd bought a ticket, I'd emailed her to say I was looking forward to meeting her. During the event she came along with her dad. She told me she was part of a collab channel with some friends — each person made videos on a specific day of the week, and her video was the day of the event, so she asked if we could film something together.

'Sure,' I said. 'It's pretty noisy though.' We were surrounded by hundreds of people playing cards, cheering and chatting with each other. 'Let's go into the back.'

She got her camera out, we chatted some rubbish for a few minutes, and as soon as we finished we went back into the main room. Her dad met us at the door. He looked nervous and pulled her aside.

'Did anything... happen?' he asked her.

'No!' she said, gasping. This became her anecdote of the day. She was telling everyone who would listen how funny it was that her dad thought something could have happened between the two of us. (On my part, I found it strange that he could ever have thought that — quite apart from anything else, I was at work, and in public.)

A few months later, she started writing unfriendly things about me on Tumblr and Twitter. I can't remember if I saw them myself or if they were pointed out to me by someone else, but knowing my keen sense of detachment from online negativity, I can guess it was the latter. I didn't know why her opinion of me would have changed and contacted her, interested to know why. I don't remember what she said in response, but that was the last time we spoke.

At least that's how I remember it.

i was targeted by him… he would organise events specifically to meet me, and found my email address without me explicitly giving it to him and would email me often.

at an event… we made a video in private (which was odd seeing as everyone else made one in the main room) and he tried to be inappropriate with me but i managed to get out of the situation before it escalated.

we spoke for a few months after, during which time i learnt that he (not a tumblr user at that point) was keeping up with my blog and twitter account, as he confronted me about a passing comment i made on one and about unfollowing him on the other.

i learnt from a mutual friend that he was still asking about me months after we last had contact, and on the day that his girlfriend posted about being newly single he attempted to make amends with me.

i was left feeling threatened and exposed by his actions, and worried that it wasn't an isolated incident. i have since heard from mutual connections that it is /not/ an isolated event. alex day is not safe and should be avoided.

i'm scared that if he sees this he'll trace it back to me and contact me which is why i'm anonymous, i'm not prepared to attach my identity to this.

I organised events specifically to meet her? Did I invent the card game to meet her, too?

The video we made in that back room was still online when this post went live. I tracked it down and watched it. She uploaded it without any editing, meaning our entire interaction was on camera, and the only thing I could even tenuously describe as inappropriate was that, at one point, she said she didn't like her nose, and I said she had a nice nose. Either she was lying about what happened between us or — as before — there were vast differences in the way we both interpreted (or remembered) the event. My memory couldn't be *that* off.

'I need to say something about this,' I said.

'Good,' said Marilyn, her shoulders loosening the moment I told her. 'That's good.'

John and Hank had convinced a generation of internet-loving kids to 'imagine people complexly', so I figured they'd be my most considerate allies. I invited Hank into a Google Doc (an online document that can be edited by multiple people at once) and drafted a response for his opinion:

> I don't consider myself a particularly good person, although I am trying to be better. There are definitely things that I've done in the past that were not good things to have done. I have, sometimes, treated people badly, manipulated people, been rude or mean to people, even cheated on people in the past. It's awful. Of course it's awful. I'm telling you about it because it's in my past, because people are flawed, some much more than others, and because I believe the mark of a good person lies in that person's capacity to apologise for what they've done, take responsibility for their actions and make sure they learn from the pain they've caused in order to make sure they never do anything like it again.

At no point in my life have I ever had a sexual relationship with someone under the age of consent.

At no point in my life have I ever undertaken any romantic activity, sexual or otherwise, without being sure the other person wanted it.

I'm sure there are other people on the internet — and in the world — who have had problems with things I've done in the past. I know this because I myself have many problems with many things I've done in the past. But to reiterate the bold points once again: I have never had a sexual relationship with someone under the age of consent, nor have I ever undertaken any romantic activity, sexual or otherwise, without being sure the other person wanted it.

I feel incredibly ashamed to have mistreated people in the past, and for the unhealthy relationships I have previously instigated or allowed to carry on when I should have been more responsible. I've been honest about that in the past and will continue to be honest about my past failures, as well as my attempts to make amends for them. Honestly, right now, I'm absolutely terrified of losing everything in my life that I care about because of this. I'm terrified that I've misinterpreted signals from people who didn't want things to happen like I thought they did, and that I've caused genuine harm to people without meaning to. But I also can't help acknowledging that this discussion is good. People should **always** be encouraged to speak up in cases where they feel uncomfortable or mistreated, and the signal boosting of such cases are necessary to help other people that have been mistreated to a) speak up themselves to make people more aware of how their actions are interpreted and b) feel more empowered to voice their concerns next time before things go too far.

Ultimately, the decision to believe me, or continue to support my work, is yours alone.

After reading it, Hank shared his thoughts with me:

Hank: it's good...you will get a lot of people asking for specifics...you will get a lot of backlash...you should probably talk in future posts in a somber tone about serious stuff, even if it's not this, and avoid being funny for a long while in videos or on Tumblr.

Hank: This is the most emotional google doc of all time. It was really heartbreaking to watch those words appear on the screen. This is a bad bad day. But I think you're handling it well. John and I, unfortunately, will need to stay out of it.

Me: No worries. Thanks for taking the time. I really needed it.

Hank: OK, I've gotta get going. I hope this all works out soon.

Me: I'm really scared, Hank.

Hank: It's really scary.

I posted my statement. The first anonymous person — the one I suspected was Crystal — responded:

> I'm so angry. This is absolute bullshit, and people are going to believe you. You've just enabled every sexual abuser in a position of power to get away with this, as long as they say they didn't do it.

> I hope you realise how many people are going to be taken advantage of, abused, or raped because of this post.

In the aftermath of my response, Crystal started writing on her own personal Tumblr account: 'I really didn't want to get involved with this,' she wrote, 'but I feel like Alex's post is super damaging to anyone who wants to speak out this kind of thing in the future and I can't really just let it slide.' She told the internet she 'wasn't okay with the fact he was cheating on his girlfriends' (not mentioning she once high-fived me over it) and went into detail about how her experiences with me were 'pretty similar' to those described on the anonymous account, even writing, 'They both sound like I could have written them,' which, if she did, indeed, write both of them, is pretty fucking bold of her. (The anonymous account went from vitriol to silence and, to this day, hasn't been used again.) Her post gave that first one a lot more legitimacy; now two accounts from 'different people' said I did the same things. Having said that, Crystal offered me a caveat: 'I think — and this one is important — if I had outright said, "No, stop, I don't want this and I don't consent," I would have been able to walk away. The thing is, I didn't feel like I could have said that without him cutting me out of his life entirely and/or being mocked by him, either to my face or to his friends.'

Crystal was the least of it. The floodgates were opened and it seemed everyone I'd ever hurt was out for my blood, using Tumblr as the vessel of their vengeance.

'I was emotionally manipulated and lied to for a good portion of our relationship,' wrote Laura, who had clearly learned the truth about my treatment of her since our breakup two years prior.

Freya joined the fray too:

> We texted constantly. He sent me the clichéd, cute good morning and goodnight texts, and he told me he'd fallen for me. In the February, he came and stayed with me at uni. We didn't have sex, I said no, but my god did he make me feel guilty for it. He continually told me (and had been for a few months) that it wasn't working with Marilyn and that he was going to end it, so we might as well... I found out about all of the other girls he was doing this to and tried to stop him. He said he couldn't. I was exhausted. By the May, all inappropriate contact between us stopped.

One weekend in 2011, Danny and I had gone to the Midlands to spend the weekend playing Sopio with some girls Danny knew. The house contained only one single bed and two doubles, and one of the other girls claimed the single earlier in the night, so I was left to crash in bed with a shy girl with dyed red hair called Kiera. Nothing happened between us.

We left the next day and I forgot about Kiera until friends started bringing her up. 'This girl Kiera was asking where you lived,' someone told me. 'Apparently she hangs around Mile End station cos she thinks you live there,' said another. At a house party, Danny left his phone charging and went to check it later to find Kiera going through it, reading our texts and looking for my contact details. She turned up at one of my Lady Godiva signings claiming she had a dentist appointment in the area and had no idea I'd be there.

'Can I talk to him?' she asked Danny.

'No, he has to get to the next signing,' he said.

'But the next signing's at 6,' she objected, giving away her prior knowledge of my schedule.

The last time I saw Kiera was at the same Sopio event where it's claimed I preyed on a girl while her dad waited outside. When I left, Kiera clung to me and said, 'I miss you. When am I going to see you again?' and refused to let me go. Crystal had met her and we'd had long disbelieving chats about her unbalanced feelings towards me. She called her "Crazy Kiera".

On Tumblr, Kiera wrote that I 'traveled 3 hours (seriously.) to my house which is in the middle of nowhere along with a couple of others who were friends with me at the time to stay over'. She discloses that we shared a bed and adds: 'I'd never experienced anything like that before, especially when someone kind of ends up on top of you in the dark.' This vague nod towards a nighttime something is as explicit as she gets. I suppose she didn't want to accuse me of anything specific, because that would have been lying, but she embellishes with this: 'I hadn't been kissed or anything before, so this was my first exposure to *this kind of thing*' (emphasis mine).

Crystal reposted Kiera's story. Soon after that, the Swedish girl I cheated on Marilyn with put her story up too. 'When we met and actually hung out, and I realised that this could potentially go somewhere,' she wrote, 'I figured that I might as well. I was in a very bad place, and I did whatever I could to bring pleasure to my own situation, even if it only lasted for a short while. I made a bad choice, and I do regret.' Crystal reposted that as well.

To help everyone follow along, another Tumblr user created a 'masterpost' — one post to rule them all — linking to every anecdote the user could find about me. All of my posts were there too, but with follow-up links to other people picking them apart, attempting to show how dishonest, manipulative, and cold-hearted I was being. Having all the anecdotes and accusations in a serial list gave equal weight to every story, so while the one labeled 'first anonymous person talking about Alex' is about me allegedly touching someone in their sleep, the one labeled 'fourth person coming forward about Alex' is from an old friend of mine who said this:

> i sent him an email, telling him that i maybe kind of have feelings for him... he says something along the lines of "why didn't you tell me before vidcon? i would've made more time for you. and we could've hooked up." needless to say, my "feelings" weren't exactly returned, and i mean, it wasn't a big deal, really.

The more people wrote about their experiences with me, the more ridiculous the things they shared were becoming. In 2008, I'd spent all day at a YouTube gathering holding hands with a girl who now recounted:

> as I was leaving the gathering by myself, Alex walked with me and tried to kiss me when I hugged him goodbye. I rejected the kiss, and to this Alex accepted and didn't try to make a move again. In fact I have a clear memory of him saying "It's your choice, don't worry. You've made your decision." I'd like to really express here that in no way did he try anything again physically or show a disregard for my decision.

> However.

> Soon after this the Facebook messages started... below I have attached just a selection of the (not very long) Facebook conversations we had over the course of a few months.

What followed were a few cringey teenage boy messages I'd sent her, like 'you suck for being gorgeous' and 'you're insanely hot *smile* xx'. She'd edited out her messages back so it looked like I was bombarding her with flirt after flirt with no response.

'I don't feel affected emotionally by these incidents now, as it was an awfully long time ago and it was strictly flirting and not physical,' she concludes, and up she went on the list, the next person to come forward.

As I was reading all these, I got a text. It was from Penny. The last time I'd seen her was a year ago (when we were part of a photoshoot for the cover of *WIRED*).

'In your post you say you have never done something without being sure the other person wanted it. How do you explain in 2010 when you tried to kiss me even after I said no?'

My eyes were heavy. I couldn't stand to read any more about myself.

'You'd just broken up with your boyfriend,' I sent back. 'I knew you felt strange because of that and I thought it was something I could make you feel better about. I thought you did want it but just needed help getting that issue out of the way. I'm so sorry, Penny.'

'I see,' she said. 'I appreciate the apology.'

> In 2010, I went to Alex's flat to stay for the week as we were still close friends. Alex kissed me, and I stopped him and told him I didn't want to as I was recently getting over a break-up and wasn't ready. I told him I just needed him to be my friend. Alex ignored this, and continued to try to kiss me despite what I'd said. He later asked me to sleep in his bed and was very frustrated with me when I refused. I slept on the sofa and then went home. A while later, once I'd eventually realised that what Alex and I had wasn't a genuine friendship and that his

behaviour towards me generally had been unacceptable, I cut ties with him.

I confronted Alex about this today... he has apologised to me for his past behaviour and clarified that... despite the fact that I made it clear I wasn't consenting to a kiss, in his mind he was still sure I wanted it because he thought my reasons for saying no were something he could 'make me feel better about' or that I 'did want it, but just needed help getting that issue out of the way'.

I fell asleep late in the night and woke up to my Canadian friend Kerri expressing public horror that I'd approached her so recently. 'I liked him,' she wrote, 'and I thought about meeting up with him — and what if I had? He might have hit on me. I might have let him! Thank goodness now I know what he's like!'

Marilyn woke up beside me. We played around for an hour or so, being silly and childish with each other, making each other giggle. I enjoyed the morning as much as I could, savouring every moment of what I knew would be the final day of our relationship. This was worse than the hollowing-out I'd experienced with her before. Everything I believed had been broken. Only the truth was left. We sat down and I outlined all of the other people I'd cheated on her with.

For a little while, it even seemed like we might get through it. She understood why I'd lied. She knew all this was part of the person I used to be. She believed — correctly — that I'd been faithful to her for the last year. The past was worse than she knew, but it was just that — the past. I finally gave her the right to choose, and even as our hearts broke, she still chose me.

Things changed when I told Marilyn about Freya. They were good friends and she took that one hard. She sent a text to Freya:

I've just found out what happened with you and Alex and I am absolutely disgusted that you never told me. Delete my contacts from everything. I expected that kind of thing from him in light of everything that's happens in my years of knowing him which does not excuse him in the slightest but not from you. Do not contact me again. X

A short while later, Freya took to Tumblr and turned on Marilyn, disclosing the message and commenting on it: 'if I'd found out my partner had abused so many people, and one of those people was a friend, I'd feel sick for that friend as well as angry at them. It's victim-blaming... apparently, my views are null and void.'

Marilyn read the post in shock, then turned to me, and I saw in her eyes the moment she let go. 'I can't do this,' she said.

All of this — from Alan's email to Marilyn leaving me — happened over about twenty-four hours. I phoned my book editor in tears, asking to be put in touch with the publicist they'd assigned me.

'I've lost ten thousand subscribers overnight,' I wailed into the phone, 'and it keeps going down.' Abusive tweets were lighting up my pocket every few seconds. I emailed Hank again.

'I don't know what to do. Marilyn broke up with me and I just want this to stop. Please tell me what to say to make it stop.'

I'd forgot that Hank was friends with Penny.

'You have to admit to everything,' he said. 'You have to tell people you thought it was your job as a man to push and their job as the woman to play hard to get.'

I couldn't believe someone who had known me so long would think me capable of this kind of behaviour — but then, he'd known them just as long. I'd introduced most of those girls to the community in the first place. He had no reason to doubt them. Even I didn't doubt them. I couldn't think of any reason they would lie about it. They must really feel like that. They really did remember it that way. If that's how I made them feel, then that's how I made them feel. My side of the story didn't matter.

'Thank the victims for speaking up,' said Hank. 'Repent. Openly. That's the only way things can move forward.'

Hank, John and I jumped on a Google Doc to collaborate on a second post. (It had been a dream of mine to write something with John. A public response to allegations of sexual and emotional impropriety wasn't what I'd had in mind.) When I referred to these events happening in the past, writing about 'that period of my life', John wrote: 'Don't act like it has passed. You don't know if it has passed for sure. Life is long. Just say what happened.'

'Only "no" means "no" is not a model of consent,' said Hank. 'It is a recipe for abuse.'

'You must acknowledge the bravery of the victims,' said John.

'"I am deeply, deeply ashamed,"' suggested Hank.

'"Now begins the long process of making amends,"' John added.

'I know you just want this to go away,' Hank said when I objected to their suggestions, 'but that's not going to happen super fast.'

I ended up posting this:

> Until yesterday, I thought that I had had only appropriate, though occasionally manipulative relationships with women. However, the model of consent that I followed, not that I specifically thought about it at the time — was that only "no" meant "no." That is not what consent is.
>
> The result of that belief that 'only no means no', is that I spent a long part of my life doing shitty things to good people and barely ever realising or acknowledging that I was doing the shitty things.
>
> I'm grateful that victims have come forward to help me recognise how awful that was. And, to clarify — it **was** an awful way to treat the people in my life. I

became an incredibly manipulative person and didn't really care about people's feelings. In my sexual experiences with people, nobody ever outright told me "NO, STOP" or pushed me away, or I'd immediately have stopped doing whatever we were doing; everyone I've done stuff with has been above the age of consent; and, in all the cases of me having sex with people, everyone says they consented to it.

But there were clearly times where I would try to initiate something, because I thought the other person wanted it, and I trusted my own read of the situation ("they agreed to stay over/they said they wanted it earlier/etc") rather than paying attention to what the other person was doing and saying in that moment. That's where I massively fucked up.

It's only in the last 24 hours that I'm realising how much I created situations that put people under enormous pressure. I wasn't being responsible enough to be aware of it, and that's my fault entirely. I want to be clear that I'm not blaming this on my lack of awareness or knowledge of consent and boundaries. I'm blaming myself. I'm deeply, deeply ashamed of this.

Thank you to the people who have shared their stories. I know it was very difficult but it helped me realise how terrible my actions were, and I want to respect their bravery by reiterating that only yes means yes.

'Today we removed Alex's products from DFTBA,' said Alan, 'following his post acknowledging he has hurt many people.... Additional posts did reveal a pattern of manipulation, treating people badly, and forgetting to be awesome.'

'I have no doubt,' wrote Hank, 'that Alex and [Steve] took

advantage of people and knew what they were doing. Thank you for the victims for coming forward.'

'To be honest, I'm absolutely disgusted,' Penny tweeted. 'It's amazing too that now Alex Day claimed he DOES know that no means no. When I said "I don't want to kiss you" he took it as a "yes"... He emotionally manipulated people the entire time I knew him, and now he's doing it to all of you.'

'Just when I thought Alex Day couldn't do anything worse than release more music,' someone else blogged.

Then I heard from Charlie.

He sent me an email telling me he was shocked and dismayed by my new post admitting to all the horrible things I'd been accused of doing. He said he was facing a lot of online calls to speak out about the situation — people assumed he must have known something — and would be writing a public blog post distancing himself from me.

In my reply, I asked him to meet with me or speak with me over the phone so we could discuss what happened. I needed to tell him how this all felt from my perspective and didn't want to do it in a way that could be copied and pasted online.

'That would make me feel uncomfortable,' he sent back. 'If you want to talk, we can do it over email.'

Charlie had an email assistant at the time. In fact, I'd introduced them. It was Crystal. So I said no.

He never spoke to me again.

> In the time that I knew Alex, I never had any notion that the girls he was with were anything other than happily consenting to being with him. The idea that anything contrary to that was going

on behind closed doors makes me incredibly unhappy, and with that, I just don't feel able to call Alex a friend of mine anymore. Simply put, I don't know if I can trust him.

I was baffled when — despite my attempts to clarify things — Charlie added:

> The frustrating reality is that I just can't know for sure what's actually happened. As much as I wish I could know the truth, I have just the same information as everyone else and so all I can do is make assumptions based on that.

I didn't blame Charlie for reacting like this. He must have been terrified. Still, even after seeing him drop videos he'd poured his heart into because he didn't think they were good enough, I didn't expect him to do the same with me. He blocked me on his phone, took the music videos for 'Here Comes My Baby' and 'Forever Yours' off his YouTube channel, made a video about sex and consent, and wrote a post on his blog giving instructions on how to block my videos from showing up online, a move he said was designed to 'help remove [me] from the website'. Charlie's damnation of me gave all those posts an extra sense of authenticity. Onlookers assumed he must have had some insider knowledge to be disowning his best friend with such confidence.

I've only seen Charlie once since this happened. We were in the same place by coincidence. About a year had passed. When he caught my eye — just like his favourite monsters from *Doctor Who*, the Weeping Angels — the sight of me turned him to stone. I wanted to run at him and shake him, yell at him, babble my side of all this, make him understand how it felt when he turned his back on me in front of everyone we knew and the millions of people who watch us online. But there was no point. The boy was scared enough. In the end, I offered him a slight smile, looked at my feet and shuffled past him while he continued staring through me like a ghost.

'Only yes means yes?' one of my remaining friends raged. He'd come to visit me at my flat, fuming about the whole thing. 'Only yes means yes?! People don't just see each other across a crowded room, walk to the middle in unison, strip their clothes and yell "I consent!" One person putting slight pressure on the other is how *all* sex happens!' For my part I just nodded and smiled, too tired to offer an opinion of my own lest it be overheard, dissected and destroyed by the mob of strangers who lived in my computer.

His furore was interrupted by the arrival of a package.

'What's that?' he asked. My chest weighed down on me as I realised; the package was huge, about the size of a television, and almost too heavy for me to lift.

'It's my plaque,' I told him. 'From YouTube. For getting a million subscribers.' I was 24 years old, I had a million subscribers on YouTube — and almost all of them hated me. I tore away the cardboard packaging and looked upon the golden play button, tilting it to my friend with considerable lack of gusto as he delivered me a sardonic round of applause.

OFFLINE

After my friend left, I locked the door; threw out a lot of personal keepsakes and mementos from my subscribers; deleted my emails, texts, and Twitter and Facebook messages; put passwords on my phone and my laptop; changed my passwords for all my online accounts; unfriended all the girls I'd ever met through the internet; turned my laptop off; sat cross-legged on the floor; looked out the window and waited for the police to knock on my door and arrest me.

I understood I was now an abuser. Tens of thousands of people had told me so. That was a crime, so it was only a matter of seconds until I was taken away for questioning, if not charged outright. With that in mind, I didn't want any additional evidence being used against me in court. I didn't want the police to ask why I had girls on my Facebook that I'd met online. I didn't want them asking why I had keepsakes from them in my flat.

After about an hour of sitting and waiting, I stepped outside to buy some water (leaving my phone, and the scrolling hate machine it carried, at home). The woman at the checkout smiled at me.

'How's your day going?' she asked.

'Yeah, alright,' I said in a daze. I didn't understand why she was being nice to me. *Haven't you read what I've done?*

Three days passed, and I started to suspect maybe the police weren't coming for me. I couldn't understand why. I wanted to go to the station myself and turn myself in. *Apparently I'm an abuser,* I would say. *Please arrest me and give me a trial so we can determine what happened and I can move on with my life.* At least I would be treated as innocent until proven guilty, with the rights to a fair trial and to face my accusers, not locked in the stocks in the town square having tomatoes thrown at me while I festered in the mess. I longed for a thorough, impartial process to delve into all of this. Instead I just kept waiting, my name never clearing or being conclusively mudded either.

'How was Greece?' I asked Mum. I'd gone over to Essex to meet her.

'Ooh, relaxing!' she replied. 'How've you been?'

'Alright,' I said. 'Wanted to chat to you about something.'

'What's wrong?'

'It's fine,' I said. 'I just thought you might hear about it from someone else at some point so I'd fill you in. Basically I'm not making videos anymore.'

'Whyever not?' she frowned.

'Well, some people online wrote about me and things we did together and said they didn't want them to happen, and loads of people read it.' This was a kind reading of the internet's current mood; it would have been more accurate to say hundreds of thousands of people now believed I raped my fans, or at the very least, cheated on my girlfriend with twelve girls at the same time. Fewer and fewer people were showing an interest even in what the actual allegations were. Someone would tweet 'so what happened with Alex Day?', someone else would respond 'he sexually assaulted his fans, some were underage', the first person would say, 'Oh wow, what an asshole' and that would be the end of it.

'Which girls?'

'Penny, Crystal, that girl Freya,' I listed. 'Laura.'

'*Laura?*

'Well she has every right to be annoyed at me,' I said, trying to diffuse my mum's rage, but she'd already yanked her laptop towards her to unfriend them all. She wanted to burn down their houses. 'How could they,' she said.

'Well, they were upset,' I shrugged. 'It makes sense.'

'We have to go,' she said. 'On the run. We'll pack a bag and get going.'

'I'm not in danger, Bean.'

'They're calling you a rapist, Alex,' she croaked.

'No,' I said, '*they're* not.'

'What about Charlie?'

'Oh yeah, he's gone as well.'

'Well,' she huffed. 'Let he who is without sin cast the first stone.'

In the fallout of my reputation going nuclear, I'd messaged anyone I'd been involved with in the past to ask if they'd ever felt uncomfortable and to apologise if they had. It was the least I could do. Some didn't respond; some blocked me. Some replied that they thought the whole thing was unfair and they'd always been fine with me. Others said they had felt uncomfortable, but tried to explain it to me instead of telling the internet: 'It's a bit overwhelming to have someone be that into you that quickly when they happen to be big on the internet but you're not sure if you're ready but they're nice but but but but — yeah,' one girl said. 'That was kinda my brain.' I learned far more from talking to her than from the internet, who just admonished me for not already knowing better.

I made the mistake early on of trying to engage with people about the allegations. My intent wasn't even to discredit the allegations — I just wanted people to know what they actually were. When I posted on my friend Myles' Facebook wall saying we should hang out soon, another of his friends replied, 'he sexually assaulted and emotionally manipulated underage girls,' which wasn't even what I'd been *accused* of.

'Sexually assaulted underage girls?' I wrote back, my patience snapping like an old rubber band. 'Is that what they're saying now?

Can you give me ANY proof of that? Can you even show me anyone who's ever claimed that? I thought I was accused of having emotionally manipulated overage girls, not raping children. Fuck, if you're going to vilify me can we at least agree on what I'm being condemned for? I'm asking you, since you seem to be the expert.'

The guy responded with a link to the story about my supposed seduction in the back room of the Sopio event. 'That would be underage sexual assault.'

'Oh,' I spilled out, 'so you're basing your unshakeable beliefs on one anonymous Tumblr post that accused me of how I very specifically "tried to be inappropriate" with her and you haven't heard my side of that account at all and you don't know who that person is and you haven't seen any proof of said account and you haven't spoken to the person who wrote the post or to me to try and clarify any of the facts of the situation?'

'You're a scumbag, that's all there is to it.'

'Brilliant.'

I didn't hear from Myles. That hurt the most. Though it infuriated me that people were being so ignorant (especially the Nerdfighters, who claim to prize intellectual discourse), I didn't care what strangers thought of me. They didn't know me. I knew I wasn't a rapist, so they could think what they liked. What really got under my skin were the friends who dropped like flies when I tried to reach out to them.

'Yes, boss,' Ciaran said when I rang him.

'Hey, mate,' I breathed, 'I'm so relieved to hear your voice.'

'Why, what's up?'

'All those things being said online.'

'Oh, I haven't looked into it.'

That was the last time I heard from him. He obviously looked into it after I hung up.

When I phoned another friend for a chat, she took my call and was courteous and polite. Again, it was a relief to hear a friendly voice.

That night, she posted this on her blog:

Alex has been a friend of mine for around a year now and in that time has never done anything to suggest abuse, contrary to what a lot of people told me he would act like. In fact, when we spent time together, he would only talk of [Marilyn] and his fondness of her.

He made a video talking about his need for change and recognition of his selfishness... all of my interactions with him have led me to believe that he genuinely wants to be a better person.

Then, of course, people came forward about his abuse and he went into hiding. The only contact I had from him was having him on Facebook, which I decided not to act on. I may be wrong for that, but I hate the idea of shutting people out. If he needs help changing and not continuing to do horrible things, then what good does shutting people out do?

After having not spoken for months, he rang me. Just for a chat, catching up. He made no attempt to meet with me. Just wondering if I was okay.

I felt weird for a good hour or so after that phone call. I felt like a betrayer of so many people.

I'm frightened.

I never heard from her again.

People were falling over each other to disown me. Marilyn's friend David sent me a message saying he could no longer consider us friends, not asking for my side of the story or replying when I offered to share it. My ex-bandmate Liam wrote a public post distancing himself from me. Most others suffocated me with silence. They stopped answering my phone calls and replying to my emails and texts. I would send a message to someone on Facebook, wonder a few hours later why they hadn't replied, and check to discover they had unfriended or blocked me. Facebook reminds people when it's your birthday to encourage well-wishes, but on my birthday, it served as a reminder for people who hadn't rejected me yet to get on with it. I woke up on the day I turned 25 to find a record number of 'friends' cancelling me like a Netflix subscription. If anyone publicly showed they were still my friend (or even associated with me), they received an immediate flurry of messages from concerned followers and made a swift disappearance from my life.

I needed my friends more than ever. I messaged people over and over again, begging for thoughts and advice or at least some kind of acknowledgement to stop them feeling so much like detached lifeboats floating out to sea. What friends I still had were friends only in private. When an occasional friend did stand with me — 'I don't know what you or I would get out of us not being friends anymore,' said an old bandmate of mine, 'I don't know how that would help reinforce you to be a better person.' — I'd think, *That's so wonderful to hear*, followed soon after by, *Now tweet it*.

'I started a Twitter friendship with one of those YouTube people,' a stranger told me in a video comment, 'and she scrolled super far back into my Instagram feed and saw a picture of me wearing a Nerimon shirt. She then sent me a message saying she couldn't associate with me anymore and then blocked me.'

To try and take some measure of control over my abandonment, I ended up deleting half my friends from Facebook in a pre-emptive strike. I couldn't bear to log on every day and wait, not knowing who my friends were, watching them disappear one after the other.

To everyone's shock, Marilyn stood by me for three more months. When someone wrote to her on Tumblr to say I was a shitty boyfriend, she replied, 'He was a crappy boyfriend the first time around. He admitted it, apologised and changed. That's all I asked of him and since then, he treated me with nothing but love and respect.' In those first few months, it was her and me against the world.

That changed when we were spotted together at a shopping centre by some of her fans. They took pictures of us and put them online to share with their friends — at which point the collective will of the internet Hulked out against Marilyn for still spending time with me. There seemed to be no way forward. She felt the burden of being close to me, and — understandably — felt like she'd suffered enough where I was concerned. I felt she should take a stand against her audience if she was going to support me. We got into raging rows, crying down the phone at each other, hanging up and then insisting the other person ring us back. I started despairing about August, the imaginary child we were to have that I'd become so attached to, and that now might never exist. I couldn't cope with that. The week after the accusations were made, I was in the studio recording a new album (the aptly-named *Nowhere Left To Hide*) and, in the midst of a full-on grieving period, wailed a song into the microphone about how August would be brought into the world somehow, even if I never got to meet them. (I then wrote what I thought was a brilliant original piano part, and Oli had to tell me — in the middle of my breakdown — that all I'd done is write the introduction to 'Candle in the Wind' by Elton John.)

Months before, I'd bought tickets to what I thought would be Marilyn's last show in *Les Misérables* (not knowing she would then renew her contract). Marilyn told me she couldn't make time for me in between shows or see me after, but I went along anyway and sat in the best seat in the house. After the show, I went 'round the corner to the stage door and found the road crammed full of fans, friends and family. All the same faces I'd seen a year earlier were swarming to adore her. I couldn't get anywhere near, and I knew I wouldn't be welcome there even if I could.

I spoke to her on the phone the next day and we ended things for good. The end of that show was the last time I ever saw her: on stage, in costume, grinning, applauded by thousands of people — including me — while I watched from the shadows.

A few weeks later, she uploaded a song to YouTube about being in love with someone and never getting the chance to see where it would go.

She didn't specify who it was about, but one of her fans found David's name in the tags.

'New look?' said Susi over lunch. I'd shaved my head the week before.

'Yep,' I said. 'I love not having to worry about what strangers think of me anymore.'

'So how are you?'

'Fine, mate,' I said, and I believed I was. 'I'm free. I just use YouTube the way normal people do, watching music videos and clips of comedy shows. I sold my video camera.'

'You sold it?'

'Yeah,' I said, as though she hadn't been listening. 'I've got so much free time. I'm reading way more. I started learning French.'

'You're not making videos anymore,' she said. I wasn't sure if it was a question or a statement of alarm.

'Nah,' I said. 'I'm done. I denied what happened *and* admitted it and they both made things worse. I don't need this shit in my life. I started YouTube cos I was bored and it was fun, and I'm not bored now, and it's not fun.'

'What are you gonna do?'

'What do you mean, "What am I gonna do"?'

'Without YouTube, what will you do?'

'I'm gonna do what I've always done,' I said, stunned. 'Work on my card game, write scripts, come up with business ideas. I just finished recording a new album. I've got a book coming out in the summer. I'll be fine.'

'The book's not going ahead,' said Ivan.

'What?'

'The feeling at Random House is they wanted to work with you because you were a YouTube personality. They were interested in seeing how old media could work with a social media star.'

'I'll make videos if I have to,' I said.

'The truth is, Alex, they were excited to work with you, and that excitement is just gone now.'

'But I thought they couldn't cancel the book?'

'It's not in the contract,' he said, 'but we shouldn't hold them to that.'

There was a short silence.

'You can keep your advance,' he said.

'We can approach other publishers.'

'Nobody else will want to take this on.'

'Then what do *you* suggest?' I asked.

'Well,' he said, 'I look forward to reading your next one.'

My book was scrapped, but there was still an appetite for a book by a vlogger at Penguin Random House. To fill the gap I'd left, they signed up the YouTube duo Dan and Phil, whose book they called 'The Amazing Book Is Not On Fire'. The book's description says it will allow you to 'learn how to draw the perfect cat whiskers, get advice on how to make YouTube videos and discover which of our dining chairs represents you emotionally'. The first line of the book is 'Hello. Well that's five characters out of the way.' It has large fonts, lots of pictures, and it became a *Sunday Times* Bestseller.

Even though Marilyn and I had broken up, my friends and family continued following her, subscribing to her and continuing to let her augment their personal info streams, thus knowing everything about her the moment she chose to share it and forgetting I didn't, because I wasn't plugged in like that. It was hard to move on from her when I got weekly reports on her life from people who assumed I already knew. Even when they didn't tell me, I had to resist the urge to check, because people share their whole lives online (especially Marilyn) so I was able, at a moment's notice, to find out what she was doing and who she was doing it with. It turned out Marilyn was delirious with joy as a result of her new boyfriend — someone who didn't seem to have any problem being showcased all over social media — writing blog posts about how loose and light she felt. To distract myself, I downloaded a new app called Tinder. It was horrible. Pictures of girls (selected to look as appealing as possible) would appear on my screen, and then I would thumb them off my screen with a judgmental swipe like a Roman emperor. I deleted it after an hour.

Every day I reflected on the hate people felt towards me. I was scared not just of what they'd said but that, maybe, they were right. Most of these girls had been good friends of mine. I'd sought their opinions and shared my art with them. I trusted them. If they said I manipulated or abused them, I saw no reason (other than my own subjective experience) to doubt them. I knew them too well to believe they would make it up. With that on my mind, I started to doubt my own sanity. I began to believe I was the worst kind of predator: the kind who not only abused people but didn't even realise he was doing it and, therefore, didn't know how to stop. I must have been an awful person, since it was so clear to everybody else. I figured I was devoid of critical emotional faculties. Probation officers and psychotherapists (who were also Nerdfighters) analysed my statements on their blogs, pointing out how they proved I was manipulative. They called me a psychopath. I took a test for autism and learned about what was called, in psychology, the Dark Triad — the combined traits of sociopathy, narcissism and Machiavellianism. If I couldn't change, I would have to embrace it. I designed a Dark Triad tattoo and planned to get it on my chest, over my heart, so I wouldn't ever forget the truth.

'Here's my script for life,' I wrote in my diary. 'You fuck things up. You do your best and it doesn't work. You try and learn from it and it still doesn't work. The people you love get hurt by you or bored by you and you are unable to prevent it.' I wrote charged lectures to myself on the subject of monogamy: 'Everyone fancies people. The trick is you don't fuck anyone you've said you're not going to. There's nothing wrong with you if you feel otherwise. You're just not trying hard enough or being honest with yourself about which of these obviously conflicting things you want. Yeah, sex can be great, and so can a relationship be, so fucking pick one.' The progress I'd made over the last year was being replaced by bitterness and self-loathing.

Here's a message I sent at the time to one of my few remaining friends:

> I don't understand how I keep hurting people. I just want to feel normal. It shouldn't be this much effort just to feel normal things.

> If you're not interested or you don't wanna hear from me again, just... please don't block me on here. Just don't reply. Ignore me and I'll try my best to let this go and leave you alone, I promise I'll do my best, but please don't block me. I really don't want to have to deal with one more person who means something to me shutting the door in my face. I hope that's not unreasonable.

So I continued for several days. Sometimes I'd wake up early, put Rumours on the record player and glide around the flat sweeping the hardwood floors, and the world seemed like it might make sense again.

'I spent hours sweeping today,' I texted Ed.

'We need to get you some new video games, mate,' he sent back.

A couple days later I would crumble again: not bothering to get dressed, staring at my computer screen, ordering a takeaway online from a shop I could see from my window and seasoning all the chips with my tears. Though ChannelFlip were still paying me, not enough people were buying or watching my work for me to afford my rent, forcing me to move out of my dream flat and back in with my mum. I had a moving-out party and four people came. I read a comment online from someone who worried I might be suicidal. That felt like too much work. Wanting to kill yourself is an active thought — it requires effort. I didn't care enough to do anything about my feelings. I just lay there, watching the seasons change.

'Hello, darling,' my nan twinkled. One side of her face was sagging a little, slurring the words out of her mouth. It had been quite a trip to visit her; finding the right ward took nearly ten minutes. My grandad was there too, holding one of her hands in both of his.

'Hey,' I said, sitting in a chair the colour of bland and shuffling up next to her. 'How are you?'

'Yeah, alright,' she said. A vacancy crossed her gaze. She leaned out of the bed she was in and started yelling for Eric — my grandad. He frowned next to me.

'Have you spoke to Mum?' I said.

'Yes, love,' she said, fixing her focus back on me and smiling. 'She's off on her holidays soon.'

A few seconds' pause, and her eyes shifted away again. 'Eric!'

'I'm learning a new song on the piano,' I said.

'Are you?'

So it went, with me trying to anchor my nan in the present, watching her slip every time I lost her attention. I was there about an hour.

'Look at this,' said my grandad during one of her moments of lucidity. 'I got this done, look.' He rolled up the left sleeve of his coat. On his arm was her name, Hazel, tattooed in an old Celtic font. He'd had it done the day before. His skin, already straining around his bones, had swelled and bruised where the needle had punctured him, patches of purple colouring the name. 'Got this for you,' he said, squeezing her hand.

My nan sat up a little. She peered at his arm, then at him.

'What the bloody hell d'you do that for?' she said.

My grandad laughed, then coughed, but I kept laughing.

'What you all laughing at?' grinned one of the nurses, plopping down beside us. 'She being cheeky?'

'Always,' I smiled.

The nurse placed a cup and ball on the bed.

'Okay, Hazel,' she said, 'could you just put that ball in the cup for me?'

My nan lurched forward, squished the ball in her fingers, concentrated, and dropped it six inches to the left of the cup. She released the ball, staring at nothing. The nurse nodded and made a note.

'I'm gonna have to go,' I said to my grandad. 'I'm sorry.'

'That's alright, fella,' he said. I leaned in and hugged my nan goodbye. She clasped her hands around me.

'Nana,' I whispered in her ear. 'Who's your favourite person?'

She didn't say anything.

'Remember the game?' I encouraged her. 'Is it me?'

Nothing.

'Am I your favourite?'

I held her against my collar and I heard her mumble an answer into me.

'We know that, don't we.'

I pulled back and inspected her. Sure enough, I spied a glimmer of that play-along smile.

By morning she was gone.

BREATHING OUT

My interest in meditation began when I saw footage of the monk who was lit on fire — the one on the cover of that Rage Against the Machine album. The video is an incredible thing to witness: a man sitting on the floor, cross-legged, hands relaxed, not moving or making a sound while he is doused in petrol and then set ablaze. Only a few seconds pass before his life leaves him and the body slumps forward like a liberated marionette. I became obsessed with figuring out how that monk sat so calmly, because if you set me on fire right now you'd damn well hear about it. Mindfulness seemed nothing short of a modern superpower, strong enough to override the very will to live itself (along with the pain of being immolated, which must be — if you'll forgive me — searing); obtainable to anyone of any political, economic or social background; and all you have to do to get it is sit still and be nice.

I gotta get me some of that.

I dragged myself to an open day at the School of Meditation in West London to find out what it was all about.

'I was hoping a theme for this discussion would reveal itself to me,' smiled Nigel, a soft-spoken man with grey hair and a tall, beam-like frame. 'I'm a bit like Pooh Bear in that way; I just wait for things to blow in.

The sea's natural state is to remain still,' Nigel explained. 'Its movement is only caused by outside influences, but even though we know that, we don't try to hold it down or smooth it out when it crashes around. Our minds are the same. You don't meditate to quiet it; that would be to tame what is untameable. What you do is let the waves keep undulating, but move beneath them.'

'So we're trying to tune out our thoughts?' a woman asked.

'You might think you're thinking right now,' said Nigel, 'but you're not. It just happens. It's an ancient, mechanical process. You don't choose it, and you can't choose not to. Just observe what's there. It's not something to do; it's something to undo. It's not a technique to be learned but a fact to be understood: just that the space exists beyond the surface. We don't abandon ourselves. We just acknowledge the deeper self and learn from observing it.'

'So what's the main benefit?' a guy called out.

'I am deeper, and more subtle,' said Nigel. 'I understand myself better than I ever have. The person I always thought I was took a back seat and allowed something more universal and real to emerge.'

'And how often do you recommend doing this?' I asked.

'Twenty minutes, twice a day.'

'I wouldn't have time to meditate twice a day,' one guy replied. 'I'm too busy in the morning.'

'A daily rhythm is important,' Nigel smiled. 'If you need time to meditate, you'll find it.'

'I'll tell my boss that,' he smirked.

All this talk of subtlety and deeper selves was appealing, but Nigel taught Transcendental Meditation, in which you are given a secret Sanskrit word (called a mantra) that you repeat to yourself, and to get it you partake in a ceremony Nigel said would include 'offerings of rice, fruit, blossoms, linen cloth, and one week's net income'. It was a bit too secret-society for me. And repeating a word didn't make sense to me when I could just focus on my own breath, which is already there, waiting to be noticed. Breathing meditation is the practice taught by Thich Nhat Hanh, the monk whose books on mindfulness I'd been reading — and whose YouTube videos I'd been watching — for the last year.

'How do you change people's perception of you and ignore the reputation you already have?' someone asked in one video.

'I think misunderstanding is a problem for everyone,' the monk replied. 'Not only the other person misunderstands us, but we misunderstand ourselves also. We don't know exactly what we are, so how do we expect the other person to know exactly what we are? We have to be humble. If we do not have the time to observe ourselves, we will not understand who we are and our own value. We don't see our strengths and our weaknesses so we have a wrong perception about ourselves. And then we want the other person to have a good perception — a correct perception — of us? This is difficult. So we have to listen to our feelings, perceptions, body, to really understand ourselves. We have to see our strengths and our weaknesses. And then we can see the strengths and weaknesses that have been transmitted to us by our father, mother, ancestors. Understanding the self is very important. After that, you can begin to understand the other person. If you don't understand yourself, it's hard to understand the other person. So do not trust your perception of them too much. Do not judge. Do not criticise too quickly.'

A quick google told me Thich Nhat Hanh resided in Village Des Pruniers, his Buddhist monastery in France. He wouldn't be coming to London anytime soon, but I could visit him: Plum Village (as it's called in English) hosted retreats throughout the year for people to live amongst the monks and nuns. Their autumn retreat began in just a few months.

At the same time I learned all this, I got a text from Marilyn. She'd seen some comments I'd made defending myself online.

'Stay away from the internet,' she said. 'Stay away from me and my fans. You make people feel vulnerable.'

As I processed the message and dwelled again on the reality of how monstrous I was, one sentiment careered towards the centre of my mind. As my ears ring after loud music, so it felt like my mind was reverberating with one droning thought which silenced all others and bounced around in the cavernous space it had created, making sure I recognised its presence. It addressed me like a sports coach, dragging me up by my shoulders and pushing me in front of the tyre-torn path of the road ahead, and it said: *Enough. You have to get over this.*

I needed to find a way to continue onward, and I couldn't do anything without further guidance. I'd spent all my life looking outward — it was time to face whatever lay within. Most of all, I was bored of feeling defeated. Those were the thoughts that got me to Plum Village.

> Dear Alex — we are very happy to share that your room has been confirmed. We hope that you will feel at home in Plum Village from 19 Sep to 03 Oct 2014.
>
> You will be practicing with us in the Upper Hamlet — home to the monks and laymen — known for its joyful and laughter-filled atmosphere.
>
> There are a few logistical details that we would like to share with you. Please take a few happy breaths and some moments to read the attached information.
>
> With joint palms,
>
> The Upper Hamlet Registration Team

That autumn, my mum offered me a lift to the airport for my trip to France. I was ready to be woken at six every morning by a loud bell, ushered to a temple hall and taught the intricacies of Buddhism by a quiet old bald man.

I crammed enough basic French to speak entirely in — as my nan would have said — 'foreign' while travelling to and from Plum Village. The problem was I had only learned half of the useful information, so I knew, for example, that 'Quel heure est-il' meant 'What time is it' but didn't bother learning the numbers and had no idea how to interpret any possible answer to my question.

You can imagine my joy when I heard an English voice — a Londoner no less — asking the way to Plum Village. Accepting that my grasp of the native language would inspire little in the locals beyond pity — or, as they say in French, "pitié" — I latched on to the voice and the man who wielded it. He was wearing a beanie and a beaded necklace draped around a t-shirt he'd bought in Thailand. His name was Gregg. This was not Gregg's first retreat.

'I'm Alex,' I said. He took my hand, shook it, looked deep into my eyes and smiled.

'Nice to meet you,' he said, and he fucking meant it. 'Would you like a date?' He produced a fruit pouch from some hitherto unseen place of compassion.

'Nah thanks, mate,' I said. Plum Village only serves vegan food, so that's what I would be eating for the next two weeks — I didn't need to start now. I'd thought a bit about what two weeks of vegan food would be like and I'd concluded I would be hungry. I pictured us eating small bowls of rice for a fortnight. And perhaps leaves.

'Suits me,' smiled Gregg when I brought it up. 'I've been vegan for three years.'

'Why are you vegan?' I asked.

'Because I can be,' nodded Gregg.

At the train station, a bald and brown-robed Vietnamese monk met us with a smile and two palms pressed together. Then he whipped out a set of keys, jumped in a Renault and drove us to his monastery.

It was clear from the outset that Plum Village's schedule was in no way mandatory or even expected. A huge gong rang about fifteen minutes before meditation started and the monks would 'invite' us to join them, giving us time to make one last drink in the teahouse, wrap up our conversations and amble to the meditation hall at whatever pace suited us. There were three or four lazy periods per week when even the optional meditation and daily schedule were abandoned and the monks drove into town for the day or played football with neighbours. I was surprised at how many of the visitors were on their smartphones. I had thought I'd be seen as a spoilsport for bringing an electric toothbrush.

Our first meditation session took place at 8pm that evening. One of the monks led us in a guided chant.

'Enjoy this wonderful moment,' he said. 'A half-smile forms on our lips. Tomorrow is a new day. I vow to go through it in mindfulness. There is nothing to do. Nowhere to go. Breathing in, I feel like I am a mountain.'

It surprised me how tempestuous meditating can be. Once you start observing your wayward thoughts, you realise the battle required to focus on the present time and place. I'd be focused on my breath, and suddenly I was with Marilyn, signing Lady Godiva CDs, with my dad when I was eight, flying through the TARDIS, back home in two weeks' time — and then I'd return to the room, like coming out of a blackout. My legs got pins and needles from sitting cross-legged so I kept fidgeting around. I yawned and scratched itches. I opened my eyes and peeked at the monks as they sat. I scrunched my face together to try and deepen my inner journey. I lost myself in the hurricane of my thoughts. After about half an hour we stood up to bow and, still out of it, I bowed in the wrong direction to everyone else. Then we staggered out into the sunset like the survivors of a horror movie.

Everything in Plum Village was a sign. I don't mean it was all symbolic and transformative, I mean they had stuff written everywhere. Imagine a polling station if the signs were done in calligraphy. Above the dining hall were the words, 'This is a happy moment.' Above a piano was written, 'Joy within, joy all around.' In the bookstore a sign said, 'You have enough.' The shower said, 'The most ecological shower is the one you don't take.' The toilet had a whole poem stuck to the door: 'Defiled or immaculate, increasing or decreasing, these concepts exist only in our minds; the reality of interbeing is unsurpassed.'

Interbeing is Thich Nhat Hanh's central belief and it's essentially Mufasa's teaching from *The Lion King*: we are all connected in the great circle of life, and when we die, we become the grass, and the antelope eat the grass. Meditating was only a small part of the retreat. The rest of the time was designed to encourage awareness in everything you did, so you can make walking, working or eating into meditative exercises. The food served at Plum Village was grown on a nearby farm (called the Happy Farm), cultivated by the monks and nuns and prepared in their kitchens. After I ate it, it was composted and recycled back into the earth. Before that, if you'd asked where my food came from, I would have said, 'Tesco'.

For dinner we ate curries, pizza, cakes, stir-fries, soups, pasta bakes, noodles, roasted vegetables and more. For breakfast we had fruit, porridge, cereal, and bread with jams, peanut butter and margarine. Before each meal I would spend a few seconds thinking about where the food came from and how grateful I was to have a place in the cycle of it. It became much harder to eat the fluids of animals, or their flesh, after I started thinking about it.

'But what about pizza?' I lamented to Gregg.

'Have it without cheese, mate.'

'Oh yeah. What about chocolate?'

'They have loads of chocolate. Most vegan food is junk food.'

'Wait — Krispy Kreme! I love Krispy Kreme. What could possibly not be vegan in a Krispy Kreme?'

'The cream,' smiled Gregg.

'Fine,' I pouted. 'I do think it's worth it.'

'The animals think so too,' Gregg grinned.

There wasn't much talk of Buddhism. The Buddha, it turned out, was just a bloke who found a way to help people relieve their suffering and wanted to share it with others. He said thousands of Buddhas came before him and thousands would come after (*Buddha* is a word meaning 'enlightened one'), and he never wanted a whole religion built up around him. He detested the rites and rituals happening in his name. All that mattered to him was his ideas. He said they were universal, applicable to anybody no matter your race or religion. The monks, therefore, taught not Buddhism but mindfulness, accessible to all at a moment's notice.

The monks themselves were silly and smiley. They had a basketball court, played table tennis, and wobbled along on a slackline tied between two trees.

'What's your favourite moment of the days here?' I asked one of them.

'The present moment!' he chirped back.

'Here ah Plum Village,' said another monk in a thick Malaysian accent, 'we have a three-wur motto. The furs wur is "relax". The secun wur is "enjoy". An the thur wur is "be at peace with yourself".'

The monks weren't born that way. They were lawyers, architects, engineers, businessman, university students, war veterans. One of them travelled around the world with a chamber orchestra. Another had considerable success in finance prior to ordaining. Phap Dung, a monk with missing teeth and a flare in his eyes, pursed his lips with attitude and walked with the hint of a swagger not quite eradicated from his prior life.

'I'm from Los Angeles,' he said. 'People move so fast. So many people in traffic — they all move so fast, they get stuck. In certain parts of the city, if you're not careful, you get shot. The gang members have shaved heads.' He rubbed his own shiny scalp as if divining a crystal ball, then gestured to the monks. 'I think we're like a gang. We used to be big business people. We had a taste of success. But we rebelled. We thought there must be more to life than just "work, sleep, work, sleep" and we wanted to find a different way. If you're here, maybe you feel that way too.'

I shouldn't have selected a favourite monk — it goes against the Buddha's teaching of detachment — but mine was Phap Chieu. All the monks are given a new name when they join the monastery, but when working with some children who couldn't pronounce it, they insisted Phap Chieu explain what his name meant.

'Phap Chieu means "Dharma Radiance", or Dharma Shine,' he said. (*Dharma* is an old name for the Buddha's teachings.)

'Can we just call you Brother Shiny?'

'Yes!' he said, thrilled. That evening, when all the monks were asked where Brother Shiny had gone, the name stuck.

Shiny was about my age and sounded like a Californian Valley boy. I first met him in the Plum Village bookstore where he worked behind the counter. He saw me pick up one of Thich Nhat Hanh's books and called out, 'You can get it cheaper on Amazon.' Later, when I was under a tree playing a borrowed guitar, he came to sit with me and I taught him how to play 'Blackbird' by The Beatles.

'Every monk is supposed to give up all their possessions,' he told me. 'All we have is our robe and a bowl for food.'

'Shiny,' I said, 'you have an iPod.'

'Oh my god,' he gushed, 'iOS 8 just came out and it's so awesome!'

During one of the lazy days, Shiny and I were sat in a tree drinking herbal tea when he asked, 'Have you seen *Dead Poets Society*?'

'No.'

'What? That's my favourite movie! You haven't seen it? You ain't lived half a life, bro! I have it on Netflix!' That evening, Shiny set up a projector in the meditation hall and a group of us lounged on the floor watching a stream of the film.

'So you're, like, huge on YouTube?' said Gregg. We were sat in the teahouse, watching the sun rise.

'I guess,' I said. 'But now people hate me cos of all this shit I've done.'

'Wow. That must have been hard for you.'

'I... yeah, it was,' I said, raising my eyebrows. 'It feels a little unfair to acknowledge that.'

'Well, everyone suffers, mate.'

'Yeah I know, but they're so angry about it,' I said. 'I don't know what to do. Like, my ex, she sent me this horrible text out of nowhere and I don't know whether I'm still causing her suffering or whether she's causing her own suffering.'

'She's causing her own suffering! Absolutely!'

'Isn't that arrogant?' I asked. 'To wash my hands of it and leave it with her?'

'We have five precepts here,' said Shiny, who'd drifted over and offered us a flask of tea. 'You can't kill, steal, lie, take intoxicants or commit sexual misconduct. But your actions break a precept only when breaking it causes suffering. If your intent is pure, whatever you do will come from a good place.'

'My intent wasn't pure.'

'But it is now,' said Shiny.

'Yeah... but if I know I'm gonna upset people more, I shouldn't be online.'

'I dunno,' said Gregg. 'You can't lock yourself up in some tower, mate. You can't avoid the internet forever just cos some people don't want you there. Anyway, I like you.'

'Yeah, I'm gonna subscribe,' grinned Shiny. 'I'll reply to everyone, "He's nice. I'm his monk friend. Be nice."'

'Thanks guys,' I smiled.

'You still have an audience, right?' Shiny asked.

'People are still subscribed,' I said, 'but even if they like me, they'll just be told not to by the people who don't. It's no use.'

'It sounds like they're suffering a lot,' said Shiny. 'You should make videos to try to help them.'

'It'll just piss them off.'

'Our teacher pisses people off,' said Shiny. 'He re-wrote one of the Buddha's sutras to make it more modern and accessible.'

'What?'

'I know, right?' said Shiny. 'It's like rewriting a bit of the Bible. People said all sorts of things about him for that.' He flashed me a mischievous grin. 'They were horrible. But you have to do what you think is right. People don't always want to be helped. Some people will always oppose you. It doesn't mean you shouldn't try.'

We sat and watched the sun grow larger. I took a deep breath in, then out.

A guy limped to a bench beside us a few minutes later.

'You alright?' I asked, nodding at his leg.

'I sprained my ankle a while back,' he said. 'I was hiking up a mountain.'

'That's nothing,' I smiled. 'When I breathe in, I *am* a mountain.'

CEMETERY PARK

My time in Plum Village had provided me with the perfect getaway from the world of YouTube. I wasn't to know it, but it would be the last chance I'd ever have to escape it. When I got off the train back at London's Waterloo station, I looked up and saw a huge banner stretching across the wall for a YouTuber called Zoella.

Zoella's first novel, *Girl Online,* debuted with the highest first-week sales for a first-time author since records began. Around the same time, her boyfriend Alfie released his own book, *The Pointless Book,* which sat at number one for eleven weeks. The two of them now have their own waxworks at Madame Tussaud's and the BBC commissioned Zoella's brother to make a documentary about a road trip across America. (I don't know if they ate burgers in every state.) Marilyn got offered a deal of her own to write an advice book for teenagers; posters of her as Éponine were plentiful throughout the London Underground as I went home. They were displayed next to adverts for Summer in the City, now a ticketed event for ten thousand people organised by MCM, the creators of London Comic Con. VidCon that year hosted eighteen thousand people (with vloggers staying in a private security-manned floor of a nearby hotel). A larger-than-life Emma peered down at me from a screen in Piccadilly Circus;

her music was featured in an Apple product launch. The top YouTuber had fifty million subscribers and appeared on the cover of *Variety* in America. John sold over ten million copies of his new book *The Fault In Our Stars* (which was then made into a film by 21st Century Fox) and had a conference call with Barack Obama, during which the President said, 'tell [your daughter] not to forget to be awesome'.

Susi was right. YouTubers were mainstream.

I had an email waiting from Brother Shiny when I got home. 'I just checked the comments on your videos,' he said. 'It was so funny! People are so angry with you and they can't let go of it at all!'

The next morning (after explaining to my mum why I didn't want a bacon sandwich for breakfast) I meditated, did some writing and headed out for a stroll along the green outside our house. It took me about twenty minutes to amble to a small hill surrounded by trees, where I sat down and crossed my legs.

I got my phone out of my pocket and flipped it around to face me. It had been six months since I last showed my face on the internet.

'I feel very happy right now,' I said. 'I feel very content. I hope that you're having a really nice day also and that you watch this with open-mindedness and compassion and a lack of judgment.' I told the camera I was scared of Tumblr, who seemed 'militantly liberal and intolerant of anyone else who doesn't share their opinion', before apologising to anyone who thought that wasn't a fair assumption, and clarifying this has just been my experience with it.

'I don't feel like my defence will even be listened to, because — as the perpetrator — it will instantly be made invalid, and a lot of people accusing me of manipulation just write off everything that I say by saying, "Well, we've said that he's a manipulator, look, he's manipulating you again; he's doing it right now, don't fall for it," which sort of renders anything I say pointless.

'But what I've learned over the last two weeks is... there's a lot of anger and fear and pain in our community right now and I am a person that can reach a lot of you and maybe I can decrease some of that — and misunderstanding, particularly, maybe I can decrease some of that by just explaining my side of it, and even if you don't agree with my side of it or you don't believe my side of it or you think that I'm just trying to preserve myself — because, you know, being famous on the internet has always been *so* important to me — then maybe you can just write it all off, but I think it's still better that I said something. Even if one person who watches this comes away from it feeling a little bit more reasonable about the whole situation then I feel like that's good. I feel like I've reduced the overall misunderstanding and fear and anger in the world by one person and that's a good thing to do and I think that the attempts to decrease it will outweigh the inevitable increase in anger that this will create. I just want to speak honestly, or to the best of my abilities, anyway, like, as honestly as I can given that I'm biased, I'm only one person in this story, and these are my recollections, my memory is as faulty as anybody else's, and so on.'

I spoke for about half an hour, letting my thoughts flutter in and out. I didn't go into detail about my perspective on most of the accusations, because I didn't see the value in offering another rebuttal: 'All that would achieve is that they would then go back to Tumblr and say, "Oh my god, he's being a manipulator, he's an awful person, that's not what happened," and then you guys would just argue in YouTube comments till you all die about whose side you're on and that's not the point. It's not going to get us anywhere.

'All I can say,' I went on, 'is that I didn't mean to make anyone feel pressured and that I'm really sorry for making anyone feel pressured and it was not my intention, and the only thing I can do at this point is think about it, as I have already, a lot, and learn from it, as I've already started to, and make sure I don't put anyone in a situation like that ever again.'

I uploaded the video straight from my phone without editing it, went to have lunch with my mum, and when I came back, I was trending on Twitter.

There were many differing opinions on what I'd said (though a common thread was that people were obsessed with why I'd shaved my head, most assuming I did it as the result of shame, disease, or religious fervour, as though the only shaven-headed people they'd ever seen were the Buddha or Britney Spears). One person dismissed my video and said I should instead show my remorse by committing to 'a year long video series about abusive/predatory relationships where [I] received counselling'.

Opinions weren't restricted to strangers — my old friends all weighed in with their take, each one thriftier than the last. 'I watched all 30 mins of Alex Day's video,' tweeted David. 'I'm not convinced of any development & I don't agree with his choice to continue making videos.'

'Alex Day has apparently uploaded a new video,' shared Penny. 'I've said it many times, but I'll say it again: abusers aren't welcome in this community.'

'"Sorry if you felt pressured" is not an apology,' said Hazel. 'This sounded like a lot of empty words.'

'I. AM. FURIOUS.' wrote Marilyn.

A mutual friend came to me as an envoy of my ex-bandmates Charlie and Liam, telling me they were uncomfortable with me receiving any more money from Chameleon Circuit's albums and that I should publicly donate my share to a sex abuse charity from now on.

'Tell Charlie I will consider this if he agrees to talk with me in person or by phone so we can have an honest discussion about my side of the allegations,' I replied, and was unsurprised when I heard no more about it.

As the fallout from the video continued, I got a phone call from Susi.

'I'm phoning to let you know we're terminating your partnership with ChannelFlip,' she said. 'We didn't know your video was going to go up and it's caused huge debate among the people we represent.'

'I won't go to the party then,' I replied. (ChannelFlip had just invited me to their Christmas party at Warner Bros. Studios, on the set of the Great Hall from the Harry Potter movies.)

'The internet's basically exploded at me,' I emailed a friend.

'You picked a hell of a time to come back,' he replied, 'what with Jason.'

'Who's Jason?'

'You don't know?'

'I've been in a monastery.'

Two vloggers, Sam and Jason, had separately been accused of violent rape and sexual abuse acts, sending their viewers into a storm of anger and condemnation right at the moment I'd decided to pop my head through the door and try to make everyone feel better.

'If you don't think Alex Day has noticed that he might benefit from the contrast between his accusations and the ones more physically violent and specific in nature then you're being naive,' someone wrote on Tumblr, figuring that my ill-timed comeback was part of some cunning master plan. 'It was a deliberate and opportunistic choice to return to YouTube at this moment. Notice how he emphasizes the lack of physical force during his incidents of coercion. Notice how he carefully selected which accounts he would address. Notice how he casts himself as the victim of a vitriolic tumblr community.' I saw this post because it was shared by Liam, who added, 'This is the most succinct issue I have with Alex's new video, which I have not watched and encourage you not to watch.' I was blown away. This was a thought leader in the Nerdfighter community boasting about the fact that he didn't get his information from a firsthand source — he instead read a transcript and suggested others do the same, which is problematic not least because the transcripts being passed around read like this:

um yeah if youre upset by this or youre offended by this or youre angry about this then im really sorry um I think the best thing to do would be to not watch my videos again because it's probably not gonna get any better for you um but I didn't mean any harm

In response, I made a video a few days later and, halfway through, interrupted myself and said, 'Open bracket. Hi. This is the person writing the transcript. This is no longer Alex talking. I just wanted to let you all know that I'm having a really good day. I'm very peaceful and happy and I'm enjoying watching Alex's video and typing it out for you. With lots of love, The Transcripter. Close bracket.'

The transcripts stopped after that.

I'd known, of course, that my return to YouTube would open old wounds and hardly expected to be welcomed back with open arms. In fact, I'd done enough damage to my former friends and colleagues that I didn't think they would even listen to what I had to say, let alone showcase it to their own followers (through the prism of their own views, granted). All I wanted to do was reconnect with anyone still interested in hearing from me while doing my best not to bother anyone who didn't. The easy, selfish decision would have been to keep my head down and stay away from trouble, but I knew if I was going to rebuild anything in my life I had to open myself back up to that anger and confront it head on. Amongst the din of reproof and naked rage, I accepted who I was now, understood how people would continue to see me, and found I was able to pick myself up from my past and set a better example with my present and future.

Despite — or perhaps because of — the controversy it caused, my long video in the park got half a million views. The day after, I got a phone call from a number I didn't recognise. It turned out I'd deleted it.

'Hello?'

'Hey, Alex.'

There was a short silence.

'It's Mark.'

'Oh,' I said. 'Right.'

'You sound angry.'

'I'm confused,' I said. Mark was a vlogger I'd met once or twice. When the allegations began he was one of the few acquaintances I had who sent me a message of support, saying he didn't think I'd done much different from any other young stupid guy, that if all his exes lined up to write accounts about *him* on the internet he'd look like a dick as well, and that if I ever wanted to catch up or have a chat he was always available for a drink.

Then he unfriended me from Facebook on my birthday and that was the end of Alex and Mark.

'What can I do for you?' I asked.

'Well, mate, I just wanted to apologise,' he said. 'We don't know each other that well, and I always thought we'd be good mates if we ever got to know each other, but on your birthday I was in the YouTube Space and they saw me on Facebook where your name came up. Hazel started having a go at me, saying you tried to hit on her when she was at your house once, and everyone else started giving me hassle, saying I shouldn't support you, and I figured I didn't know you much anyway and couldn't be bothered with the hassle so it was easier just to delete you.'

'I hit on Hazel in my house once?' I said, baffled.

'I dunno, mate. Anyway, I was never into the whole YouTube thing. My girlfriend always followed the drama and couldn't get off her Twitter and I didn't get why she was so into it.' (Mark's ex-girlfriend is now one of the most popular YouTubers in the UK; at the time of writing she has over a million subscribers and broke a record when — as an unsigned artist — her EP charted at number 6 on the UK Albums Chart. She has since implied her relationship with Mark was abusive.) 'Since we broke up,' he continued, 'I've been more and more distant from it all and realised how small and stupid it all is. And I've always felt bad for abandoning you and wanted to say sorry.'

Mark wasn't the only person who reached out. While many responses conveyed malice, I found myself on the receiving end of a secret burst of positivity. In private messages and emails, where people couldn't see or judge them, old friends and strangers reached out to express their sympathies.

'How is your well-being?' said someone on reddit. 'Some of us over at Australian Nerdfighters are concerned that Tumblr is taking this too far and there is potential that you could be facing depression and suicidal ideation. No matter what you do, please don't end your life. You have done shitty things in the past, but in essence I think you are a good person. There are always numbers you can call.'

'I think it's horrible how you're being treated,' a girl messaged me on Twitter. 'By the way, if you ever want sex, no strings, I'm down.'

My friend George even went so far as to make a public video titled 'Why I Don't Hate Alex Day' (and later told me that, for his own well-being, he'd stopped replying to the comments on it).

The next video I made was about my nan. Because her name was Hazel, I set up a charity page for whoever still liked me to donate money to plant hazel trees in her memory. Each tree cost about five pounds to plant.

'I asked online if anyone wanted to donate to plant a tree for her,' I told my mum.

'Oh yeah,' she said. 'Any takers?'

'Yeah,' I smiled, my eyes glistening. 'We're gonna plant 150 trees.' The company planting the trees said it was the biggest donation ever made on behalf of an individual. I insisted I plant a few of them myself, and the owner of the company took my family to Tower Hamlets Cemetery Park in East London ('round the corner from my old place with Charlie) where the trees would be planted. So many were donated that, when we asked where in the park we would find them, he smiled and replied, 'Just think of this whole park being for your nan.'

When I self-published my book a few weeks later, I sold a thousand copies overnight, and my mum and I spent days in her living room surrounded by boxes, signing books, hand-writing the addresses and giggling as we lugged sacks of envelopes to the post office 'round the corner. My audience, however, were losing interest in my ongoing rambles about mindfulness and compassion. They'd subscribed for snarky comedy, *Doctor Who* rants and *Twilight* readings, and weren't interested in hearing how much more tranquil they'd be if they observed their breath.

I did, however, get a kind comment on one of my videos from Marilyn:

> Not that you need my approval for anything you do, but I do massively approve of you using the platform you still have to encourage kindness and as unsure as I am from past experience, I do hope it's sincere. From a purely selfish perspective, it will always sadden and frustrate me that you didn't learn any of this sooner to save a lot of heart ache and trauma, but even so I'm still glad you've got to a point where you understand some of the things I used to agonise over trying to explain and I hope you and the people around you are far better off because of it. xxx

I was also surprised when I had the chance to reconnect with Ellie, one of the girls who wrote about me online. We spoke on Facebook and then met up in a cafe, both a bit nervous at what the other might think of us.

'It was all so much,' she said. 'It was out of control. I'm sorry for the part I played in all of that.'

'I don't blame you,' I said. 'I'm sorry for treating you so badly.'

'Fair enough,' she said, and smiled, and we got some tea. We're still in touch and I remain in awe that she was able to forgive me. Nobody owed me forgiveness, or a second chance, or a renewed public platform, or the chance to continue doing what I love. I haven't done as much wrong as people have said, but I've done *enough* wrong; I held a position of public scrutiny and I fucked it up. I didn't want to reclaim it. But I didn't just blink out of existence. I still had thoughts that I suspected people might benefit from hearing, and I believed there to be enough space for me to exist alongside others, living in my own little corner of life, contributing to the world in whatever small way I was still allowed. We were all in agreement that I shouldn't be looking for forgiveness or redemption — I wasn't. I didn't want to be forgiven. I just wanted to be.

I used the remainder of my savings to buy a flat in Kent which I rented out to help sustain me (not wanting to rely on income that came from as unpredictable a place as popularity). My commitment to putting better things in the world was all well and good, but I couldn't figure out how to make a living from it. For a while I thought Russell Brand was the answer: like me, he was controversial, anti-establishment and born in Essex, and I spent the summer attending weekly events he hosted in East London. This was deep in his revolutionary period — about a hundred of us would listen to the comedian reading from Naomi Klein or Noam Chomsky and answering questions about community living and the unsustainability of current worldwide economic distribution.

'You're wearing toe shoes,' he said, spying my feet in the front row. I'd started wearing shoes with separated toes to give me the feeling of walking barefoot without the dirt and dangers of city ground.

'I knew you'd notice those.'

'Don't sit in the fucking front row, then,' he said. 'Now we can learn things about you because you prescribe to a particular set of ideals that you call your identity.' He looked me up and down. 'Into the mic, are you... a vegan?'

The room erupted as I confirmed his hunch.

'Oh well, he's been humiliated, give him a big hand.' I grinned and waved at the room.

I walked into the space the following week to find my seat and saw Emma and her boyfriend across the room. I tiptoed round them, hoping she wouldn't smash me into the ground with a nearby box of Hare Krishna cupcakes. It was getting easier to deal with the hate — I knew it didn't relate to who I was now, leaving them livid at nothing but a dead memory — but friends and loved ones found it more difficult. One friend of mine, Joni, was in my life for years but never introduced me to any of her friends, in part because they'd heard of me by reputation. They'd warned her about me when she'd first mentioned me, made clear their disapproval, and though she adored me and wanted to make up her own mind about me, she couldn't change theirs. It was a hard conflict for her — nobody wants the people they love to be in pain with themselves or each other. Being my friend was like telling people you were a member of UKIP, or a fan of U2, and there was little I could do about it, no matter how good 'Beautiful Day' is.

'Why do you have to be so controversial?' she pouted at me. With my baggy trousers, loose-fitting t-shirts, toe shoes and shaved head, I certainly wasn't the figure of a man trying to fit in.

'I'm not being controversial,' I said, 'I just want to be myself.'

'You don't care what people think of you?'

'Yeah,' I said, 'but not people I don't know.'

'Why?' she said. 'That seems selfish. I know you, you're not a selfish person.'

'I don't care what strangers think,' I smiled, 'because if I did, I wouldn't get out of bed in the morning.'

Four months later I turned 26, sold everything I owned that didn't fit into a small bag (ending up with exactly 40 items, including clothes, toiletries and an iPad to work from) and flew to Egypt. (I had believed the Pyramids of Giza were stranded in a vast desert, but it was a myth created by clever camera angles — they were on a roadside at the desert's edge with a Pizza Hut on the other side. It was the same with the statue of Rameses, which they moved from the centre of town to the edge of the airport so the tourists couldn't miss it.) From there, I got a plane to Tokyo and spent a week with the monks of Plum Village, who hosted a meditation retreat at the base of Mount Fuji. We spent days singing songs like 'Happiness Is Here And Now', 'The Island Within Myself' and 'Here Is The Pure Land'. I participated in a two-hour ceremony to welcome aspirant Buddhists, during which I peeked and caught one of the younger monks yawning. In the evenings I sat in an outdoor hot spring where nakedness was mandatory and swimming was banned. I sat back in the heat, kicking my legs and sighing with contentment in the April dusk.

Then Phap Dung, the gangster monk, did the backstroke past me, completely nude. I sat up in shock, and he stopped, grinned his toothy grin, pointed at his naked body floating on the surface, and said, '*Here* is the Pure Land.'

When I returned to the internet from my second monastic absence, I saw this in my Facebook messages:

> I want you to know that there are people out there (such as myself) who think very highly of you and who miss seeing your face on the Internet. If you would ever like to chat it would be my biggest pleasure to speak with you. That's really the only reason I wrote to you. If you'd ever like to, I'll do whatever I can to prove you can trust me. In case you care to know, here's a bit about me... I'm Sarah. I'm 22. I live on an island in Canada. I like pizza and hiking... I am afraid to send this message because maybe I'll never get a reply. Fingers crossed. Take care. You're awesome.

'I have to ask,' I sent back, 'have you googled me recently?'

'Yes. Of course. And? I know about what 'happened' but I also know there's two sides to every story. I'm leaving my house to go climb a mountain so I'll text you later.'

I began a cautious discourse with Sarah, suspecting every online contact at some point of being a mole designed to catch me out and reveal my wicked ways to the masses. (Which never happened. Obviously.)

'I'm planning a two-month trip around Europe in the summer,' she wrote.

'That sounds so fun. I'd love to be part of something like that.'

'I'd be happy for you to join me.'

'Sarah, this is how Tumblr accounts get started.'

I didn't want to make anyone else ever feel lured or pulled in or coerced. After many attempts over several months to reassure Sarah that I wasn't joking, but I didn't have to go with her if she didn't want me to, and many attempts from her to reassure me that she wouldn't mind my company and that I wasn't hijacking her trip, the two of us flew to Portugal and began a relaxed two months of travel across Europe, meandering from restaurants to escape rooms across the continent, hanging out of train windows, peering through museum glass and flexing our muscles in the sizzling sun. Every day, we went wherever we wanted and laughed the whole way. Sarah reminded me I was allowed to be happy.

'I had a whole thing figured out,' Sarah said once, 'if it turned out you were gross.'

'Oh yeah?'

'I was ready,' she nodded. 'If you were not nice I was ready to, like, get on a train without you and peace out.'

'No way!'

'Yeah. You'd just have to make your own way home and I'd go off without you.'

'You gotta do what you gotta do, mate,' I grinned. 'It's good you had a plan in place.'

'It was a whole plan,' she said.

'I'm glad you didn't have to use it.'

'Me too! I'm hungry. Where is food?'

To reconcile my desire for mindfulness content with my audience's objection to it, I told people on main channel that I was done, retiring, ready to move on, but that I was setting up a new dedicated channel for daily mindfulness videos called The Daily Day. It would allow me, I figured, to rebuild from scratch and develop a new brand for myself online. After a month or two, though, I noticed nobody shared the videos, though engagement was high. I realised the best way to get people to take up my message was to remove myself from it, freeing it from the things people felt about me, so they could allow it to grow without also making a moral statement in doing so. With that, I set up an email address for people to submit their own videos to and reached out to people to run The Daily Day's Twitter, Facebook and Instagram accounts, posting the community-made videos every day on my behalf. In effect, I handed the channel to its community and gave them equal ownership of it. It was my idealised version of YouTube, made real one last time; a channel with no hierarchy between the creator and the people watching it.

The whole thing died a slow death over a few months. People who didn't like the user-submitted videos as much as mine made their feelings clear — I'd assumed the joy of it was they could just make their own, but they didn't do anything apart from complain. The people who did make stuff felt hurt and attacked by the rest of the community. The videos stopped coming in, and The Daily Day — like Nerimon — was left dormant.

I intended to return to London only as a pit stop to see friends and family before jetting off again, but I checked my bank balance as I landed and found myself scraping the bottom of my financial barrel. I couldn't afford to go anywhere else.

Eager to make it on my own again, I found a company who managed abandoned or private buildings being renovated or awaiting demolition. For a cheap fee you could have a room in a school, a library or an office building in the centre of the city, all expenses included. You'd have to move every year or two (when the building was redeveloped or destroyed) but in the meantime it was a unique opportunity.

'So you're a squatter,' said a disapproving Jonathan, sighing. 'Alex, you're in your mid-twenties. You're middle-aged. Living in an old fire station is fun at sixteen. It's not fun at twenty-six.'

'It's a police station,' I corrected.

I was paying four hundred a month for what amounted to a one-bedroom apartment; two rooms in a police station with furniture donated from neighbours nearby with space to read, sleep, work and meditate, and huge shared kitchen and shower blocks for use amongst the fifteen other people who lived across the building's three floors.

'Alex Day!' said my new housemate Dylan, an eighteen-year-old boy with spiky gelled hair and his phone camera trained on me. 'Oh my god, it's fucking Nerimon!'

'Yeah, alright, mate.'

'Fuck me!'

Dylan had watched my videos for several years and relished in sharing photos of me to Snapchat, often when I least expected it. (Snapchat was a new photo-sharing app with a twist: the photos disappeared a few seconds after you looked at them. It earned its notoriety when people used it to send naked photos of themselves and others figured out they could screenshot the images before they expired.)

'Mate,' he said, 'I just went in Chino's and Eddie Redmayne was in there having a panini!'

'No way! You say anything to him?'

'Nah,' said Dylan. 'Probably busy, innit. Learning scripts or whatever.'

'Let's go back,' I said, grabbing my coat. 'I wanna see him.'

'He'll be gone by now,' said Dylan. He often told stories like this — as exciting as they were hard to prove. He told me he was the lead in a movie that would start filming in January and that he'd found a bargain-price house in Baker Street he was planning to move to. Then he mentioned — in the company of my friend Lizzie, who I'd befriended after she stopped me on the Tube and complimented my new album — that he was planning to move to New York to live with Matthew Perry.

'I've been DMing him on Twitter,' he told us. 'He said I can go over there and stay at his.'

'But don't you need to be here for that feature film?' Lizzie asked, slipping me a glance.

'Oh I'll work it out, mate, fuck!' said Dylan before changing the subject.

Lizzie crashed in Dylan's room that night and burst with excitement when she saw me the next morning.

'You're not gonna believe it. You know that digestion thing he's got?'

'Sure,' I said. Dylan was suffering from some kind of intestinal pain; the doctor had put him first on a vegan and then a gluten-free diet to determine what might be the cause.

'He said it was cancer.'

'What?'

'Wait,' she grinned. 'He said he had cancer. I said, "Oh my god, what kind is it?" and *he* said, "They're not sure"!'

'What?!' I said. 'So it's bollocks? Who lies about cancer?!'

'He said that's what his stomach problems have been but he doesn't wanna tell people!'

'What doctor is this?' I blanched. 'So he has some kind of intestinal pain, the doctor says, "Try not eating dairy." He goes back and says it didn't help and the doctor goes, "Oh, it's cancer then"!'

When I began to distance myself from Dylan, he responded by bitching to my housemates and friends about me at every opportunity, relaying conversations that didn't happen and passing gossip that never existed back to me. He's since told mutual friends that he found out how horrible I really was after he ran into Charlie at a party, and

Charlie "opened up" to him. When I checked up on Dylan on Facebook recently, I was baffled to see he'd changed his name to Alfie. Even his surname was different. I have no idea what's real anymore.

I moved out after six months and into a houseshare with a woman in Waterloo called Stacey whose staircase was covered in shoeboxes and who had a huge framed portrait of herself at the top of the stairs. My days of thinking this would be better than living with 'Dylan' were short-lived.

'You woke me up this morning,' she told me the first day I was there. I'd woken up at about eight in the morning. She'd stayed in bed until the late afternoon.

'What time did you go to bed?' I asked.

''bout five,' she said.

'Have you thought about shutting your bedroom door?' I asked. I'd had to walk past it on the way to the bathroom and noticed it was ajar. 'That way I won't disturb you.'

'No,' she said. 'I want to hear what's going on.' That seemed weird. It got weirder.

Stacey didn't want me making too much noise or putting any of my food in the fridge (or my blender in the kitchen), refused to let me have friends stay over and wouldn't even allow them through the door without her approval, and when I left my half-empty bottle of soap on the side of the shower, she threw it away.

At one point during my stay there I had a horrible fever, incapacitating me for days to waste away in bed. On the way back to my room after getting some water from the kitchen, I stumbled due to dehydration and fell against Stacey's budgie cage. I pulled myself up, checked that the bird and the cage were fine, shuffled back into my room, and collapsed on to the bed.

From the other side of the door, I heard, 'You broke my bird cage.' She hammered on the door. 'Alex!'

I grunted some kind of reply.

'You broke my bird cage. Come, look.'

'I can't move,' I moaned. From my room, I heard a friend of hers insisting that the bird cage was fine.

I only lasted a month there. Just two weeks after moving in, she texted me with no prompting, 'You can't use the washing machine. You have to go somewhere else. There's a launderette 'round the corner.'

'Okay, I'm gonna move out,' I sent back. 'This will be my two weeks notice.'

On the day I moved out, Stacey said fraud had been committed against her bank account and — what bad luck — my £700 security deposit had been taken out of it. I might have believed that if she hadn't asked me to lend her a hundred pounds at least twice in the month I lived with her, and if she didn't have another housemate besides me paying rent. I took her to small claims court in the end, as did the other housemate when she moved out. Neither of us saw our money again.

From there, I wasted even more money on security deposits and agency fees when I moved into a tiny room near Canary Wharf with some European guys who slipped towels in their cupboard doors so they could see from the way they'd moved whether someone had used their crockery or spices. When I moved out (six weeks later), they'd upgraded to padlocks. I'd found an even smaller room on the outskirts of the city, close to Heathrow Airport, and was set to live there for the long-term when I got a text from Gregg.

'Hey brother! I'm moving to London. You in?'

THE PURPLE SPACESHIP

'It's not gay!' I heard as I let myself into the flat.

'It's a little bit gay, mate,' grinned Gregg.

'What am I walking into?' I asked. My housemates — Gregg, Maryn and Georgia — were chuckling on stools around the purple-tiled kitchen table that had inspired us to dub our place the Purple Spaceship. They were talking about Maryn's plans with his girlfriend, Red.

'Maryn's saying he wants someone to do him in the bum while he's having sex with Red,' said Gregg.

'That's not it,' smiled Maryn, fetching himself another slice of avocado on toast. 'You want one, A-Day? I've got the crunch. I need my proats!'

'Sure thing,' I said, never refusing food as a rule. Maryn served me two doorstop-sized slices of sourdough bread with a generous helping of avocado and balsamic vinegar on top. The three of them were all vegan, loving food as much as they loved to share it.

'I want to have anal sex with Red,' Maryn explained, 'but I want to feel what it's like for her. So I want someone else to have sex with me at the same time and match my rhythm.'

'Yeah,' I said. 'I get what you're saying, but it is pretty gay, innit.'

'How is it gay to want to be closer to my girlfriend?' Maryn argued.

'In that another man is doing you in the bum!' Gregg cried.

'Wait, would he cum inside you as well?' I thought to ask.

'Of course,' insisted Maryn. 'I want to feel everything she feels.'

'And then what?' asked Georgia. 'You just cuddle Red and the other guy rolls away?'

'Yeah, he's not involved after that,' said Maryn. 'Anyway she's coming over later—'

'I am *not* putting it in your bum,' laughed Gregg.

Maryn was our gentle giant, towering over us with smiles and stories, always full of oddball schemes and plans, but he spent so much of his time at Red's he was rarely around to share with them with us. He would swan in with a huge bag of organic food, pull us into tight hugs, make us all lunch, stock the cupboards and the fridge with produce, and then go away again for so long we ended up eating all his food to stop it going off, only for him to drift by a week or two later with another huge bag and with no acknowledgement of the prior supply. Our rent was essentially subsidised by his regular grocery shop.

Georgia was compact and scatterbrained. She blew through the flat like a hurricane, as happy as if she were bouncing on a trampoline, and breezed along the streets of London on long, barefoot walks. She often engulfed the kitchen in a cloud of flour and diced herbs as she improvised her latest recipes for our enjoyment, combining flavours in new ways and never making the same thing twice. The two of us hit it off, and the moment we acknowledged it to each other, Gregg (who'd known all along) encouraged us to share a room to save on rent.

'That's a bit quick,' she said.

'Up to you, mate,' I smiled at her.

'Well,' she said, 'whether it's gonna work or not, we'll find out either way pretty quickly.' With that I became her roommate and her partner.

Gregg and I spent the summer sitting in parks, climbing trees and meditating together. We ate raw food for a whole month, an undertaking I christened 'Rawgust', and followed it up with 'Steptember', a challenge to walk everywhere for the following month. We monitored our progress with fitness trackers.

'We should start a blog,' said Gregg, 'called Get Lost, about our adventures in London and the value of not being connected, and about getting lost in life and the world around us.'

'Sounds great!' I said. By that evening I'd signed up the domain name, started the blog and was nagging Gregg to write the first post.

'I'll get to it, mate,' he smiled, lounging on the sofa.

Late in the summer, Shiny flew over to visit and we wandered around East London together, me in my baggy jeans, him in his brown monk's robe. We met my mum that evening for a meal at Vantra.

'So nice to meet you!' she said, hugging him.

'Let's stay in touch,' Shiny smiled, pulling a smartphone from some secret monastic pocket. 'Are you on Whatsapp?'

'Of course!' said my mum. (Whatsapp was a service allowing people to send text and media messages to each other anywhere in the world for free.)

I smiled, pulling my phone out. 'What is *that*?' said Shiny when he saw it. I'd sold my iPhone that summer as a result of Gregg's preaching of the 'analog life' (and also because I needed the money to pay the rent), replacing it with a simple Nokia phone that cost about forty pounds. It does calls, texting and Snake, and when the battery wears down I would think, 'Ooh, the battery's low, I'd better charge it sometime in the next few days.'

'Dude, you gotta get with the times,' said Shiny.

'Let's have a selfie,' Mum said, leaning towards us with her phone out and her smile prepared. (The first time I ever heard the word *selfie*, it was from my mum asking to have one with me. I thought it was a cute mum-word she'd invented.)

'How are you my dear?' asked Lizzie the next time I caught up with her.

'Great,' I grinned.

'Wonderful,' she smirked. 'And how are things going with you and Gregg?'

'Oh, we're very happy together.'

'Splendid.'

'Yeah, thanks for asking.'

Gregg introduced me to a menagerie of London friends, all of whom were happy to take me under their wings. I was part of a supportive and loving community based on compassion instead of success. We marched on animal rights protests together, then sat down over a pizza and chatted in earnest about our favourite types of nut milk.

The vegan community in London had its own group of YouTubers who had nothing to do with my former lot; they made recipe videos, video diaries documenting what they ate in various situations, and educational videos about nutritional sources, animal welfare and the environment. Like my old friends, they hooked up with each other, made videos calling each other out on their shit and showcased their petty squabbles to an eager audience. While my new friends gossiped about the drama, Gregg and I rolled our eyes and ate figs.

More and more, though, my old life crept into my new one. In the autumn I got an invite to a pool party screening of *Finding Dory* for press and media types. I assumed I'd been struck off those kinds of lists, so I was flattered to be included. Since Georgia was working, I invited Gregg as my plus-one.

The screening took place in a hotel pool, with tiered seats on one side of the water and a projector shining the movie across the water onto the opposite wall. I walked in with Gregg and stiffened as I took in the scene.

Around the room, I caught sight of Tomska, Hazel, David and Penny, plus many other former friends who I knew might now have a problem with my existence. It was a small screening and the place was packed with social media people. I had strolled right into the lion's den.

'You alright?' said Gregg, seeing my body change.

'Yeah,' I said. I wouldn't have gone if I'd known, but I was there now. 'All these people hate me.'

'Want me to go talk to 'em?' he grinned.

'I'm not doing anything wrong, am I?'

'No, you're just standing here, mate.'

'I just wanna see the movie. I *did* get an invite.' I decided to enjoy the film as though I were the only human left alive in Jurassic Park, keeping my head down, not looking anything in the eye and making as little noise or movement as I could muster. I expected, if there was a problem, that one of my old friends would come up to me, tell me I was making them uncomfortable and ask me to leave. I would have done so. But nobody did. Perhaps people hadn't noticed I was there or, even better, had reached the point of being able to share a room with me without kicking up a fuss. Two years had passed since the allegations were made. Perhaps we were all starting to move on.

Pleased with our collective civility, I grinned as the lights went down, munched on my complimentary popcorn and settled into the movie.

'Wanna stay for the afterparty?' asked Gregg afterward.

'Better not,' I said. 'I'll end up being thrown into the pool.'

The following afternoon, in the midst of a catchup session with Lizzie, I said, 'I went to see *Finding Dory* yesterday' and she said, 'I know.' I frowned.

'That's creepy,' I said. 'What do you mean you know? How did you know?'

Lizzie got her phone out, tapped the button for Twitter, scrolled a little and tilted the screen towards me, pointing at a tweet from Penny.

'Was having fun at the #FindingDory party until I saw they'd invited a widely known YouTube abuser.'

'I had anxiety the entire night,' David had replied.

'He just doesn't care,' Penny continued. 'There's been zero remorse/acknowledgement for the worst things he's done. I had a minor panic attack and had to leave.'

Shocked that they were sharing their feelings on the official hashtag, I messaged my friend at Disney to apologise if I'd made her job difficult or given her any problems.

'It's fine,' she said. 'Let's just say the YouTube community hasn't forgiven you.'

Despite this, I was still making the occasional video if an idea struck me, using the front camera of my iPad (which I used in lieu of a laptop) to do so. One evening when Georgia came home from work, she found me bent over my iPad, tapping lyrics into the keyboard.

'What you doing there, A-Day?' she asked, throwing her keys on the kitchen counter and her arms 'round my neck.

'Writing a rap,' I said, 'using every spell from the *Harry Potter* books. It's about a guy who runs a kebab shop.'

'That sounds well silly,' Georgia grinned.

'It's called "Avada Kebabra".'

I filmed with my friend George's high-end camera for the day. He sent me the footage and I added the names of each spell in text beside my head. I couldn't resist doing some token promotion — old habits die hard — sending the video to a few sites and news outlets on the off-chance it could catch someone's interest. I got a response back from a London newspaper, who featured it on their site and tweeted the link.

'So do you get more money for that?' asked my mum when I phoned her about it.

'No,' I said, 'they've uploaded it to their website so it doesn't affect me...'

I trailed off. I was looking at my video, reading and replying to comments. 'It just went up by a lot. About ten thousand views out of nowhere. Wonder why that is.'

'Probably cos you're so bloody talented,' my mum said.

'No, it's not that,' I said.

It didn't take me long to track down the source of the spike. It originated with a tweet from Marilyn.

> The man who sexually abused young girls and emotionally manipulated/cheated on me making a comeback? No thanks.

Marilyn had just — with nothing to back it up — told her half a million impressionable young followers that I sexually abused young girls.

Her fanbase detonated.

Sixteen hundred people retweeted the attack to their own audiences. Thousands of raging tweets were fired at the paper by Marilyn's followers and friends, blowing up their timeline and mine. Sarah, my lone ranger (the one friend of mine who straddled both my online and offline worlds), rode against the onslaught to tweet at Marilyn defending me and challenging her audacious accusation, only to be dismissed: 'The fact he's still publicly pushing his image without regard to those he abused shows he hasn't changed at all,' Marilyn shot back at her, at which point Sarah was pushed back by Marilyn's fans advancing on her, unleashing a secondary barrage of abuse. It was gang warfare, with Marilyn's troops and mine clashing in the slums of the internet — and mine hopelessly outnumbered.

'Leave it,' said Emma, doing the online equivalent of holding Marilyn back by the shoulders. 'Anyone who defends an abuser isn't worth your time.'

I closed Twitter and opened an email to a defamation lawyer. I didn't know how Marilyn came to believe I'd sexually abused young girls. I started to think maybe everyone just believed everyone else's story, everyone corroborating each other to generate some pretence of credibility. In any case, it wasn't true. I'd never seen anyone even suggest it.

'You have a good case,' the lawyer sent back. 'Phone me and we'll talk.'

If winning a lawsuit worked like that stick in *Men in Black* that makes everyone forget you were accused of sexual abuse if you prevailed, maybe I would have done it. As it was, chasing Marilyn's money wouldn't make me feel any better, nor would it change what people thought of me. Maybe it might make her think a little harder next time about what she tweets, but Marilyn was far from the only one saying these things. 'He sexually abused a lot of young women,' Freya had tweeted the same day. It only took a minute to set up a new Twitter account, or get a friend to slander me on their behalf, and I didn't want to spend the rest of my life in a lawsuit. There would be too much unpleasantness. It was, I suppose, the reason my accusers had also shunned official legal channels in favour of the instancy of the internet.

For their part, the newspaper's response to this backlash was non-existent; in fact, I was as amused as my detractors were furious when they tweeted about the video again that afternoon.

In the evening I received this email:

Hi Alex,

We just wanted to get in touch to thank you for your video subscription which we posted on our site today.

We thought we would let you know that the article did well for us with 13,000 views and 500 shares and the video had 11,000 views with more than 50% of the viewers watching until the end.

So thank you very much and do send us any other videos you think would work well for us.

Many thanks!

I should point out that I was not a big deal on YouTube at this point. I no longer had a million subscribers; I'd lost nearly half a million since the allegations were made. My videos averaged around 10,000 views each. It was astonishing, then — and almost certainly the result of the publicity garnered by my former friends on Twitter — that 'Avada Kebabra' was spotted by 'Viral Thread', a Facebook page that showcases viral videos to millions of people. With my permission they posted it to their page. And then another. And then another.

Across all platforms, and against all odds, with me being hated more than ever and accused of more heinous crimes than I'd ever been before, the video got over three million views in one week and became my most-viewed video ever.

Successes like these, I'd gathered, were now the exception to the rule. Every now and then I got a glimpse of my previous life through some news story about YouTube, and even I'd noticed that the quirky viral videos of my youth didn't really happen anymore. Nowadays, top-trending clips were all music videos, movie trailers and talk-show interviews. Moreover, when it was reported that major institutions in the UK and US — including the *Guardian* newspaper and the British government — ran ads that were played on extremist videos, they all pulled their ad campaigns from the site in protest. Under fire, Google unveiled restrictive new guidelines tightening their policy of what constituted an advertiser-friendly video. They specified many things that would stop a video from being able to make money from then on: 'sexually suggestive content, including sexual humour'; 'inappropriate language, including swearing'; and 'controversial or sensitive subjects and events'. Those three alone covered almost every video I've ever made.

I've never believed Google owes me a platform or a living — having always maintained that I'm not YouTube's target user, just someone who works there — so I wasn't angry about the changes even though they impacted me, but I felt like I was the only one as scores of creators howled in protest at what they called the 'Adpocalypse' and how much harder it made their lives, seemingly unaware of the transient nature of the internet and all things on it. I've always been concerned about the impact this negativity has on the people watching, and this time my fears were founded; after watching videos on the unfairness of YouTube's changes by vlogging heavyweights like Casey Neistat, a small-time YouTuber called Nasim Aghdam drove over 500 miles from her home to Google's headquarters in Mountain View, California, whereupon she shot three members of YouTube's staff and then herself. Police placed the motive for the shooting on "Aghdam's feelings of persecution regarding YouTube policy".

I still had the money from the tenants in the flat I owned, but it was only just getting me by. My mum had been lending me money every month to help me live, on my word that I would pay it back as soon as something worked out. Gregg and his underground network of vegans were helping too. When Gregg's friend Damien organised a conference called Vevolution (which he billed as 'TED talks for vegans'), he signed me up to speak and then suffocated under an avalanche of online nastiness. The people choosing not to eat animals were still quite happy to devour my reputation.

I'd also been introduced to the editor of a vegan lifestyle magazine and landed a gig writing freelance articles for them. For the first time in my life, my name was in print in a physical thing that was endorsed by a third party — and it was among good-natured, wholesome articles about being kind and compassionate, to boot. The editor loved my writing so much she only had me change one word of my first article. 'It was a joy to read,' she gushed.

The magazine tweeted about the article that day.

'Please don't tell me this is Alex Day from YouTube, he's a known sexual abuser,' read a tweet in response. It only takes one observer to alert the hive mind; the abusive messages began swarming in their thousands.

'Can you call me?' read the next day's email from the editor, and that was it for my burgeoning magazine writing career.

After that I released a new album, *Split Infinities*. I had all my friends singing and playing instruments on it, put all our faces on the cover, and watched it sell about thirty copies.

'So you're not pushing your music?' Mark asked me.

'Nah,' I said, 'I don't wanna be famous. Why is the music industry so concerned with making artists instead of songs? I wish I could post my music into a pneumatic tube that would send it to a label, they would push it to radio and make it big, and I could just stay at home and work on the next one.'

'The problem you have, then,' smiled Mark, 'is that you wanna be a globally successful musician but you have the temperament of a librarian.' It was true; I'd lost my fight. Whenever I popped my head out, it was stomped back down. I'd given up.

'Time to move on,' Gregg sighed, stretching out in the morning sun. 'What do you reckon, A-Day?'

'Time to move on,' I nodded.

'I'm feeling Toronto. Canada's amazing in the summer.'

'Yeah?'

'Mate, the food is *incredible*. You should come.'

'I dunno,' I shrugged. 'I gotta get some work. I've just borrowed another grand from my mum.'

With Gregg moving out and Maryn not having been seen for several months, seemingly lost in the London fog, Georgia and I looked for a place to stay that wouldn't set our bank accounts on fire. I took to a Facebook flatshare group to put the word out:

> Hey all,
>
> I'm looking for a vegan place in the vicinity of Bermondsey station; budget is about £600 a month but if a few of us pull together I'm sure we can get a three or four bed place to split the costs :) Message me!

'Before any of you consider living with this man,' wrote a bystander, 'you might want to read this.' She accompanied her post with a link to my allegations. When I protested, she replied, 'I believe people should know they are moving in with someone who manipulates women, before they do it. It doesn't matter if you've changed, they should still know.'

Thanks to the internet, I was soon to be without a job or a home. My only remaining option was a room above a pizza place. The room had just enough space for a wardrobe, a single bed, and the door. The bed stuck me with loose springs and the shared shower was disgusting. I didn't invite anyone 'round. I didn't want them to see it. Georgia (who'd moved to Brixton) spoke to me about renting a small place of our own, but we could only afford it if we didn't mind spending the occasional month without food. While mulling over my options, Georgia headed up to her grandma's place in Yorkshire for New Year and I went to a meditation retreat Gregg had recommended.

'It's intense, mate,' he said. 'All you do is meditate for ten hours a day. But it's *so* good. You let go of so much baggage.'

Vipassana retreats (*vipassana* being an old word meaning 'insight') embody the principle of putting on your own oxygen mask before helping others. You're alone with yourself, so you have nothing to do but work through things, breaking down your own resistance. It's a bit like trying to overcome your gag reflex for ten days straight.

The first day began at four in the morning. After I'd dressed myself, I meditated for two hours. Breakfast was served. After a break to have a shower (or, in my case, get some more sleep), I meditated for three hours. Lunch was served. After another break. I meditated for another four hours, taking me to what would be "dinner" in the real world but at the centre consisted of a small cup of tea and two pieces of fruit. Then, after one more hour of sitting, the day would end with a discourse from the teacher, a grinning Indian guru with a penchant for Pali (the language of the Buddha) who told stories about his life and the life of the Buddha. He was the sort of person (like Gregg) who's so peaceful it makes you angry at your own shortcomings, speaking with a voice like Jafar had reformed. He finished his talk, I sat for thirty minutes more, went to bed just before 10pm, woke up again at 4am and started again. It was a meditation marathon. Whereas Plum Village felt like putting on a warm blanket, Vipassana felt like putting on a warm blanket because you'd just experienced trauma and might go into shock.

The centre want you to feel comfortable, so you're allowed to take extra cushions or blankets for your time in the hall. Though I found one of each sufficient, some of the people around me built thrones and monuments for their sit; the man to my left ended up with eight cushions, sitting on four and placing two more under each knee. You weren't allowed to communicate with anyone else on the retreat even by gestures or glances, which caused problems in our rooms when someone adjusted the heating and someone else found it too hot or cold. On the third day, the third guy in our room left the course — my roommate and I came back from a meditation session to find his bed made and his stuff missing — and the two of us were left pretending nothing had happened for another week. It was only on the last day that I was able to run up to him in the dining hall and turn heads by yelling, 'Mate, Chris left!'

Every hour during our sits, a gong would ring, and the teacher would open his eyes at the front of the hall, throw an indifferent glance across the room, say, 'Take a five-minute break and then start again,' and then walk off as though it weren't agony. When our five minutes had passed, he would return and begin a series of ancient chants that sounded less like a divine language and more like I had put the responsibility for my forthcoming enlightenment in the hands of the Swedish Chef. The teacher was available for daily interviews if you needed guidance but, given the individual nature of the work, the only response to 'I'm struggling a lot' was 'Okay, keep trying'.

On the fifth day, I paced around the outside of the meditation hall as though gearing up for a boxing match. I tore into the hall with my eyes boring into my cushion, and at the end of the hour I kicked it as I left. I went back to my room and threw my pillows against the wall, flung my limbs against the bedsheets and hollered wordless noise into the air.

Silence fell. I stormed off to the teacher.

'What can I do for you?' he whispered.

'I'm just… I'm finding this so hard,' I said, surprising myself by bursting into tears.

'There's obviously a huge sadness that is within you and you have to let go of that,' he said. I composed myself, nodding. 'I wish I could help. But you can only help yourself.'

I realised (while the teacher said some other stuff about misery and enlightenment) that I'd been holding on to the idea that I don't deserve success because of my past mistakes. In my efforts to prove I was a good person, I'd crossed the line from being remorseful to being a total pushover, standing out of the way of people who'd spent the last few years calling me abusive, dangerous and remorseless. I'd taken it all lying down. Without even paying attention to it — or, more likely, *because* I wasn't — all my personal and professional goals had withered to nothing. I used to look back at my earlier life and think it was a good start. Now I looked back in awe that I got anywhere at all.

Everyone has made mistakes. Yes, some are a lot worse than others. But we all deserve the chance to pick ourselves up, accept responsibility for what we've done, make amends to those we've hurt, and then get the fuck on with it.

When the course was finished, I got chatting with a guy who also lived in London.

'Whereabouts are you?' I asked.

'Oh, all over,' he said. 'I live on a boat.'

'No way!' I said, and then for our entire three-hour coach and train journey home I grilled him on every aspect of life on a boat. By the time I was back in the city I knew how boaters keep warm, where they get their post, how they vote, what sort of toilets they use, how often they have to move, what they spend every month, how easy it is to cook, where their water comes from, how they get power and what happens when they break down.

'Take my number,' he smiled, 'and maybe I'll see you on the water.'

Living on a boat would be cheaper than a flat since I could buy one outright, and we wouldn't have to share with anyone, but I'd have to sell my flat to pay for it and it wouldn't retain its value. I'd never even stepped aboard a boat before, let alone owned and run one. I had no practice at steering one, knew nothing about engines or electrics or plumbing, and I couldn't swim.

We bought our boat three months later.

ANOTHER ADVENTURE

The first time I moved our boat, I started careering towards one side of the bank. In a panic, I smashed the engine into high-gear and pulled hard away from it, causing us to crash instead into a stationary boat on the other side.

'You alright?' the owner called out, poking his head through an open window.

'Something up with the steering,' I gestured (not mentioning that the problem was it was being steered by someone who had no experience).

'Can you drive it?' he frowned.

'It'll be fine,' I replied, answering a different question. I drove our boat away from his and towards the open water. 'There we go!' I called back, grinning and waving. 'Cheers!'

We were exhilarated, spending the next half an hour pointing at patches of the canal bank and yelling, 'Let's live there!' We pulled up a couple miles later to fill our water tank, Georgia at the front end of the boat while I steered the back up against the bank. We bumped against the side of the canal and I stepped off to tie the boat up when I saw Georgia stepping across from the other end. It was very odd. She was coming from far lower than I'd expected, almost as though she was climbing out of the canal. I looked at her feet and, sure enough, one was soaked. *Ahh, she must have slipped when she stepped off and dipped her foot in the water as she regained composure.* I panned up her legs. How were both her legs sodden with canal water? When I made it up to her face I realised her entire body was drenched in water. When I'd bumped against the bank, it turned out, Georgia was crouching on the front tip of the boat and had tumbled promptly into the deep. (Or, to use a more appropriate term for a canal, 'the shallow'.)

'So are you enjoying it?' asked my friend Scarlett a couple months later. (I'd met Scarlett after she made a video for The Daily Day.)

'Imagine everything that can go wrong with a house,' I said.

'And then imagine everything that can go wrong with a car,' said Georgia.

'Yeah, and then imagine you're on water and you can sink,' I finished.

'So... are you enjoying it?'

'Yeah,' I grinned as Georgia slinked her arm around my waist. 'We're enjoying it.'

We took Scarlett for a trip through Regent's Park that afternoon to confront our very first lock — Camden Lock, where hundreds of people thought, 'Ooh, look, a boat' and took photos of our nervous faces. Over the next few hours we endured torrential rain, looked on in horror as our tomato plant was decapitated by a low-slung tunnel roof and — at the moment I said to Scarlett, 'This is about as bad as it gets on a boat' — heard the engine cut out and leave us drifting in the middle of London Zoo because a tent — a *tent* — got caught up in our propeller.

'How long have you had the boat?' we shouted to another boater as he passed.

'Three winters,' he puffed. 'This your first?'

'Yep.'

'We'll see if you can hack it!'

'It'll warm up again,' I smiled.

I'd taken to watching a few 'boat-tubers' — vloggers who uploaded videos about life on the water — to help me learn the (ahem) ropes. My favourite was a girl called Jasmine who later gave me advice in a boating forum I'd joined to find answers to my questions. I spoke to her on Facebook one afternoon before a cruise.

'It's hard the 1st year but you'll get there,' she wrote. 'What's your YouTube channel?'

'My name is Alex Day and that's also my channel,' I replied. 'I just chat about boating and meditation and veganism and other things.'

'I now know who you are and do not wish to have any further contact.'

Jasmine's abrupt response still surprised me — you think I'd be used to it after four years of slander — but I realised it was never going to change on its own. If I was to apply the lessons from my meditation retreat, I needed to start sticking up for myself. It might feel unfair when people block me from getting flatmates on Facebook, but how would you react if Harvey Weinstein showed up on *your* timeline asking for a place to live? In their minds, there was no difference between him and me. People can't help but believe what they've heard if they're never offered anything different.

I had lots of reasons for not challenging the narrative about me until then: I felt I'd already tried, I felt it sent the wrong message about sex abuse cases in general to have the guy defend himself, I wanted to be kind to the people who accused me because I still cared about them, I thought it would all blow over, etc. It was my fault for following the path that led me into trouble in the first place. But it was also my fault I hadn't done enough to put it right. If you don't take charge of your own story, you can bet someone else will.

When I was in Plum Village, I wrote this in my notebook: 'We are like ships, and if we allow ourselves to be carried along the ocean, sooner or later we'll find we've been washed up on the shore. Life moves. You have to steer your own ship, even if it means you move against the tide, because your journey at sea will be much longer.'

I fired up the engine, loosened all the knots, and started moving forward.

'Is it fair for me to say you were using the power of being a YouTube star to have sex with women?' the radio presenter asked me. Once I started speaking with more candour about my experiences — leading to an interview with *Mashable* — I caught the attention of a radio show on the BBC. They'd invited me to share my story.

'No,' I countered, 'I thought I was getting girls *in spite* of the fact that I was making videos on the internet. I didn't think that was a selling point in the slightest.'

'Yeah, but some of them were your fans—'

'No they weren't! They started off as people that had seen my videos, and we got talking, but they ended up as my friends. In a lot of cases I'd been seeing them in person, hanging out regularly for months — if not years — before anything happened.'

'So where does it end for you?'

'All I can do is try to take responsibility for it,' I said. 'Try to figure out what led to that happening and make sure it never happens again.'

'Well, you seem like a decent guy,' the interviewer said, to my delight.

'I don't think I should be the moral standard for YouTubers,' I replied. 'But thank you for the compliment.' It was a good start.

Penny refused to listen to the interview, which didn't stop her objecting to it. 'Pretty horrified that the BBC decided to give him a platform to defend abuse,' she tweeted, prompting the show's producer to email me:

> Hey Alex, thank you again for taking part in our story. I think it was really important to hear from you and I'm grateful for the candid way you shared your experiences with us.

I've had a bit of flack on Twitter today. Apologies
if our coverage opened floodgates to you again.
Hope it was alright.

Thank you again, hope we can keep in touch.

Even now, I'm still getting accused of things. My friend Maria sent me
this recently: 'One of my fellow volunteers at the theatre told me
tonight that she knows you, that you were quite good friends, that you
then tried to sleep with her 14-year-old friend after getting her drunk
at a party in a hotel room and that she hasn't spoken to you since. She
seemed quite angry. I tried to defend you and after a while she asked
me to stop talking about it because the conversation was getting her
quite upset. It was a pretty surreal experience.' It was surreal for me
too, because it didn't happen.

'What was her name?' I replied. 'If we were good friends I should
know her.'

'Isabelle,' she said. I wracked my brain for hours trying to think
of an Isabelle, a Belle, an Izzy, a Bella or any other derivation.
Sometimes I still try. There's no-one. I had no idea who would say
something like that, or why.

Likewise, I saw a video just the other day of a girl (who I've never
met before) saying I approached her and her friends at VidCon and
invited them up to my hotel room for a party 'with alcohol', and that
when I was told they were underage, I replied, 'We don't have to tell
their parents.' I don't drink, I don't like parties and I don't wanna hang
out with kids in my spare time; I don't recognise any of myself in any
of this. I don't know where people get this stuff. Maybe she's got an
actual memory of someone and didn't know who it was, declaring it
was me later because it made sense to her, or maybe someone told her
a made-up story and she's forgotten she wasn't part of it because she
can picture it so well, or maybe she's just lying. All I know is it isn't
true, and people just listen and believe it.

Still, every now and then, people surprise me. After I announced this book, I received an email from the girl who wrote perhaps the most damning accusation against me — 'Alex Day is a sexual predator who targets underage people'. This is what she said:

alex,

feel free to tell me to fuck off. saw you posting about your new book and it's basically the book i've tried to wish into existence for so long so i thought i'd say fuck it and send you an email. it's been a long time.

sorry for being a slightly (totally) unhinged teenager, but tbf, i was literally a kid lol

i'm not proud of the ways i acted back then. i lied to myself so many times i genuinely don't really know what happened any more. yes, this is an admission that some of the shit i said about you was exaggerated. also the reason i never say, took you to court, because i knew i couldn't even rely on my own testimony. i guess.. i thought the same as everyone seems to have thought. that somehow the hurt would disappear without too much critical thought on anyone's part. that it was possible to apply a quick fix to the situation. that i was helping, somehow. i've never admitted to anyone else that some of what i said was exaggerated. i thought i would never have to because it was ,anonymous' but i was dumb to think i could hide behind that even for a moment.

that being said, i still think some of the ways you acted were inappropriate, but i'm a massive fucking hypocrite to hold that against you.

It was a cathartic email to receive — but of course, the damage had already been done.

I met a nun a while back. Her name is Sister Frances Dominica and she founded a children's hospice in Oxford. She ran it for thirty years and was awarded an OBE by the Queen for her work. She is 75 years old. A few years ago, two women made allegations of 'historical sexual abuse' against her. Frances has always maintained she is innocent and those who know her best have supported her throughout, but she was barred from her hospice effective immediately and wasn't allowed any contact with the residents or staff.

I met Sister Frances at a church service for FACT — Falsely Accused Carers and Teachers, an organisation of which she is now the patron. She took my hands in hers and thanked me for coming with the kind of gratitude one feels from people who have sometimes wondered if anyone will ever smile at them again. She was meek, her skin barely covering her; I felt lucky I'd been through all this so young. Though she was never prosecuted, her ban from the charity she founded is permanent, leaving her unable to continue any of the work to which she'd dedicated her life.

'If you don't go to trial,' her voice quivered from the lectern, 'you are never found innocent.'

Even in a trial, 'innocent until proven guilty' is a hard thing to come by these days, as anyone who's watched *Making a Murderer* can tell you. I saw this discussed a while back in the *New York Times* article 'Ever Heard Of Bill Cosby?':

> Under the Constitution, he is entitled to an impartial and local jury trial. The problem is that after decades in public life everyone knows him, and from months of news coverage almost

> everyone knows he has been accused of sexual
> assault by many women. How can a court find fair
> jurors in an age of media overload?

On October 15th, 2017, the actress Alyssa Milano tweeted: 'If all the women who have been sexually harassed or assaulted wrote 'Me too.' as a status, we might give people a sense of the magnitude of the problem.' This one tweet gave rise to the global 'MeToo' movement which sought to expose widespread sexual harassment and misogyny in Hollywood and other industries. The movement — the result of sexual harassers being in positions of power for far too long without being culpable for their actions — had a huge positive impact on sexual education, consent and respect around the world, along with toppling some of the media's most abusive juggernauts. *TIME* declared 'The Silence Breakers' their People Of The Year in 2017. But it also eliminated an important level of nuance. In court, even individual murders -- let alone other types of physical abuse — are sentenced differently, each verdict being based on the details of that individual case. The MeToo movement has been outstanding overall, but it also carries a lot of collateral damage, like when a controversial article about the comedian Aziz Ansari added him to the world's no-fly zone by detailing what amounted to a pushy date.

Jon Ronson put it best when he said — I'm paraphrasing — that there seem to be more and more people in the world today who value ideologies over human beings, rather than the other way around. And if 'innocent until proven guilty' is out the window, we might as well throw the rest of the justice system out with it. Taking proof into our own hands makes us more empowered but it also enables us to say anything to ruin anyone else's life at any time with a Thanos-style finger snap. Indeed, one politician in the Welsh Labour Party, Carl Sargeant, was so distraught by accusations made against him last year that he killed himself.

Late last year, an independent British judge released the Henriques report, a damning review of the way police handle sex abuse cases. 'A contributory factor', Henriques wrote, 'was the nationwide requirement that 'victims' must be believed... the policy of 'believing victims' strikes at the very core of the criminal justice process. It has and will generate miscarriages of justice on a considerable scale.'

A while after I read the report, I got a call from a senior police officer who phoned to ask if Jonathan had ever touched me inappropriately. I laughed at the idea and said no.

'Forgive me for being ignorant,' I said, 'but, if he had, wouldn't it be me that comes to you with an allegation?'

'Yes, normally,' he said, 'but we're doing it the other way around.' I dread to think what would have happened if someone more vulnerable or in need of money had got that call.

The Henriques report went by unnoticed. By what I'm sure was a complete coincidence, it was decided that it would be made public on the same day Donald Trump was elected President of the United States.

While writing the chapters in this book about the allegations against me, I came across the term 'ghosting'. It's defined in the dictionary as 'the act or an instance of ending a relationship by not responding to attempts to communicate by the other party'. The word was invented the year it happened to me.

Ghosting is not a new problem — people have always been able to sever their ties with others — but in the internet age, where you can always be in touch with people in some form, the feeling of being cut-off is that much more severe. I'd always found my friends' sudden lack of interest in my well-being to be the hardest part of my experience over the last few years but never knew the phenomenon had a name, or that it was recognised by professionals. *Psychology Today* published an article titled 'This Is Why Ghosting Hurts So Much' in which the author writes:

Ghosting is the ultimate use of the silent treatment, a tactic that has often been viewed by mental health professionals as a form of emotional cruelty. It essentially renders you powerless and leaves you with no opportunity to ask questions or be provided with information that would help you emotionally process the experience. It silences you and prevents you from expressing your emotions and being heard, which is important for maintaining your self-esteem.

Regardless of the ghoster's intent, ghosting is a passive-aggressive interpersonal tactic that can leave psychological bruises and scars.

Other articles I found by googling the word described ghosting as creepy, awful and victimising, and helped me understand why, to this day, I have frequent dreams in which my old friends ask how I'm doing or give me the chance to explain myself.

A short while ago, I tweeted one of these articles. I thought people would be interested, as I was, to learn this was an increasingly common phenomenon and give people an idea what it was like on the receiving end. My words sat dormant for several days, until Emma noticed it and lit the fuse through several tweets:

Hooooooly crap I just saw the biggest example of a shamed YouTuber trying to play the victim and I'm ready to go off.

I'm fairly sure having your girlfriend find out publicly that you cheated on her dozens of times was 'emotionally cruel' too, to be honest.

You are DAMN right we ghosted you. It's because we were all fucking disgusted by what you did to her and the people you pressured.

Ghosting is NOT nice, but sometimes, when you're a right cunt, it's absolutely justified. If we all did it, perhaps YOU are the problem.

Sorry. Drama isn't nice and it's unnecessary, but I've had to see one of my closest friends still cope with what he did.

No you're right, I shouldn't apologise. His tweet trying to get people to feel sorry for him proves despite his claims, nothing has changed.

That's not even all of it but I'll spare you the rest. In summary, she spent some time with her friends explaining what ghosting is (and why it doesn't apply to me), tweeted Sarah saying that 'as a woman' she shouldn't be my friend, and made a whole YouTube video about me that she titled 'if you fuck with my friends, you fuck with me'. After this, she turned green, ripped all her clothes off and yelled "VLOG SMASH" at the ceiling, grew to four times her normal size, climbed the Empire State Building and was shot down by military fighters.

('Thanks for telling me about Alex Day,' one guy tweeted at her. 'You're quite the promoter.')

Emma has half a million followers and, over the next twenty-four hours, I got hate tweets from what seemed like all of them, but I had no idea it was happening. The first I knew of the uproar was when someone texted me, 'I'm so sorry for what's happening to you,' which is an ominous thing to read without context.

'Why, what's happening to me?' I messaged back. I log in to my Twitter about once a week, so people were just shouting into space. Upon opening my account, the first thing I saw was, 'You are one massive cunt.' That was pretty representative of the general mood, although five tweets down from that I read, 'Hope you are having a good day Alex! :)' That's the good thing about my little audience now: Whenever hate comes my way, it's always followed by a huge influx of 'chin up' and 'stay strong' messages.

Aware that thousands of people were hovering at my Twitter like drunks on the day their team lost the game, I sent out a couple things in response:

> Just because I suffered doesn't mean other people didn't. Having sympathy for one side doesn't mean you lose sympathy for the other side.

And:

> In my opinion it doesn't seem very useful to practice kindness if you're only using it on those you find it easy to be kind to.

This being the internet, some people found it necessary to argue even against kindness:

> angry43: Of coouuurse you would adopt a philosophy which requires you to be kind and compassionate to willfully shitty people

> Me: doesn't Christianity also offer this? 'Forgive them for they know not what they do', turn the other cheek etc?

> angry43: Your point being?

These people aren't horrible in their hearts. We all express ourselves online with somewhat of a blind spot in our sense of compassion. It feels ironic that Hank recently started a video production company called Complexly. We seem to forget that people change. As Emma was so eager to point out, all my friends ghosted me — which means they have no idea who I am now. It's like seeing a banana when it's hard and green, and saying it's disgusting and bitter, forgetting with time it'll get softer, and bruise.

Even when we do remember, we sometimes let our biases get in the way. Shortly after Pewdiepie (the most subscribed YouTuber in the world) suffered backlash in the media after a very public mistake, Marilyn commented, 'I'm all for calling out those who have done wrong but it's unfair to drag someone's name through the mud continuously for the same mistake, especially after there has been an apology and a promise not to do the same again. One person can only be held accountable for one mistake so many times.' Yet in response to my ghosting tweet, she replied, 'if you intentionally do something bad, no one owes you sympathy when you suffer the consequences.'

I went to a great talk recently at the London Buddhist Centre about how forgiveness is a 'spiritual death practice'. The woman giving the talk said that, by not forgiving someone, you hold on to your identity as a victim, but by allowing yourself to feel forgiveness, you kill that prior identity of yourself and give rise to a more complex, empowering idea. And the truth is that all my former friends agree with me on the importance of focusing on light instead of darkness, to the point that Marilyn and I both retweeted the same thing from Gigi Hadid: 'Please, as social media users & human beings in general, learn to have more empathy for others and know that you never really know the whole story. Use your energy to lift those that you admire rather than be cruel to those u don't.'

One of the few friends I still have in common with Charlie went to VidCon in 2017. Not being in the YouTube scene anymore (despite my haters' best efforts to keep me relevant), I asked him what it was like these days.

'In the beginning, everybody wanted more people to become internet creators,' he said, 'the more the merrier. Everyone had the motivation and patience to be helpful to everyone else. Now that there's money and people's livelihood at stake, success of others can come at the cost of your own success, or your own ability to put food on the table, so there's much less motivation to keep the new media party open to the public, where everyone is welcome. It's in everyone's own best interest to turn platforms into walled gardens where the people who are already successful can continue being successful without added competition.

'I saw Charlie,' he added, 'and at some point our conversation turned to the Chameleon Circuit days. I preached the importance of forgiveness, and said something about hoping someday all of us could at least be on speaking terms again. He became visibly uncomfortable, so the conversation ended, and he hasn't responded to any of my texts or messages since. It makes me both mad and sad that, for some people, the price of their positive feelings for me is me having negative feelings for someone else.'

Today's most popular YouTubers appear to me somewhere on the spectrum between a kids' TV presenter and a wasted groomsman at a stag do: getting together with mates to answer questions and attempt dangerous stunts and then gurn about how meaningful it all is. The big new thing on YouTube is "story time" vlogs, in which — as one friend described it — 'you film yourself sharing an anecdote from your life.' I'd thought that was just what YouTube *was*, but people are going further and further away from that for clicks and likes. A vlogging couple lost custody of their children after mistreating them in videos. Another vlogger accidentally shot and killed her boyfriend after 'one of the most dangerous videos ever' went wrong.

Of course, there have always been shit YouTubers. In our day we were frustrated at the likes of Smosh and Fred being the most-subscribed and, therefore, the public face of something we thought had much more creative merit than their antics implied. Similarly, now that I only see the public face due to my lack of involvement with the community, Logan Paul and Pewdiepie are the sum of what I see to be YouTubers, but I shouldn't fall for that, just as I wouldn't have wanted people to fall for it all those years ago.

It's difficult to find the truly creative content, though. My old friends seem paralysed. Liam recorded a beat poem about his increasing unoriginality and irrelevance on the site. Charlie made a video saying he'd been diagnosed with anxiety and depression, which he said started around the time he began his exposure to the world of the internet. Zoella graced the cover of *Cosmopolitan* with the headline, 'The secret life of a social media star — Rule No 1: Get therapy. Lots of it.' The article outlined Zoella's struggle with "crippling anxiety", part of which might have been a result of the criticism she faced when it was discovered that her best-selling book, *Girl Online,* was ghostwritten. Many YouTubers, despite never having expressed any desire to be an author, have accepted book deals with titles like — and this is true — *They Let Me Write A Book!*

My agent was thrilled to hear I was ready to write a book about YouTube. When I sent him the first draft, he called me in for a meeting.

'I have to say,' he said, 'you have a real chance with this. It's fascinating. I'm sure you can get it published.'

'Really?' I beamed.

'Absolutely,' he nodded. 'Of course, I'm not the right person to represent you. I'm too old. I don't understand these things. I'm completely wrong for it.'

'Wanker,' said Jonathan when I told him.

I spent a few months researching and writing to agents across the country. Of the hundreds of people I approached, I was rejected by all but one: a young woman called Tessa who saw merit in my work, looked into all the details surrounding my past, and agreed to represent me.

Tessa approached editors with all the major publishers in the UK. They all loved the book. They all went to their sales and marketing departments with it, and then all their publicity people googled my name and threw my book out the window as though it were covered in shit. So it was that I lost the second book agent of my career.

'Can't we approach small publishers?' I pleaded. 'I'd still love to have your support.'

'Well it's not as simple as that,' said Tessa. 'The foreign rights agent here is uncomfortable with me representing you. It's hard for me to move forward when not even my whole team is on-board.'

After I lost my agent, I spent the evening at Ziferblat, a co-operative space in Hackney for the public to hang out and work in. The only other person around was the host, Cori, so we poured a cup of tea and sat together for a chat.

'How's it going?'

'Alright I guess,' I shrugged. 'I lost my book agent today.'

'Why?'

I sighed. Every time someone asks me what I do, I have to wonder how many things I can say before they google me, or ask why I don't do it anymore, or why I don't seem excited that half a million people are subscribed to my channel.

'Well, three years ago...' I began, and told her everything I'd been accused of.

'Wow,' she said at the end. 'That must have been hard. Thank you for sharing it with me.'

'It's all good,' I said.

'I have to say,' said Cori, 'I already knew all of it.'

'What?' I said, wondering how she was still sat here if she hadn't heard it from me.

'A few times when you've been here, people have come up to me or one of the other hosts and asked about you,' she said. 'To ask what you were doing there.'

'How come you never told me?'

'Because this is a safe space for everyone,' she said. 'You as well. We didn't want you to feel unwelcome here. We looked into what happened and decided it didn't make sense with the Alex we know. If anyone has to leave because they can't stand to be in the same room as you, that's their choice.'

Not everyone shares that attitude, of course, and my past isn't going anywhere. My cousins are now twelve and thirteen and I worry one of them will, at some point soon, get into YouTube. (Kids are getting into YouTube younger and younger. In a recent survey of a thousand young people aged six to seventeen, when asked, "What do you want to be when you grow up?", over 30% answered, 'A YouTuber'. It was the most popular answer — with blogger/vlogger coming second.) If my cousins get into YouTube, they might at some point be told their cousin is a sex abuser, or someone in their class who watches YouTube will rub it in their faces. Even them googling me would be enough. I don't know how to explain all this to them.

The internet seems like a foreign country to me now — and it's impacted the whole world. I've gone from feeling like the only person on the internet to the only person who isn't. Everything seems to be pigeonholed as either shit or amazing; every politician is Hitler, Jesus, or irrelevant. Pop culture has become a tumble dryer of things we already know, rife with sequels, prequels, spinoffs, adaptations and remakes. Social media is the same: if you run out of things to post, Facebook offers up posts from previous years so you can reblog yourself. Our lives have reruns now. Dan and Phil made a video not too long ago with the title 'Dan and Phil React to Teens React to Dan and Phil'.

People expect the internet to be filtered for them, ready to burst into flames if it isn't. I tweeted recently about a new episode of *Doctor Who* and my timeline was filled with angry followers reacting as if they'd just stepped on a landmine. They said I'm not allowed to talk about it until they'd watched it for themselves. A well-crafted big budget piece of art can't be ruined by a 140-character plot summary. As John posted once, 'People knew how Titanic would end, and they still liked it.'

When my detractors talk about me, they write 'Trigger Warning: Alex Day' at the header. The idea of the trigger warning originated with Vietnam War veterans suffering post-traumatic stress disorder, with flashbacks triggered by various ideas or sensory input, but usage of the term surged online through Tumblr and is now seen on anything that any person could find objectionable — which is to say, anything. I've seen trigger warnings for rape, sexual abuse, domestic violence, misogyny, Islamophobia and war. I've also seen them on pictures of food to protect people with anorexia, and on one website where a photograph of a dog was preceded by the words, 'Teeth are bared in a way that may be perceived as aggressive', added after a guy commented he'd suffered a dog bite and would have appreciated the heads-up. A piece meant to offer help with depression might have a trigger warning for depression at its header, warding off the very people it's designed to reach. A TV drama about a woman's brave recovery after a rape could be criticised if they show a rape scene. I even read that the word 'trigger' was being reconsidered because — these were the exact words — 'the word "trigger" itself might be triggering for people who have experienced gun violence'. This is about as antithetical as things could get from the wild early internet of my youth, when we were surrounded by adult or offensive content but learned to navigate the space with appropriate deftness. I find it bizarre that anyone could expect the internet — or the world — to bubble-wrap itself just so they can have a less challenging Monday afternoon.

To be fair, I want the internet filtered too. A few years ago an EU law was passed known as the 'right to be forgotten'. It stated that search engines had to allow people the right to have certain webpages — like, for example, blogs that make unfounded accusations of rape — be deleted from search results. My request was denied by Google when I asked them to scrub my allegations from its results, but I was far from the only one asking. More than two million people have submitted requests since 2014, and a whole industry of 'reputation management services' has emerged to assist those who need it. This kind of problem isn't reserved for the rich and famous. It can happen to you. All it takes is a person with a phone and an axe to grind.

In my day-to-day life, I spend most of my time offline and these things don't come up much. The hate is there but I'm not overwhelmed by it. I'm too busy working on new projects. Donald Glover defines an artist's job as 'to make something beautiful out of chaos', and that's what I'm trying to do now. I want to make art that's better than I am. And I no longer feel bad for wanting to achieve great things, because I know the best way to support the people I love and who love me (and the world in general) is from a place of success. If I do well, I'll make sure it benefits everyone. I'll admit I still shoot out a thoughtless tweet every now and then when I feel frustrated or challenged by someone, but I've come to think growing up is just the process of making sure the mistakes you make now are smaller than the ones you made in the past, and I think I make smaller mistakes than I used to.

Thanks to the direct support of my audience on Patreon — a site that functions like an online tip car for independent creators — I earn about £1500 a month from my online endeavours and I have a loyal YouTube audience of about five thousand people. I'm far more grateful for them than when I had a million. It's the quality of an audience, not the size, that matters, and by doing my best for them, I'm cultivating a group of compassionate people who inspire and push me forward. Success means nothing if I'm pursuing it at the expense of the people around me.

On balance, if I could start from scratch, I'd pick the internet again. It enables anyone to choose what they want to do with their life — anything in the world — and can help them start doing it. Of course, that rabbit hole is also the dangerous thing about it. I recently saw an ad on YouTube that said, 'Your screen is your window to the world' and I thought, *No. My* window *is my window to the world*.

I first went on the internet all those years ago because it helped me connect with people, and now I come off it for the same reason. My only lasting hangup is that whenever I see a teenage girl with dyed hair or a Gryffindor scarf I assume she hates me, and even that is fading. But although it's tempting to imagine what life would be like if we put the genie back in the bottle — if we were a little less distracted, a little less reactive and a little more aware — the tech's out there now. This is the world we have. And I'm glad I get to live in it.

FURTHER READING (AND LISTENING)

I like reading and, given that you just finished my book, I hope you do too. Here are my top ten recommended books for people who enjoyed this one:

1. *You Are Not A Gadget* by Jaron Lanier
A manifesto about what the internet is turning us into and what it — and we — could be instead. A short but strong read.

2. *So You've Been Publicly Shamed* by Jon Ronson
I was nearly invited to be part of this book. It shares several case studies of people whose lives have been ruined by internet shaming and offers a bit of insight as to why we participate in it. (His TED talk on the subject is also outstanding.)

3. *Modern Romance* by Aziz Ansari and Eric Klinenberg
A look into how technology has affected our dating lives and created new problems. Written by Aziz Ansari, who has become one of the most controversial symbols of the MeToo movement.

4. *Dataclysm* by Christian Rudder
The title doesn't work in my accent but the book is from one of the founders of dating website OKCupid. The book discusses some amazing ideas he's learned about love from the statistics generated by the site's users.

5. *Trust Me, I'm Lying: Confessions Of A Media Manipulator* by Ryan Holiday
Ryan wrote the *Forbes* article 'Is Alex Day the Future of Music?' in 2012. This is a great exposé on how the media work in the modern age. (Bonus reading: I used ideas from his recent book *Perennial Seller*

to market this one, it's a must for anyone who wants to make lasting art.)

6. *The 4-Hour Workweek* by Tim Ferriss
This book motivated me to finish my first album and focus on generating passive income and liberating my life from my work. A must-read if you could be happier in any way.

7. *Peace Is Every Step* by Thich Nhat Hanh
For an elderly Vietnamese monk, Thich Nhat Hanh writes in a remarkably engaging and relatable way. A great book with lots of moments of insight— I love the 'traffic light meditation'. A calming, easy read.

8. *The War Of Art* by Steven Pressfield
A book about the struggle of making art and how urgent it is for you to overcome it and DO SOMETHING. A motivational read (though I'm not into the end where he talks about angels).

9. *A Million Miles In A Thousand Years* by Donald Miller
I read this in Zambia and it's my favourite book. It's about what happens when you view your life as a great story with scenes that pop. As a professional storyteller, I connected a lot with this.

10. The Henriques Report by Sir Richard Henriques
Not a book, but fascinating to read how the police in the UK handle sexual offence cases and how our modern morality is guiding them in a specific direction.

And finally, here are ten songs Jonathan has introduced me to, all of which he says are smash hits. Don't worry about searching them all: I've shared them in a playlist on Spotify, which you can find by searching 'JK's Hits'.

1. 'Summertime Girls' by Y&T
The 'Don't Stop Believing' that could have been

2. 'Shoorah! Shoorah!' by Betty Wright
I don't know anyone who won't feel better after hearing this song

3. 'Free Your Mind' by En Vogue
The ultimate progressive anthem

4. 'Beach Baby' by First Class
McFly from the Seventies

5. 'Just The Girl' by The Click Five
The most modern track on here

6. 'Euphoria' by Loreen
An absolute dance smash from 2011

7. 'Time Of The Season' by The Zombies
So good it was sampled by Eminem

8. '(I'd) Wait A Million Years' by The Grass Roots
Because The Proclaimers didn't go far enough

9. 'Aicha' by Cheb Khaled
A French song with heaps of melody

10. 'Great Is Thy Faithfulness' by Avalon
A Christian hymn from the early 20th century; the Avalon version is
my fave

A NOTE FROM THE AUTHOR

This book is credited as written by 'Alex Day', which — having read it — you'll have figured out is a bit of a simplification. In fact, this book is written in part by friends, strangers and detractors, all of whom had valuable things to say about my life as it ebbed and flowed in front of them. The book wouldn't be what it is today, nor I the man, were it not for their respective support, criticism and bile. I'm grateful to them all for their assistance as they helped me grow through almost absurdly different methods.

Even the bits written by me were not accomplished by me alone. After I wrote the first draft of this book — an odd, emotionally detached treatise detailing the last ten years of my life with bemusement and a deep lack of accountability — I sent it to Georgia, Rebecca, Maria, Poppy, Sarah-Grace, Charlotte, Jack, Michael and Jonathan, all of whom provided valuable feedback. (My thanks to all of them — especially Poppy, who said she rated this book higher than *The Great Gatsby*.) Jonathan helped me when he highlighted the reservedness with which I shared personal information, to which I said, 'I don't want to write a personal story,' to which he (quite rightly) said, 'Don't write a book then.'

With that in mind, I opened myself up a lot with a more painful second draft about my personal experiences, which Michael and Jonathan very kindly re-read for me (although Jonathan skipped through the second draft up to the moment he first appeared). I also sent the draft to Fiona, who gave me the eye-opening feedback that I showed no growth and that by the book's end she wasn't on my side (a sentiment echoed by Jack when he first read it and said he didn't believe the ending), leading to a total overhaul of the last 25% of what I'd written. Looking back, my second draft was an absolute sob story, designed to defend myself from premature criticism and justify the existence of itself. I'd let the negativity in my head too much and had to flush it out.

By that point I'd recruited my wonderful editor, Edi González (whose rates are very reasonable and whose work is unsurpassed if you're in the trade and you're looking for an editor). It is because of her that you are reading the polished, professional manuscript she enticed from the mess of words I'd committed to each page. Her guidance and support helped me unearth the courage within what I'd written and give the whole thing the tone it needed.

It was only near the end of my time writing this book — all the while asking, 'Why the hell am I writing this anyway?' — that I realised I wanted to put it out there not to defend myself or win people over, but to help people. I wanted to provide a personal blueprint of success and failure, something that could motivate people to achieve their own unrealistic goals while also taking heed of the lessons I learned along the way. I hope my story stops others from causing unnecessary pain to those around them, in all the various ways I've depicted it here, and liberates people to pursue their dreams, even if their dream is to direct a music video in the TARDIS and cradle Miss Piggy's head. I also hope you have a better understanding of the weird and wonderful world of social media stars over their first decade of life in the spotlight. I've struggled to find an accurate account of our strange and exciting community as we learned to navigate this new world and watched it reform around us, so I did my best to write one. I trust that it will remain a valuable reference into the future.

The final draft was sent to Tessa, Fiona and Georgia, who read the complete work and helped me highlight final adjustments that needed to be made. Their support meant the world at a time when I wasn't sure if this book should ever see the light of day, and I'll always be grateful to them for helping me across the finish line.

The cover was designed by J Caleb Clark, and — being unsure about the boldness of a coffin on the cover — I messaged some friends about it when I first saw it. I'm so grateful to Michael, Georgia,

Brighton and Rebecca for helping me find the courage to put that beautiful design on my book.

My friends — Scarlett, Lizzie, Danny and many others — have been patient with me, not questioning why after two years my answer to 'What you up to?' was still 'Writing the book'. Polite smiles and I-look-forward-to-reading-its were offered many times. Thank you, all of you, for sticking with me.

Many people have been kind enough to support me on Patreon, which has literally kept me alive and with a roof over my head while I finished this book. To that end, I want to thank the following people for their belief in me: Aaron Kiely, Abbey Jaques, Adam Seage, Adam Stoner, Aileen Maciejewski, Alden Horowitz, Alec Lefeber, Alex Wall, Alexander Erting-Haynes, Alexandra Clarke, Alexis Rae Connors, Alice Watson, Alicia Kiattinat, Ally Hollis, Alyssa Leman, Amala Williams, Anders Kristensen Nordvik, Andie Marchand, Angel Caglar, Anna Bareham, Anna Clare, Anna Iudaeva, Aoife O'Sullivan, Aria Slippert, Autumn Kunkle, Becki Kendall, Ben Jordan, Bex, Bonnie Kzzinsky, Brogan Jones, Cassandra Gerth, Catalina Curran, Catherine Hurtado, Charlie Ambler, Charlotte Sharples, Charnell Veves, Chris, Chris Coulson, Chris McSweeney, Chris Scott, christina DJV, Claudia Merlini, Connor Holland, Daniel Morgan, Danny - We're just kids in love, Domenico Sambuceto, Dylan Bisset-Larsen, Dylan Spicker, ecchikitten, Ed Nichols, Edward Parsons, Eimear Dyer, Eloise FitzGerald, Emma Blasdale, Emma Carroll, Emma Schwallie, Erin Dacey, Erin Schloeffel, Eve Mack, Felicia Robyn DeWald, Felix, Fred Rich, Fur-Guess Dennehy, Gemma Dene, Grace, Grace Caroe, Harlan Simpson, Helen Bush, Helena Unwin Golding, The Inglorious Raccoon, Jamie Rodgers, Jamie Walton. janelle gonzalez, Jared, Jasmine Hamlin, Jeff Gillis, Jenna Lynne, Jessica Di Silvestro, Jessica harkin, Jodie Eastop, Jon Shaw, Jonna Heijke, Joseph Metcalf, Julika7, Kasper Thøgersen, Kaitlin Sabbage, Kate Anderson, Katherine, Kathryn Kruse, Keira-Louise Moore, Kieran Storer, Krystal Y. Rivera, Laura, Lauren Palumbo, Lewis Christian, Liberty Rodriguez, Linda Marric, Lockian, Louis Andrews, Luke Carvill, Margaret Moore,

Marianne Vakiener, Maribel Araque, Mary Kilbane, Matt, Matt Garrard, Maureen O'Daly, Max Lopez, Megan McMahon, Michael Nonya, Mio Geire, Miss00000, Molly Kusznier, NinjaFace, NJ Levy, Olivia Kitson, Oxygen Halo, Patrick Kirby, Peter Child, Philip Sharples, Pierce Moore, Quincy Gaines, Raphaela Edelbauer, Ricky Billings, Robert Bray, Robert Lee, Robin Dearest, Roman Ross, rubbydubby, Saffron Webb, Samantha McCrae, Sara Kugler, Sara West, Sarah Elizabeth May, Sarah Nicole, Sarah Walters, Sarah White, Scott McCracken, Sebastian Pontin, Shaunessy McKay, Shino Kelly, SF, Sienna Lee, Soul Journey, Stephen Spinks, Steve Hodge, Stroma Sutton, Tanner Jones, Thomas Fairbrother, Thomas Lock, Toby Roberts, Tom Hawkins, Tom Tremayne, Tünde Molnár, User#2283, Vince Sackey, and Zmac808.

There are plenty more people I could thank, but that would be at the detriment of those I've hurt. Though I hope this book will be useful to many people — and I'll no doubt gain from it being out there — I regret that this had to be the story I ended up telling, as I'm sure many others do too. I'm sorry to anyone who feels let down by me, and I hope this book goes some way to redressing the balance. I'm sure it's not the book you would have had me write, but I can only do my best with the life I've made for myself, and I hope for your understanding in my attempt to open up and show others how destructive our actions can be for ourselves and the people around us.

This book was self-published. Whatever you thought of it, I'd be hugely grateful to you for posting a review of the book on Amazon. This only takes a minute or two and pushes the book higher in their mythical and mysterious ranking system, putting it in front of more people like you who might enjoy it.

Thank you for reading. I'll see you on the internet.

-A

ABOUT THE AUTHOR

Alex Day is a twenty-nine year old student of the Open University, currently studying French and Chinese. He has written and released five albums and two books, including this one. Since he believes in the concept of interbeing — which suggests all things exist as one without the dualistic separation of self — he is an eighty-nine year old Vietnamese zen master who lives in the south of France and founded a Buddhist monastery where he lives and works to promote and cultivate mindfulness. He is also Elton John.

Sign up to Alex's mailing list at alexday.ninja for a brief once-a-month email about latest projects and recommended books.

Lightning Source UK Ltd.
Milton Keynes UK
UKHW01f0614270718
326381UK00002B/175/P